What the reviewers said about the 1992 Lambda Literary Award nominee, *The Erotic Naiad:*

"Make sure you have fresh batteries for this one!"
The Empty Closet

"A signature collection with irresistible appeal ... Stock up on this perfect end-of-the-year gift book, it will sell like potato chips"
FBN

"A welcome addition to any library by some of our favorite authors"
Linda Ingram

"Sure to entertain you"
Golden Threads

"Sexy, funny, sometimes warm, often hot, always a pleasure"
Bay Area Reporter

"Quickly draws readers in"
Washington Blade

"Has winner written all over it ... sure to be a collectable and welcome addition to your library"
AM/bush

THE ROMANTIC NAIAD

Love Stories by
Naiad Press Authors

EDITED BY
KATHERINE V. FORREST
and **BARBARA GRIER**

THE ROMANTIC NAIAD

Love Stories by
Naiad Press Authors

EDITED BY
KATHERINE V. FORREST
and **BARBARA GRIER**

The Naiad Press, Inc.
1993

Printed in the United States of America on acid-free paper
First Edition

Cover design by Pat Tong and Bonnie Liss
   (Phoenix Graphics)
Typeset by Sandi Stancil

Library of Congress Cataloging-in-Publication Data

The Romantic Naiad : love stories by Naiad Press authors /
edited by Katherine V. Forrest and Barbara Grier.
      p.   cm.
   ISBN 1-56280-054-X
   1. Lesbians' writings, American.   2. Love stories, American.
3. Lesbians—Fiction.   I. Forrest, Katherine V., 1939–   .
II. Grier, Barbara, 1933–   .
PS648.L47R66   1993
813'.085089206643—dc20   93-24252
                                                              CIP

ABOUT THE EDITORS

Katherine V. Forrest

Author of the novels *Curious Wine* (1983); *Daughters of a Coral Dawn; Amateur City* (1984); *An Emergence of Green* (1986); *Murder at the Nightwood Bar* (1987), which has been optioned by film director Tim Hunter; a short story collection, *Dreams and Swords* (1987); *The Beverly Malibu* (1989), (Lambda Literary Award winner); and *Murder by Tradition* (1991), (Lambda Literary Award winner). Her novel *Flashpoint* will be published in June, 1994.

Articles and book reviews have appeared in a number of publications, including *The New York Times* and *The Los Angeles Times*. All book-length fiction has been published by The Naiad Press, Inc., Tallahassee, Florida. She is co-editor, with Barbara Grier, of 1992's *The Erotic Naiad*.

Fiction editor, Naiad Press.

Member, PEN International.

Jurist, Southern California PEN fiction award.

Katherine V. Forrest was born in Canada. She has held management positions in business, and since 1979 has been a full-time writer and editor. She lives in San Francisco.

Barbara Grier

Author, editor, bibliographer, writings include *The Lesbian in Literature, Lesbiana, The Lesbian's Home*

Journal, Lavender Herring, Lesbian Lives as well as contributions to various anthologies, *The Lesbian Path* (Cruikshank) and *The Coming Out Stories* (Stanley and Wolfe). She is co-editor, with Katherine V. Forrest, of *The Erotic Naiad* (1992).

Her early career included working for sixteen years with the pioneer lesbian magazine, *The Ladder*. For the last twenty-one years she has been, together with Donna J. McBride, the guiding force behind THE NAIAD PRESS.

Articles about Barbara's and Donna's life are too numerous to list, but a good early overview can be found in *Heartwomen* by Sandy Boucher, N.Y., Harper, 1982.

She lives in Tallahassee, Florida.

THE
ROMANTIC
NAIAD

Love Stories by
Naiad Press Authors

EDITED BY
KATHERINE V. FORREST
and **BARBARA GRIER**

TABLE OF CONTENTS

The Bride

Jennifer Fulton

When Georgia phoned to say she had kidnapped a bride, I was not surprised. In the entire three years I'd known her, my roommate had nurtured an unhealthy fascination for these swan-like creatures. Spotting one in its black shiny limousine, she was wont to yell dramatically, "Don't do it, don't do it!"

Like any supportive friend, I had tactfully suggested, over numerous chickpea casseroles, that she throw in her job at the Melbourne Botanical

Gardens. The place was a mecca for bridal parties. It could only be a torment to her.

But Georgia was hooked. I suspected her of nurturing a rescue fantasy. A reluctant bride hangs back during the vows ... everyone cranes and whispers, and lo, in a cloud of diesel, Georgia Simmons soars by on her mowing machine, plucks the bride from a fate worse than death and bears her off to a love nest in Fitzroy.

I should have seen it coming. A few days back she had arrived home, morbid and downcast.

"I saw one this afternoon, Ellie," declared she. "Drifting across the lawn like a wraith. I thought I was dreaming ... that maybe it was Titania, the Faerie Queen."

"And Oberon?"

Georgia sighed. "He was *gross* — the kind who thinks foreplay is waking her up before he jumps on her."

"They're only straight people," I soothed. "They probably deserve each other."

"But this one looked different."

"You always say that."

"She had a kind of quiet desperation about her ... like maybe she was having second thoughts."

No doubt she was worried about getting grass stains on her train, I thought. How ridiculous getting decked out days before the wedding ... all for the photos.

"They just had to do the suspender bit," Georgia mourned.

This was a recent fad in suburban wedding photography. The Bride wore suspenders and stockings with little bows at the ankles. Daring and playful, she would lift her dress. Kneeling, the groom would tackle a suspender, sometimes with his teeth.

"I could barf," said Georgia. "He had no idea. Imagine it on The Night."

"Don't torture yourself," I said. "Get a girlfriend."

I could think of several fetching young dykes who would have welcomed a date with a woman who had biceps, a pay-packet and her own Jeep. But no — Georgia had to have one of Them — a Bride of her own.

"You should see her," she breathed down the phone. "She's gorgeous. Her dress is cream, not white. And it's short and tight, with huge roses all around the bottom."

"Must be hell sitting down," I said.

"Her car broke down. She had to get out so her dress wouldn't crush. It was raining and so I went over to see if I could help, and . . ."

"Take her back right now," I advised sternly. "Tell them it was a mistake."

"But Ellie . . ."

"No!" I shouted. "Georgia, you can't just kidnap some woman who's about to get married. What are you going to do with her?"

"I thought I'd bring her home."

"Here! You must be crazy. What about the cops?"

I was wasting my breath. Having secured one of this exotic breed, Georgia would not surrender her without a fight.

Half an hour later they arrived. It was even worse than I'd imagined. The Bride was a bosomy woman wearing big hair and clutching a limp bouquet. She was blindfolded. I doubted this was part of her original ensemble. Her dress was splattered with mud and one cabbage-like silk rose was dangling by a single thread. With a brief triumphant look in my direction, Georgia hustled her inside.

"Fantastic, huh," she whispered, "what a babe." She eased her quarry onto our couch and informed the wretched woman that no one was going to hurt her.

The Bride sat in rigid silence, bound hands trembling in her lap. Georgia disentangled the sweatband from her own dense black mop and used it to tie the Bride's ankles together. "Can I get you something," she then offered deferentially. "Coffee, maybe?"

Appalled, I confronted her in the kitchen. "Georgia, this has gone far enough. She's obviously terrified . . ."

"But I said I wasn't going to hurt her."

"I'm sure that's really convincing for someone who's been abducted on the eve of her nuptials and is now tied up and blindfolded in some strange apartment. For all she knows, there could be half a dozen sickos sitting about waiting for show time."

"I was going to take off the blindfold," Georgia huffily informed me.

"You'll take her home," I hissed. "Right now, before any more harm is done."

Georgia's dark brows drew together. Her face was the picture of sulky defiance. "I won't," she said.

"Then what *are* you going to do with her?" I demanded, as I made the coffee. "Have you thought that far ahead? They've probably started a manhunt already. Kidnapping a bride — you'll be public enemy number one."

Georgia stalked mutinously into the sitting room and perched on the couch. Careful not to disturb the Bride's elaborate coiffure, she removed the blindfold.

Our guest blinked and gazed around, and I could see immediately why Georgia had been tempted. The Bride was the kind of stranger you passed in the street, then halted in your tracks to stare back at. There was something lustrous and wholesome about her. She seemed shamefully miscast in the drab toil of city life, her presence in our apartment the startling and magical stuff of dreams.

I fought off a bizarre desire to stroke her satiny cheek. Instead, I touched myself — a reality check — and met her eyes. They were an odd shade of amethyst grey, the color of distant mountains.

"I'm sorry about this," I mumbled.

She held my gaze. There was a poignant dignity about her, sitting there, hands neatly clasped, ankles bound. "What are you going to do with me?"

"We're going to take you home," I said, ignoring Georgia's gesticulations.

The Bride responded with a small grave nod. "What's the time?" she inquired.

"It's three."

She sighed. "I'm late."

"For your wedding?" I asked weakly. Oh, what a horrible thought.

"For the photo session," said the Bride. "We were supposed to be there at two."

"Maybe they're still waiting," I said, reminding myself of the gravity of our situation. "We could take you back . . . say you'd had an accident . . . we could forget this ever happened."

She was already shaking her head. "Randy's not

that patient. . . ." Faintly bitter. "He can't stand lateness. I'll be lucky if he wants me at all after this."

Georgia looked cynical. "Is the guy crazy?"

The Bride fidgeted. "There are dozens of girls just waiting to step into my shoes."

"It's not your fault this happened," I reasoned. "The whole thing was a mistake. Georgia's been under a lot of pressure . . ."

"Pressure?" Georgia glanced sideways at me, evidently failing to appreciate the need for a plausible defense of her actions.

"Since er . . . the loss of someone close," I blundered on. It wasn't a total lie. Our neighbor, Mrs. Cassidy, had last week abandoned her apartment for a Queensland beach condo owned by her son, a dentist.

"I'm so sorry," the Bride said huskily. "I had a loss myself, recently." A slow tear foundered its way down her cheek. Awkwardly, she lifted her bound hands to brush it aside.

I couldn't bear her stricken expression. Neither could Georgia. She scuttled off to the kitchen, her customary refuge during personal crises and the scary bits on TV.

"Here." I rustled up a tissue and dabbed the Bride's face. "Allow me."

Her mouth was trembling. In an uncharacteristic flight of fancy, I saw myself wiping away the lipstick and tenderly kissing it.

"She died in my arms," she whispered. "Two months ago."

Faced with such grief, I felt like scum. With a severe look in Georgia's direction I reached for the

Bride's hands and started loosening the knots that secured them. I wished I could think of something appropriate to say. But I was undone by the jasmine scent of her, the sorrow so candidly revealed. I wanted to take her somewhere beautiful, bathe her in milk, rub soothing oils into her body, entrance her with some melodious instrument.

This romantic fantasy disturbed me. I am essentially a practical woman, a fate I suspect I share with most farm-raised people. On a farm nothing is mysterious, and everything is immediate. The earth is too close, the seasons too long, life and death too familiar. To be romantic is to court disillusion.

The Bride was talking about her dead friend. "She just wasted away. I felt so helpless . . ."

I had obviously missed a few beats. I placed my hand on hers, hoping she hadn't noticed my lapse in concentration. "You were there for her," I declared tritely. "What are friends for?"

She stared at me, then glanced toward the kitchen. "Your friend, Georgia . . . Has she ever done this before?"

I lowered my voice. "No. But I saw it coming. She seems to have a thing about brides."

"Perhaps she should see someone."

"I've tried to tell her."

"It could be bride-envy. I've heard about it . . . women throwing paint bombs at bridal salons, that kind of thing. Randy says they must have been jilted at the altar."

"Really?"

"Did you read about that bride from Toorak? The groom ran off with the best man. She broke a bakery window and vandalized a wedding cake. Now she's getting married again. Temporary insanity — that's what she's pleading."

I nodded. In the sixties it was pregnancy, in the eighties, property. Now the excuse was insanity. "Would you like to call Randy?" I reluctantly offered.

She shook her head. "He'll never believe me. It's not the first time."

Georgia emerged from the kitchen, eyes wide. "You've been kidnapped before?"

"No! I mean the photos. I missed the last session too." She looked glum. "My heart's just not in it . . ."

"It's not?" I murmured.

The Bride cradled her head in her hands. "Oh, God. How will I ever tell him?"

"You have to," I urged. "Before it's too late."

"I can't," she responded miserably. "I need him."

I heard Georgia choke.

"It's the money," she confessed. "I know that sounds mercenary, but a girl has to eat."

"Well, that's the capitalist patriarchy for you." Georgia's disenchantment was apparently complete. "Men want something — they just buy it. Secretaries, prostitutes, wives . . ."

The Bride glanced awkwardly in my direction and started unraveling her auburn hair. "I guess I should be leaving . . ."

"You gonna turn me in?" Georgia made a half-hearted bid for lesbian martyrdom.

The Bride shrugged. "It was a lousy day anyway. The session was probably canceled."

"Well, that's something," I found myself blabbing all of a sudden. "Say, if you don't have anything else planned why not stay for dinner?" Ignoring Georgia's raised eyebrows, I continued. "Do you like moussaka? I'm a pretty good cook."

"You really want me to stay?" The Bride gingerly touched her face. "I look a mess, right?"

"No... You look... great," I croaked. "Really. You're beautiful."

I hadn't meant to come right out and say it, and having done so I felt color staining my cheeks.

The Bride was blushing too.

And Georgia was staring with interest at the two of us. Moving to kneel beside the Bride, she untied her ankles and massaged them methodically. "Feel better?" she inquired.

"I think I'll survive."

Her tone was almost teasing. Apparently our guest no longer feared for her life.

Relieved, I said, "By the way, I'm Ellie."

"And I'm Caroline." The Bride solemnly shook my hand.

Georgia was actually smirking. "And I've got a date for the movies," she announced cheerfully.

I frowned at her. But she was already pulling on her Docs and leather jacket.

"You two have fun now," she added as she vanished out the door.

Her peremptory departure was accompanied by an odd popping sound, and turning, I found the Bride pouring champagne into two glasses.

"I don't get it," I said.

The Bride handed me a glass. "Georgia was telling me you don't have a girlfriend. She thinks there's no romance in your life."

My roommate had shared my most intimate secrets with a stranger she had kidnapped? I inhaled some bubbles and coughed.

"I have exactly the same problem," the Bride went on, ignoring my spluttering.

"You're about to marry it," I reminded her.

She laughed and sipped some more champagne. "Gee. You really haven't caught on, have you? Let's try those introductions again, shall we. I'm Caroline Simmons, Georgia's sister."

I stared. "Her sister?" The gorgeous overpaid *Best Brides* magazine 1992 centerfold who had destroyed Georgia's street-cred forever and whom I had secretly longed to meet? "You're the model?" My voice sounded squeaky. "And Randy . . ."

"My photographer."

I gulped the Bollinger. "And this . . ."

"Georgia's idea," she said, with a trace of embarrassment. "I think she hoped we might hit it off . . . I've been so depressed since Becky died."

"Becky? . . ." Her friend? Her lover? Georgia's sister was a lesbian. That much I knew.

"My dog," she supplied. "She was only eight years old. German shepherds usually live much longer."

I released the breath I was holding and studied her as she went on talking about her dog. I'd been set up. Georgia had decided I was the one who needed a girlfriend, and she had dreamed up this whole elaborate farce just to introduce me to her sister. Why? So that I would be caught unawares . . . maybe demonstrate some previously unsuspected strength of character?

Well, I had not exactly swept Caroline off her feet. In fact I hadn't even untied her for nearly half an hour. She was probably wondering what her sister thought we could possibly have in common. Anyway, I wasn't looking for another fling. I wasn't looking. Period.

Wondering how I could draw the evening to its least embarrassing conclusion, I returned my attention to the conversation. Caroline was talking about how hard it was to have a big animal in a city apartment. She seemed to think it was her fault somehow that the dog had died. That maybe it didn't get enough exercise and maybe she had compensated for her imagined neglect with too much food, literally killed the poor creature with kindness.

I felt uncomfortable listening to these revelations, ill at ease with the display of emotion. "But you loved her," I managed eventually. "Surely that's what really counts."

"Do you believe that?" She sounded wary. "Or are you just being polite?"

There was something beguiling about her; an innate hopefulness I guessed was the very quality that made real brides so appealing. And in that moment I was reminded of every calf that ever nuzzled my hand as we waited for the abattoir truck, of every horse shot or kitten drowned, of every reason I had ever found for not loving.

And I was silent.

She touched my hand. "Shall we make that moussaka?" she said.

Peace and Quiet

Jeane Harris

The first day the woman with the purple hair stepped off the huge Harley-Davidson with black leather saddlebags and shiny chrome pipes, Emma knew that no one had ever said to her: "Get a life." This saying had been her ex-lover Margaret's favorite and one that had often been directed at her. Even though they had broken up six months before, Margaret still said it to Emma frequently. Most recently she had said it when she found out that

Emma had been visiting her grandmother's grave at Forest Hill Cemetery every Saturday.

"That's pathetic," Margaret had said disgustedly. "Jesus, Em, why don't you get a life?"

Emma often pondered this question from the bench by the reflecting pool where she sat after visiting her grandmother's grave. She supposed that thinking about the meaning of one's own existence in a cemetery was natural enough. Sometimes she brought along a sandwich and as she ate and questioned whether she had a life — or at least one worth living — she watched people visit the graves of their relatives and friends. It had occurred to her that observing other people's private rituals of grief and remembrance might be considered insensitive.

Margaret called it "downright morbid and weird. It's about as weird as that Coke bottle you had engraved on her tombstone," Margaret said. "I can't believe you did that."

"She loved Coke," Emma pointed out. "It was her favorite thing in the world."

"Yeah, well, I still think it's bizarre."

"It's not bizarre," Emma insisted. "People in the South put all sorts of things on their tombstones — I've seen people put food, toys, articles of clothing. Some even put photographs of the deceased on their tombstone. As a matter of fact, putting gifts on the graves of the dead is a common practice in many cultures. Mexicans celebrate a holiday called The Day of the Dead where people picnic on the graves of their departed loved ones."

"You're lapsing into your reference librarian mode," Margaret warned her. "Anyway, I don't care what you say, engraving a Coke bottle on your grandmother's tombstone is weird."

"Look, I've seen one stone of a five-year-old boy that has a teddy bear engraved. My favorite is the woman who has an engraving of Elvis on her tombstone. You know, before being moved to Graceland, Elvis was interred at Forest Hill in a mausoleum. You should go down sometime and see for yourself."

"No thanks," Margaret had said. "I don't have time to hang out in cemeteries having picnics or looking at tombstones. I *have* a life."

Emma had been thinking about this conversation with Margaret when the woman's noisy arrival startled, then annoyed her. After all, it was a cemetery — a place where one expected a little peace and quiet. For Emma Rawlins, head research and reference librarian for the Tennessee State Library System, peace and quiet, order and stability, ritual and routine, were extremely important. Indeed, they were a way of life.

But even Emma had to admit that the woman's appearance was impressive. Black leather jacket. Faded jeans with the knees ripped out. Heavy black combat boots. Black leather .gloves. Ears pierced all the way around. Violet mascara.

Emma watched the woman climb off the Harley, stride purposefully down the row of tombstones and stop at a grave site. After standing motionless for a few moments, she reached inside her leather jacket, removed a bouquet of delicate pink roses. Then she gently placed the roses on the grave, sank to her knees, and crossed herself.

The actions were unexpectedly poignant and seemed so out of character for someone dressed in black leather and riding a Harley-Davidson that Emma felt tears well up. Even more surprising was when the woman hastily wiped her eyes with the back of her hand. And even though Emma could not be sure, she thought she saw the woman's lips move, as though she were talking to someone.

More than anything else, this gesture endeared her to Emma. Because even though she would never have admitted it to anyone, Emma often talked to her grandmother. She knew it was silly, perhaps even irrational, to talk to a tombstone, but she found it comforting.

Obviously other people, even people with purple hair, found it comforting too.

As the weeks passed, Emma observed the woman visit the grave as regularly as she visited her own grandmother's. Further, the woman's adherence to her ritual was as unvarying as Emma's own. Always on Saturday afternoon, always pink roses, always kneeling, and genuflecting.

Then, one day, instead of going to the grave with the roses, the woman headed directly for her. She stopped in front of Emma, blocking her view of the reflecting pool until her presence was impossible to ignore. Finally, Emma looked up into a pair of beautiful hazel-brown eyes fringed with thick long lashes that didn't need the heavy violet mascara. High cheekbones accentuated flawless skin flushed from either the wind or anger, though if the woman's belligerent posture was any clue, Emma would have guessed anger. As the seconds stretched into minutes, Emma felt her own face growing red from embarrassment.

"Can I help you?" Emma finally said. Her voice sounded squeaky and she cleared her throat.

"Yeah, I want to know why in the hell you're spying on me?" the woman demanded, and Emma noted her drawl was deep South — at least deeper than Tennessee.

"I have no idea what you're talking about," Emma said indignantly. "I don't even know you."

"Okay if I sit?" The woman pointed to the seat beside Emma.

Emma shrugged. "This is a public place. You can sit wherever you wish."

"Well, maybe spying's too strong. Could be I overreacted a little. I do that now and again." The woman sat down and put her helmet on the ground beside her. "Okay, why are you watching me?" She touched her spiky, purple-tinted hair. "It's the hair, right? You think it's too much?" Then she smiled — a sweet, self-deprecating smile with a hint of sadness that Emma found utterly beguiling.

"Actually, I'm used to it now," Emma said, returning her smile. "I admit when I first saw it, I was taken aback."

The woman laughed. " 'Taken aback'? That's good. I thought only people in nineteenth century novels or British PBS specials used that one." She held up her hand. "Yeah, I read. Even have a library card. Hey, I made a donation to PBS during their last pledge drive."

They became friends. Every Saturday after their separate rituals they sat and talked on the bench by the reflecting pool. She told Emma she was the lead guitar player for an all-dyke heavy metal band — Serpent's Tooth. Emma had been right about her accent — she was from Montgomery, Alabama and had moved to Memphis to take care of her eighty-nine-year-old grandmother who now lived in a nursing home. Emma talked about her own grandmother and the painful decision to put her in a nursing home after the final devastating stroke. They talked about movies, books and music. They disagreed about animal rights and argued about political correctness. They both liked hot dogs with yellow mustard and watching women's basketball. They hated exercise, shopping malls and golf. They admitted to a fondness for cribbage. The next visit and each Saturday after that, Emma brought her cribbage board and they played on the bench.

Then, one night after dinner Emma sat in her recliner-rocker, a book open but unread on her lap, and replayed their conversations, reviewing everything she knew about the woman. Suddenly, a great tenderness and affection washed over Emma as she thought about their friendship and she realized that she had fallen in love with the woman. Even more surprising and upsetting was that, although they had talked about many things, there was one thing she didn't know about the woman.

Her name.

The realization came as a shock. It was her job, indeed it was her nature, to doggedly research difficult, often extremely obscure questions, the answers to which most people didn't know or care about. What, she wondered, had she been calling the woman all these weeks? The worst part, Emma thought, was that she had no idea how to obtain the information now. How could she possibly admit to the woman that she had fallen in love with her but hadn't bothered to catch her name?

She racked her brain for ideas but, short of lifting the woman's driver's license — and since she had never seen her carry a purse or bag, she couldn't imagine how to accomplish this — she couldn't think of a ploy that would enable her to discover the woman's name.

The realization that she didn't know her name made Emma realize a few other oddities about the relationship: their entire relationship had been conducted in a cemetery, they had never had drinks or dinner together, never gone to a movie, never visited each other's home, never met each other's friends. Up to this point, it had seemed natural to Emma that their friendship was confined to the boundaries of the bench and reflecting pool. Now it seemed odd. More than odd, Emma thought. It was eerie.

The next Saturday Emma went to the cemetery early and, after putting the flowers on her grandmother's grave, she stood, looking down at her tombstone.

"I know we never talked about me being a lesbian, Grandma, but I know you always wanted me to be happy. I've finally met someone I think I can be happy with. I think you'd like her too — once you got past the packaging. I haven't told her I love her yet — I don't know what she'll say. Or if she even feels the same way. But I'm going to find out. Her name? Well, that's a problem. I don't know. But I'm going to find that out too." She looked around anxiously. "She should be here any minute."

Emma went to the bench, ate her lunch and waited for the woman to appear.

The sun was beginning to set and the air had turned chilly by the time Emma finally admitted to herself that the woman wasn't coming. She felt as though her chest were being crushed. She looked around a final time and stood up, feeling in her jacket pocket for her car keys.

Then a thought struck her.

She started off down the row of graves where she had observed the woman kneel and deposit her roses every week. Suddenly, Emma stopped as another disturbing thought occurred to her.

She had no idea whose tombstone she was looking for. She had never once thought to ask, nor had the woman ever volunteered, whose grave she was visiting.

Emma stood for a few moments as she pondered this lack of information. She did know the general vicinity of the grave, and she resumed walking and looking until she spied a grave that looked relatively recent. Sure enough, there on the mound of dirt was a bouquet of faded pink roses.

What she saw on the tombstone however made her heart nearly stop.

SAMANTHA PETERSON
FEBRUARY 16, 1963—JULY 1, 1993

Beneath the dates a photograph frame was encased in plastic. There was no mistaking the hair and black leather jacket — or the Harley Davidson engraved beneath the name.

It was her.

Emma's mind reeled. The woman she loved was dead — killed in an accident. She would never be able to tell her how much she loved her. Emma closed her eyes and fell to her knees, shock and disbelief flooding her.

The second thought that crashed into her mind was the date. July. It was now September. Two months had passed since the woman's death.

Impossible. She had sat on the bench with the woman every Saturday for weeks. They had talked, laughed, played cards, become friends. Those memories were real.

There were only two possible explanations, Emma knew. She was either crazy and had imagined the whole thing or — and this next realization was even crazier and to someone of Emma's disposition, totally ridiculous — she had met and fallen in love with a ghost.

Emma leaned closer to the grave and stared hard at the picture. There was absolutely no doubt. The smile was slightly lopsided, a little cocky. The dimple in the corner of her mouth. The smile she had grown to love.

A cold gust of wind blew a paper wrapper across Emma's knees, startling her. She stood up and looked around. The sun was below the level of the trees, and Emma became acutely aware of how far from the entrance she was. Trees which had seemed solidly comforting now loomed over her, casting ominous shadows over the graves. The cemetery no longer seemed a safe place, and Emma's heart began to race.

The woman was a ghost.

In the cemetery with the wind blowing and darkness beginning to close in around her, that possibility did not seem so ridiculous. The hair on the back of her neck prickled with fear. She buttoned up her jacket and began to fumble in her pocket for her car keys. She had to leave.

Because what had seemed terrifying to her only moments before — that she would never see the woman she loved again — now paled beside an even more terrifying possibility.

That she would.

She hurried down the row of tombstones, her feet scattering leaves across the graves. The air seemed abnormally still as she raced on, running now. Finally she saw the familiar outline of her car through the falling darkness.

She had reached the end of the row when she heard it. The low, throaty, unmistakable sound. Emma didn't need to look down the road to know what she would see, but she did and there it was.

The single bright headlight of a motorcycle.

Emma stood transfixed as the motorcycle pulled up beside her car. The black leather clad figure climbed off the bike and walked toward her. Beyond fear now, Emma stood motionless as the figure approached. She knew she should put her key in the door lock, scramble into the car as fast as she could and drive away without looking back.

But she didn't. Because in the glow of the headlamp she saw the woman she loved. She didn't look like a ghost at all. She was smiling and holding out her hand and it wasn't the skeletal claw Emma had feared. The hand she touched was warm and soft.

"Hi there," the woman said. "Sorry to be so late. I —" Emma watched her face as the happiness faded to be replaced by a worried frown. "What's up? You look like you've seen a ghost."

Emma's laugh was slightly hysterical and the story came tumbling out of her — everything she had thought and felt over the past two months. When she was finished, the woman put her arms around Emma and Emma could smell the pungent leather against her face.

"It's okay," the woman whispered. "I understand — I love you, too." She pulled away and held Emma's face in her hands. "My name's Amelia. Amelia Peterson. Samantha was my twin sister." A look of pain passed across her face, the grief still fresh. "She died of leukemia in July." She motioned to the motorcycle. "She loved her bike so I had it engraved on her tombstone."

"I thought —" Emma began.

"I know," Amelia said gently. "It's kind of funny, isn't it? Samantha and I — we were as close as two people can be. We always knew what the other one was thinking and I've got a feeling that somehow, somewhere, she's happy that at least something good has come out of her death."

Over Amelia's shoulder Emma saw the moon

rising through the bare branches of the trees and the peace and quiet of the cemetery no longer seemed ominous or threatening. She held Amelia closer.

"I know what you mean, darling," she said softly. "I think my grandmother feels the same way."

Better Than Having

Nikki Baker

The check-out clerk with the bad split-ends tied back in a big, pink, plastic barrette says, "That'll be seventeen dollars and ninety-two cents," and the woman in the mink opens up her purse. She pays twenty dollars cash in a crisp bill from a smooth brown wallet; and the clerk has to check the digital read-out at the top of the self-scanning register to make the right change.

"Paper, please," says the mink.

The bagger, a polite young man with broken skin snaps out a brown paper bag and begins to fill it.

Seventeen ninety-two for the pair of grocery store pantyhose, the box of frosted strawberry poptarts, and the bottle of wine, spaced out on the long black conveyer in front of the red plastic bar that differentiates her grocery store pantyhose from mine. I have, in addition to the pantyhose, a week's worth of groceries for my lover and me, all of the basic food groups. I have also bought, in bulk, whatever was two-for-one with a clipping from the weekly coupon flyer.

The coupons I keep hidden in my pocket as I can't imagine that a woman who wears her mink to the grocery store would value this economy and I would like in my own way to make a good impression. I have seen her before, last week, and the week before that, with her pantyhose and her poptarts, with her good bottle of wine. I do not imagine the mink cooks and can only believe that she has bought the cheap grocery store stockings as a back-up to carry in her purse in case of a run in her good silk hose on some important occasion, while I plan to wear my coarse, heavy nylons to work tomorrow. With her twelve dollar bottle of Chardonnay, she is a creature of indulgences. In her fur coat, she is an aficionado of selfish pleasures. This in itself may be part of her charm, as I cannot take my eyes off the sleek black animal hair cuffed around her wrist.

Two dollars and eight cents. The checker puts it down in the mink's flat palm without counting the change out backwards. The clerk lays the money down blankly in a green knot and the mink smooths the dirty bills in her small, French-manicured hand.

I think I would like to be that money. I would like to feel her smooth-palmed hand stroke me.

These weekly treats always happen on Sundays, my encounters with this tall, black woman in the full-length diamond mink coat hanging over her warm-up suit, as if to support my childhood notion that Sundays are somehow more special than other days.

When I was a girl, Sundays were early morning services, hymns and pennies from my father placed in a flat tarnished dish, smooth wooden pews, and visits by distant relations. Sundays were stockings and hats, and the smell of pressed hair, heavy dinners eaten at three o'clock in the afternoon, and the rattle of my father's papers in the front room of our tract house. The ritual of homework, that had lain neglected all weekend, done frantically under the hard face of my mother at night.

Sunday is still a day for thick newspapers and ritual. The ritual is this woman in her mink, my having left my lover curled up in the warmth of our bed to go off to the grocery store when the sky is barely light, and the air so cold that your lungs shudder to suck it in. The coffee and the newspapers will come later.

"Why do you have to go there so early all the time," my lover asks. She is sleepy-eyed. She is a night person, not really herself until sometime past noon. This is one of the many things I know about her, along with her birthday and her favorite color, along with the sounds she makes when we make love. This dysfunction she has in the mornings has become a point of familiar tension.

"Gotta go early," I tell her. "The produce is fresher. And there aren't any crowds at the check-out." I say, "The baggers aren't as busy and they can be more careful with the eggs."

She grunts at this logic and rolls over, tucking her knees to her chest and wrapping her arms around the cat. We have had this conversation before; and we will have it again, next Sunday. Not a fight really, just a reaffirmation that with the passing week we are still, both of us, exactly who we were the week before. She is. I am. We are filled with our certainty.

But there is a seductive question mark behind every detail of this woman at the grocery store. Maybe this is her charm more even than her showy opulence, more than her beauty (although there is that too), that I don't know a single other thing about her beyond her mink coat and her pantyhose, her poptarts, her wine, and the fancy black car in which she comes and goes to the grocery store (the only place where I have ever seen her). It is never even certain that she will be there at the Jewell Store, that she hasn't varied her routine somehow, slept in with some sleep-over date, taken a vacation; and my skin prickles on the way through the electric doors in the store lobby until I finally spot her in some aisle. On the weeks when she isn't there, I miss her, feeling cheated. I wonder where she is and with whom, although it's hard to imagine, given so little information about what she does out of context.

When my lover and I were fresh and new I used to wonder about her in this vaguely jealous way, where she was when she wasn't with me, what she was doing and when I might see her. Now, seeing my lover again seems near certainty, knocking on wood, barring some freak accident going to or from our places of work. And I look for the woman in the mink on Sundays the way the faithful look for Mary at Lourdes. This winter, she is my church. She is my new Madonna, the mink lady of the grocery store with her flat-top, Philly chop, the dark lady of my everyday sonnets, glimpsed by seconds in the aisle of the Jewell grocery store at the corner of Southport and Addison Streets. Her face is shades and shadows, melting into the bronze of her cheeks and the warm orange, red, of her painted lips. It stops my breath in wonder to see her perfectly painted lips so early on a Sunday morning, at a time when my lover can barely steady her hand to hold a coffee cup.

At an hour when my lover's eyes are certainly little slits, the mink's black eyes are big and wide, ringed by mysterious circles, darker than her coffee skin, inky, heavy sun-guard where years of days have tanned her face unevenly behind her chic, rimless glasses. There is a soft, cool light behind her eyes when by some rare chance they rise above the top of her grocery cart to connect with mine. On these occasions sometimes we speak, as our two carts pass in the narrow grocery aisle, and I thrill to the odd *frottage* of metal brushing metal.

She is so close I believe I can feel the heat of her body even through the heavy fur, and smell the cologne she is wearing as it travels through the space of her open coat. I can imagine the feel of her painted lips.

"Excuse me," she says.

"Yes, excuse me." I fumble and smile, dancing awkwardly with my cart, eyes raised and then dropped away from her gaze. She finds the right angle suddenly and passes, eyes away from me, smiling now at the floor, her fur coat always trailing behind her like a dead heavy cape. I am thinking, one day she might stop her cart long enough to talk to me.

One Sunday morning. She will forget her pantyhose or her poptarts; her expensive bottle of wine will be confused on the check-out conveyor with my economy brand and I will have to go after her, running perilously over the ruts of ice in the parking lot out to the big black German car she drives. In the cold, in my little cloth and down parka, I'll knock on the passenger window and she will look across the seat with her cool black eyes as the window comes down with the sound and magic of electricity. She will be smiling her grocery aisle smile, lips parted and her breath making pale smoke in the frozen air, her hand hung out the window to take whatever it is I have brought her. The pantyhose, the poptarts. Her fingers feeling cool. My hands are damp and she says something. Her name?

She says, "Get in," and opens the door. She says, "Get in and hurry," and pulls me towards her across the camel-colored leather seat.

"Close your eyes," she says. "That's right."

Her mouth is warm and all her weight bears down against me. Her heavy coat falls over us like a blanket.

All this some Sunday, while my lover sleeps.

Or perhaps, I think, it will happen in the

produce aisle. Near the hot house tomatoes. Under the fluorescent lights. Across the bunches of crisp green onions, our hands will meet. Maybe in the cereal aisle we will reach for the same box of frosted poptarts.

There is something comforting in these fantasies about the grocery store woman in the big coat. The odd aching pleasure of senseless covet that can make fiction seem so much better than fact. The security that the woman in the grocery store and I will never quarrel. Never part, never cease to care for one another in my dreams. She will never leave me for someone else or need my unconditional support to get through whatever it is she is working out in therapy. She will never demand or expect — or lie at home on these Sunday mornings keeping the sheets warm for me and hugging my cat.

The grocery store woman's smooth hand folds around her change and the other drops to the clasp of her purse, fishes out a billfold again slowly enough for a word. As she hunts for the billfold deep in her bag, there is a space wide enough for the start of a conversation, if I wanted, while the bagger holds out her purchases for her and the checker begins to ring up mine. But instead, I look down at my watch and back up again and the woman in the mink is smiling at me, a vague smile for a familiar stranger.

I smile back.

"Come again," the bagger says to her.

I will, next Sunday morning.

Winning Tennis for Women

Hilary Mullins

My father and I have never agreed on much. Even back in high school, I was used to side-stepping his advice.

"Get yourself into positions of leadership, Lynn," he'd say. "Run the school newspaper, test your mettle. You could be the next Barbara Walters."

Or: "Learn tennis. It's a great thing to do on

dates. And it's the only sport you can learn from a book."

I never did make a move to seize control of the school paper and only played tennis twice during my entire high school career, both times with a quiet classmate named Todd who later beat me out of the closet by five years. To this day I harbor a secret aversion to Barbara Walters.

But one day, a couple of summers ago, right after I came out — a virginal baby dyke at the ripe age of twenty-five — I started having second thoughts about my dad's counsel. At least part of it.

I was working at the local food co-op that summer, partly because it's the closest thing to dyke central in our town. On the day in question, I'd been over in the bulk section all morning, filling the old tofu tubs to the brim with shiny hard beans and little stubby pieces of rice. Of course I'd noticed when Amanda came in, but suddenly she was walking right towards me, looking spiffy in her faded green cut-off shorts and hot pink tank top. The top of my head started zinging but I told myself she was probably heading for the big barrel of brewer's yeast behind me — we weren't really friends or anything though I had been crushed out on her for months. But no, Amanda stopped right in front of me, a big smile opening her face. My insides reeled.

"How you doing, Lynn," she said.

"Can't complain," I said. For the moment, it was true.

"You play tennis?" she asked.

"Sure," I said. Yeah, right.

"You want to play Wednesday?"

"Sure," I said and nodded, bending down to pick

up the next bag. On my way up, clutching the big open sack, I looked right at her, saw the line of her collar bone, her broad shoulders accented by the pink band of her shirt crossing them. Then our eyes met, and I just about lost ten pounds of garbanzo beans on the floor right there. I set the bag back on the floor, wiped my hands on my pants to stall for time. Amanda stood there smiling with a red shopping basket in one hand, pencil and scrap of paper for writing prices in the other. She didn't look nervous at all.

"I'll meet you over at North Beach Park, all right? Ten o'clock okay?"

"Yeah, that would be great. Yeah sure." I pushed my purple cap up off my forehead and tried to smile. She smiled back, the corners of her mouth crinkling. Then she walked off down the aisle. I went back to my buckets, trying to look hard at work but keeping a keen eye on her green and pink form as she went around the store. The way she looked up-close kept coming back to me in flashes — that great smile of hers with the little dents in her cheeks, the grey-blue of her eyes, those sturdy arms and her sweet little breasts molded under her tank top. I kept feeling the same tingling I'd just felt looking at her broad bared shoulders, the way I had wanted to draw my hands along them and down her sides and keep going. Inside I was just straining for the chance, pulsing towards her.

It was almost too exciting to bear, these full-bodied bursts I felt around Amanda. Up until five or six months ago I hadn't even admitted to myself I could feel that way at all. Being with men had made this pose more or less easy to maintain,

but coming out had blown my cover. I wanted girls.
I wanted them bad. And I wanted Amanda in
particular. I wanted her so much that my wanting
seized me whole, shaking me through my gut and
down into my thighs, firing the long-defended core
between my legs.

I headed for the stock room, rocking a big bag of
organic brown rice off the shelf. It was so
crazy-making to feel this way — the adrenalin
coursing through my body like a geyser lifting the
top of my head. If I didn't watch myself, I was liable
to come on to this woman spewing like Old Faithful.
The weight of the rice bag settled into my arms and
my knees bent with the load as I walked, hugging
it, out to the bulk section. Up at the front of the
store, I saw Amanda heading for the door, one arm
wrapped around a grocery bag. I stopped, watching
her go, and the tingling started again, churning,
churning. Then she was gone.

I bent down to the bag, swift, yanking on the
thick string to open it, and heaved the bear of a
thing up. The rice poured out, rattling off the sides
of the white plastic bucket. Maybe, I thought, I
should try a little creative sublimation, channel some
of this crazy energy into bringing my tennis game
up to speed. Yeah, that was it. That would chill me
out. And besides, Amanda knew I had only been out
a little while — and who wanted to look like an
amateur at everything?

When I got off later that afternoon, I rode my
big blue bike to the library, found the book I

needed, and pedaled furiously home to my lesbian group house, precious cargo bouncing in my pack. Plunking down at the kitchen table with a tall glass of iced tea, I pulled the book out and turned it over to see *Winning Tennis for Women* stamped into the dark green spine with bright gilded lettering. This ostentatious 70's guide, as it turned out, was written by some famous coach, an older woman who used to run camps for budding stars. I leafed through, checking out the photos that showed white women dressed in white tennis clothes in various poses: serve, forehand, backhand. Geesh, all that white. But it didn't look that hard. I went to the front of the book and glanced through the table of contents. It listed headings like: Serve, Return of Serve, Strokes, Female Considerations, Playing Singles, Playing Doubles. This game was beginning to look more erotic than I had ever given it credit for — obviously what my father had been getting at when he talked about dates.

Taking gulps of my honey-sweet tea, I started taking notes in the house notebook, writing down every sentence that said something important I would need to remember. After a couple of hours and three glasses of iced tea, I had transcribed a page of everything I would ever need to play winning tennis. It went something like this:

Not being powerhorses, women often concentrate on technique and finesse. Keep your serves simple and serve to the other player's weakness. Control is more important than power and depth is more important than speed. Always be in a ready position for return of service, and remember to turn and follow through in a stroke but not in a volley — with a volley you have to get in close. This means you must never stand still or retreat. Be sure to use your knees to go up and down and don't forget to use your backhand as well as your forehand; you need them both to play! Once you start to get your game down, you will have the experience known as "feel." This happens when your serves, strokes and volleys are all connecting just right and you become conscious of a tingling sensation all through your body.

Wednesday morning, after a few evenings of practice at the backboard with a thirteen-year-old racket and a slobber-faded ball I'd stolen from our neighbor's dog, I was sitting on a big boulder by the tennis courts, bike propped next to me. I was a little early but not as early as I would have been without the clothing crisis I'd had getting ready. Finally I'd settled on my black gym shorts with the Lambda symbol, topping them off with the latest women's shelter benefit T-shirt, light purple to go with the darker purple cap I wore twisted around to complete the look.

I wanted to seem cool as I sat there waiting, arms folded over my chest, but I was nearly sick with excitement. What did I really think I was doing? I barely knew this woman. What if she wasn't attracted to me at all and was just looking for a little tennis? Would I be able to keep my cool? Or what if she really did want me? Would I be able to keep my cool then? I gritted my teeth against the seething, this excitement that didn't know the first place to start. When I was with boys I had always let them figure out how to get the ball rolling. Most of them seemed to prefer that arrangement, whether they said so or not. But how did girls do it? This was like being fifteen all over again. Was I supposed to wait for Amanda to make the first move? Or was I supposed to take the lead? And then what? What?

I shook my head furiously. Christ, here I was obsessing about what we were going to do in bed, and we hadn't even gotten on the court yet. Looking up, I saw Amanda's red Toyota truck coming towards me, skimming along the blacktop. Every single thought tumbled into a washing machine spin of excitement as I bounded down from the rock and towards the parking lot. Then I stopped a little short, maybe twenty feet away. Amanda swung out of the cab, looking great in a faded red T-shirt and white shorts. Wonder of wonders, she was smiling widely at me. Something in my chest went spr-oing.

"Hey!" she said.

"Hey," I said smiling back, my palms suddenly damp. I shifted my racket from hand to hand as we walked to the court side bench and could barely look at her as she pried up the lid on a brand new can of tennis balls. The last thing I'd bought in a can like that was potato chips.

"Wanna just hit it back and forth for a while?" she called, walking out on the court. I nodded and got set, watching as the ball she whacked lofted towards me. It seemed to hang in mid-air for the longest time, a bright whirling orb, but then suddenly it was zinging over to the right. I swung and missed.

"Shit!" I whirled around to see where the damn thing had gone.

"Don't worry about it; I'm rusty too!" I turned back towards Amanda, who was grinning at me. If she only knew just how rusty I really was. I squinted in the bright morning sun, trying to remember the tennis notes I'd taken, but my mind had gone blank, the entire litany evaporated like the last inch of water in a boiling pot. I yanked my hat back around forwards and waited for the next ball, swearing I would at least make contact.

Which I did with a hard whomp, but the ball veered up towards the sky, glancing off the fence three feet over Amanda's head. I cringed.

"Sorry!" I still couldn't look at her right on.

"Hey, you don't have to apologize." Amanda was walking backwards towards the line. She hadn't stopped smiling.

But in spite of Amanda's seemingly good humor, it was hard not to apologize repeatedly over the next half hour. Playing with a partner was a whole other game from the solitary sport I'd been engaging in; it had been much easier to connect with volleys from my own hand than it was to gauge Amanda's shots spinning towards me. Somehow I couldn't line my body up right to make smooth hits the way she could. Instead I was swinging the racket like it was a baseball bat, over-hitting when I did manage to collide with a ball. My shots went everywhere; I even had to retrieve a few balls that flew out over the fence.

Every time I looked over at Amanda she was grinning and didn't seem to mind. But I was sure she was just being polite and that I had blown it. What had I been thinking anyway? Maybe you could learn tennis from a book, but you sure as hell couldn't get good at it in three days. It didn't matter that I'd had my tennis notes nearly memorized — I wasn't remembering them now in the heat of the moment and it was obvious that it was the years of practice that really counted anyway. If only I had heeded my father's words back in high school! I'd be wowing her. Instead I had exposed my true inexperience. Shaking my head, I swiped at a ball gliding in low and felt the crunch up my arm as my racket scraped hard into the court surface.

That was enough. I trotted up to the net. Amanda looked surprised for a moment and then walked up to meet me on the other side of the sagging green weave. I couldn't tell if my face was beginning to burn from the sun or if it was a blush scalding my cheeks.

"Look Amanda, I lied. I can't play this game. I got this tennis book out of the library and tried to practice up, but it's no use, I'm really lousy. I'm sorry."

"You took a book out of the library? About tennis?" Amanda started to laugh.

I nodded. "My dad always told me tennis is the only sport you can learn from a book."

Amanda was still laughing. "I can't believe this! What was it, everything you always wanted to know about tennis?" She dropped her racket, still laughing. "Oh god, that's great!" She slapped her leg and bent down to pick up her racket. On her way back up, our eyes met, and for the first time I looked, really looked at her, her face still rippling with laughter, and I saw that her grin was for me, her eyes reflecting back in mine some kind of recognition.

"We don't have to keep playing if you don't want to," she said.

"Oh, well, if you really don't mind, I, uh —" My voice trailed off.

"You want to just go for a walk?"

Had I heard right? I'd been distracted, registering her actual interest in me. Then I thought of what would be really fun.

"You want to go out in the canoe?" I didn't have to explain what canoe. Every girl in town knew that our house, perched up above the lake, kept a canoe lashed to a tree down at the tiny stretch of beach below. We paddled out all the time in the summer, landing at a huge flat-topped boulder we called "Dyke Rock" to sunbathe and skinny dip.

Amanda's head was bobbing up and down. It was settled. We gathered up the balls and walked back out to the truck. Amanda unlocked the door.

"You want to just ride with me on the bike path?" My voice came out small, but Amanda was turning towards me, nodding her head some more.

"Only if I get to pedal!" A teasing edge ran through her voice.

Who was I to argue? We tossed our rackets into her truck and she swung her leg over the crossbar of my bike. I clambered up on the seat behind her and we pushed off, wobbling along the park road until Amanda turned onto the bike path that runs high along the bluff, overlooking the lake.

"Wheeeeee!" Amanda whipped her head up, strands of the thick black hair that usually clustered

around the back of her neck blowing around in front
of me like a field of dark grass. She was picking up
speed. I moved my hands forward around her to get
a good hold as we surged back and forth, and
suddenly up through me flooded a moment of perfect
feeling, coloring everything sweet and filling my
chest as I hung on to her pumping hips. Blue sky
and sweeping motion washed over us. Amanda
pedaled, whooping.

    The canoe was lying to one side when we
reached it. I deftly twirled its combo lock open and
grabbed one end to drag it along the sand to the
water. We got her launched relatively smoothly,
Amanda up front, me pushing off and pulling myself
up and in. Then we were paddling together in
unison, wooden blades dipping in and out, and I
realized it wasn't so hard being around this woman
after all. Just had to get in a kind of rhythm. Still,
we didn't talk much as we stroked our way out into
the lake, heading south for the shore out past the
inlet. After about ten minutes, the rock emerged
from the shoreline, growing bigger as we glided
towards it.
    "Welcome to Dyke Rock!" I hopped from rock to
rock ahead of Amanda, the beached canoe behind us,
and hauled myself up the side of the boulder with
well-known foot and hand holds.
    "God, it's gorgeous here!" Amanda pulled herself
up and stood beside me, hands on her hips, looking
out over the water towards the Adirondacks, almost
smokey blue with the distance.

"Yeah." Suddenly I was nervous again. "You want to swim?"

"Sure!" She immediately started peeling off her shirt.

Christ! I turned and lifted my own shirt up over my head. Then, still turned, I stripped off my shorts and dove straight out, my body lifted momentarily up in the air and then crashing down into the water, bubbles erupting out of my mouth and streaming out alongside of me. Then another crash, this one above me, and Amanda's body soared past me in a blur through the water. My head popped up into air and I treaded water, spitting. Amanda's head broke surface a few feet away.

"This is great!" I could tell she really meant it because the words came out fast and fresh. What could I do but smile back, hoping it would show I felt the same way?

I swam back into shore, pulled myself back up the rock and sat down, legs drawn up. Next thing I knew, Amanda was sitting next to me. Little shadows of wet pooled out around our dripping bodies.

Christ, now what? Amanda was so close to me that it made my skin prickle. She sat relaxed on the rock, her elbow barely grazing my rib, her skin bared to the sun. Without really seeming to look I could appreciate the long stretch of her legs, the sculpted under-curve of her breast. The tingling started in my arms, burrowing down into my crotch. What would it feel like to press my lips to hers? The thought turned the tingling into a dull roar, broke the simmering between my legs into a roil. I had to do something! But what? Should I just take her arm, bend her down to the rock? I took another glance at her sideways, saw her squinting slightly with the sun, her forehead wrinkled as she looked out over the lake, a drop of water ambling down the side of her face. My crotch was coming to a full boil, and I shifted on the rock. What to do?! What to do?! And then the words came back to me, twirling up from the bottom like frog eggs turned into tadpoles. *Not being powerhorses, women often concentrate on technique and finesse.*

Hey, that was probably right! You didn't have to overwhelm a girl like a lot of bozo boys thought you had to. I knew nothing shut me down quicker. I opened my eyes, felt the words rising up in me again. *Keep your serves simple...*

Oh yeah, that would work too. I cleared my throat and took the leap. "I'm wondering what it would be like to kiss you."

Amanda swiveled around, arms still around her knees, her mouth open, half, it seemed, in surprise, half with a smile that looked like welcome to me. She leaned towards me and then everything was the color of her skin and her mouth was on mine, warm and wet and pushing against me. The tightening swell between my legs shuddered, some little noise escaping up out of me. Amanda pulled back and I saw her eyes, blue flecked with yellow underneath, not really grey at all. She was so close and she was looking at me, her mouth still slightly open, everything in her face soft.

"Can we do that some more?" I asked. I saw her smile open wide, but then everything was a blur as she bent into me again. My hands went reaching for her and I caught her side, reeling with the sheer drunkenness of it all, taking her in as her tongue flickered against my lips. My tongue took her cue and came dancing out to play, gently prodding Amanda's mouth open and then I was inside, darting back and forth. I could feel Amanda's little grunts shouldering their way through the thicket of our tongues.

She seemed to like this part so I did just what the book had told me, serving again and again to her weakness, running my tongue wild through her mouth until she was hanging onto me, letting her head ride back further and further. I lowered her down onto the rock, tongue still furious inside her, her hands reaching up to take me behind the neck. *Control is more important than power...* I adjusted to a more subtle side-to-side pattern, and ran my hand over Amanda's side and down her hip, trying to listen through her damp skin with my fingers and then felt it, the quivering building up in her. ... and depth is more important than speed. I slowed then, moving my still-swirling tongue deeper as if I were reaching for something down her throat and into her gut. My ears roared with her jagged breathing.

Then she rolled out from under me, the seal between our mouths giving way. She was looking at me, her breathing still hard, and she reached a hand up and ran her fingers down my side and up again, skimming lightly over my breasts, lingering at each nipple. *Always be in a ready position for return of service...* I lay down on the rock next to her, letting her hands roam the length of me, first brushing my cheekbones and then caressing the hollow of my throat, circling my breasts again and moving down, grazing the kinky hair piled at the crook of my legs. Then I felt her cool palm nudging at my thighs, a smooth circling round and up, a finger that slid in across my lips and out. *... and remember to turn and follow through in a stroke ...* I rolled towards her, my legs opening for her hand reaching in, grasping the cheek of my butt and then sliding forward through my wet. Then she was rolling my clit in her fingers, and sounds were breaking up out of me that I had never heard before, noises from a thing so ripe and good it had to be shared. I wiggled a hand under her arm, and prodded my way up through the clasp of her thighs. *... with a volley you have to get in close. This means you must never stand still or retreat.* My own clit throbbing in Amanda's hand, I inched a little closer to her, hand parting her stiff hair, lightly spreading her lips.

"You don't have to do that —" she protested, but said nothing more as my fingers found the little knob of skin, moving with the same pulse she had started on me. Her mouth fell open, and she was moaning now, her head moving back and forth on the rock. She was so beautiful and my cunt was rocking in her hand like a great engine.

Be sure to use your knees to go up and down ... I moved my hand up further, entering her to the sound of her gasp. And still her fingers gripped me, moving. Her insides were wet and clung to my fingers and I pushed from my feet, using my knees to ride up and down inside her, her cunt a cradle for the insistent rocking of my hands. It was like being back on the bike again, that same surging; it was like the cadence of our stroking through the water. Like all that but better, so much deliciously better. Something was dripping down my thigh.

. . . and don't forget to use your backhand as well as your forehand; you need them both to play! I drew my hand out, sticky with her juices and reached around, sliding my hand down her crack and finding her clit from the backside. Amanda's breathing caught in her throat as I started a steady back and forth massaging of that swollen part, but her own hand never faltered in its steady beat on me. I bent over her, finding the same rhythm and the pace quickened between us, the crescendo building in my body like a windstorm. My blood was blowing up, rushing all through me, seizing and shaking me, forcing strange language from my lips. On my hand I felt some giant squeezing rushing through Amanda and I clung to her like a coon to a tree in a storm, shaking, shaking, until the wind had subsided and we both had landed back on the sun-warmed surface of the rock.

"Oh God, girl!" Amanda turned towards me, an abashed smile glowing on her face, "you're a regular pro! That book you read must have been *The Joy of Lesbian Tennis!*"

I laughed, my insides still jelly, and leaned over to kiss her on the cheek. "Only sport you can learn from a book!"

The Light of Day

Lee Lynch

Trudy was retired now and Connie, at sixty-three, had only one year, two hundred and eighteen days until she stopped supervising her clerks at the accounting firm. This March business had all started back in January.

"They need a million people at the March On Washington," Trudy had said with zeal, reading from a flyer their women's bookstore had sent. Trudy was stretched out on the couch in her sweats, resting between assaults on the snow in their driveway. "Let's go for it."

"You sound like your skate-boarding great-nephew," Connie, looking over her half-glasses, commented with some distaste.

Trudy had laughed, made an airplane of the flyer and, sailing the plane at the cat, replied, "It's bound to be an awesome experience."

Now they were on a crowded Amtrak traveling through the gritty back side of what seemed like every industrial city on the east coast. Four cities so far, Connie counted. She leaned over her knitting to peer down the aisle and groan. "No one's going to believe we're headed for the Smithsonian. Not in this rolling gay bar." Earringed men and crew-cut women occupied every seat she could see.

"Nobody cares any more," Trudy assured her, leaning over to nuzzle her cheek. The train rushed through a tunnel. Trudy tucked in a fallen strand of coiled deep brown hair. She was a thin, smiling woman, the kind of gym teacher who made sports fun even for the awkward girls.

Trudy's nuzzle in public infuriated Connie. Had retirement made Trudy forget consequences? "Nobody cares? Nobody but Ralph Smith, senior partner at work, who came back from the Republican convention last year proud of the anti-gay platform. No one but Gary Dunston, Vice President, who calls Clinton *that faggot-lover*. It's my pension at stake here."

Trudy grabbed two balls of yarn, one yellow, one pale blue, and tried to juggle them. "They'd never believe an old knitter like you had it in you to be gay." The balls were attached to the emerging sweater and Trudy somehow wrapped the blue one around her wrist.

"That's my only hope," was Connie's dry comment as she grabbed Trudy's wrist and deftly untangled the yarn. "What a mess you've made."

The train was electric, smooth and quiet except for the passengers' surges of excited talk. The sun felt soothing through the window. Connie imagined the tulips that would be blooming all over the capitol. She'd start planting next weekend, after they'd satisfied Trudy's wanderlust, or whatever this trip was all about. Someone walked by with lunch from the club car and she got a quick whiff of hot coffee. The train stopped and she craned her neck as passengers cheered more gay people aboard.

"Look at us all," whispered Trudy an hour later, after a walk from one end of the car to the other. She had arthritis in her back and preferred wandering and chatting to sitting. Her voice was thick. Connie checked, and yes, her sentimental lover was near tears. They were so different that she often wondered why in the world she loved Trudy so intensely. "It's as if we know these people," Trudy said, accepting a tissue. "Like we're one big family, children and all. We *look* alike, for Pete's sake."

"Oh, come on, Trudy. I don't even have one pierced ear, much less three holes in each."

Trudy fingered her own earlobes, a speculative look on her face. "Maybe I'll find a jewelry store. Wouldn't my old students be surprised?"

"Maybe the March will have booths like those women's festivals we read about. You can get it done right there." She teased Trudy. "Put six or seven little pink triangles in for all the world to see."

Trudy lifted an eyebrow and got a daring look in her eye. She murmured, "And then we can go get married!"

Connie had a grumpy grunt that announced disapproval. "If you want to be part of that mass marriage, maybe we need finger rings, not earrings."

A couple about their age struggled down the aisle with luggage. One of the pair caught Connie's eye and grinned. Connie nodded briefly, then returned to her knitting. Trudy, she noted with relief, was absorbed in some scene out the window. Trudy was forever trying to make friends of every lesbian who stumbled into their lives.

When they reached Union Station she was shocked. Smiling greeters welcomed the mob of gay people, handing out schedules. Outside, in the warm wind, Trudy waved for a cab. Several gay men who'd been ahead of her stepped back and let them have the first cab that stopped. At the Holiday Inn there was a line of gays, small rainbow flags in hand, waiting to register. After receiving their keys, Trudy and Connie squeezed into the elevator, then trudged along the seventh floor hall behind two chattering couples, one in leather.

Connie leaned against the inside of their door and exhaled the trip. "I'm exhausted." The small room had a deodorized motel smell, but she felt safely anonymous here.

Trudy whistled as she snapped open her suitcase and shook out her clothing. "Then take a nap, honeybunch, 'cause *There'll be a gay time in the old town tonight!*" Trudy's singing tended to make up in volume what it lacked in melody.

Connie groaned. "After thirty-two years, five-and-a-half months, I should have known. Why couldn't I have picked a type Z personality?"

Trudy rushed at her and gently laid Connie back onto the bed. "Because," she said between kisses, "you think I'm irresistible."

"Stop that, you beast!" cried Connie. She laughed so hard she knocked Trudy's glasses askew and kissing was out of the question.

That night they stood in another line, jackets zipped against the cooling wind. Paper trash scratched along the gutters. Trudy licked ice cream as they moved toward the huge auditorium where gay choruses would perform. Overhead, plane after plane rumbled into the city, visibly jouncing in the wind.

"Ferrying in the troops!" Trudy announced to everyone around them.

Embarrassed, Connie wondered, *Is her hearing going,* though she knew it wasn't. "Remember the time we went to the Gay Pride March in Boston?" she whispered, rubbing her arms for warmth.

"The time you wouldn't march, just wanted to look? And snuck around corners like a spy out of *Mad Magazine*?"

"There were cameras everywhere and you know it. You never would have seen the inside of a high school gym again."

"Want a taste of my ice cream?"

"Of course." Connie delicately bit into the thin chocolate crust and patted her lips with a tissue.

She liked to be careful of her weight. "What I was trying to say was that I think this crowd waiting in line is as big as that whole march."

Trudy looked at her. "I would hope so. That was nineteen seventy-seven."

Connie took a second taste of Trudy's ice cream and held the cold vanilla against the roof of her mouth. "No, it was 'seventy-eight."

"And this is the first time I've gotten you to a march since then. Look at all these wonderful people!" Trudy went on. "The baby dykes in gym classes all over America never have to be afraid again."

Connie shook her head. "You know that's not true."

"Maybe not, but tonight no one has to be scared, honey." Trudy reached for her hand.

Her stomach clenched and she pulled away. "I can't, Trude."

"Not even in the Emerald City?" joked Trudy.

She heard the feeling-rejected note Trudy was trying to hide. "After I get my pension."

"But who's going to see you?"

Someone had once told her that love was a series of compromises, but safety wasn't negotiable. "We're in Washington, D.C., Trudy. Isn't this where they record everything they don't videotape? Isn't this the home of the F.B.I. and the C.I.A. and who knows what else? You know there are people who want to hurt us."

"It's our time, honey! What do those kids say?" Trudy raised her voice and looked around. "We're here, we're queer — get used to it!"

A small cheer went up in response.

"I can't believe you just did that."

The laughter was gone from Trudy's voice. "I'm telling you, they can't hurt us anymore. We won't let them."

Inside the auditorium at last, Connie admitted to herself that there was something moving about being among one's own. About knowing those were homosexuals like herself in the choruses on stage. Her ire rose as the music soared. From where she sat the singers looked tiny and vulnerable. How could beings making such celestial sounds possibly be the horrid creatures their enemies claimed they were?

She wanted to cry at the beauty of those gay voices that seemed to pour into her like warmth in winter, like water in a desert, like love after loneliness. Why did she often feel lonely? She had Trudy. Still, just the two of them all these years — had that been enough? Trudy had brought home a few other couples, but it always worried her — who would new friends tell? The friendships would be desperately intense for a while, the needs of four women converging like these voices. They'd exhaust themselves and retreat, feeling like a battle had been fought. Then, years of peaceful quarantine would follow before they threw themselves into another frenzy of companionship.

Tonight, as they'd waited for the futuristic disks of light on the Metro platform to blink for an incoming train, everyone had wanted to talk to them. In the packed cars people had smiled in greeting, wearing suits and ties or jeans and T-shirts, gowns and make-up or baseball caps and fatigues. On the escalators up to the street they chanted, "Ho, Ho, Hey, Hey, We Are in the PTA!" This was the largest family reunion in the history of the world. She felt no loneliness. A million people were expected and by her sense of numbers, on which she prided herself, they were already here with more coming every minute.

Although the urge to cry continued, she realized with a shock that she felt no fear. She sat stock-still as the singers insisted that she hope. She probed her psyche. No panic here, no anxiety there, not a hint of paranoia. She tried scaring herself with thoughts of enemy cameras, but could only believe every lens she saw to be benign, its operator as excited as she felt. It was nothing but habit that made her use her jacket for cover when she slipped her hand into Trudy's.

She felt naked without her fear.

Outside, in the windy southern night, as gay people streamed around them on the street, Trudy took her arm and led her into shadow. She heard the newborn leaves rustle as they clung to weathered branches. "I want to ask you something, hon." Trudy's eyes were dark and serious, her voice earnest. "And if your answer is yes, you'll have to stick with it even in the light of day or I'll be one disappointed old woman."

"Is something wrong?"

"No, it's right." Her crazy lover knelt, despite her arthritic back. "It's always been right and I want to tell that to the world tomorrow at the Wedding. Will you marry me?"

Connie groped for her fear, always somewhere in the air, like a hovering guardian angel ready to protect her. Had it flung a feather boa over its

wings and rushed off to Dupont Circle to party with
the rest of the crowd? It was vapor when she tried
to grab it. "Yes," she said, quickly, before the fear
returned. She felt like a supplicant who'd been cured
and cast her crutches aside. She held tight to
Trudy's arm all the way back to the hotel.

The light of the next day *was* startling. Connie
lay curled around her fear on her bed, unwilling to
open her eyes. Where was the weightlessness she'd
experienced last night? Now the word *Wedding* felt
like an iron bar through her lungs. She could not
draw a full breath. She clenched the blanket in her
fists. Would the Wedding be televised? It was one
thing to be gay — but in broad daylight? The whole
idea of marriage had to do with witnesses. She'd
always feared witnesses.

Trudy sprang upright in the other bed whistling
"The Wedding March." "How's my bride-to-be?" she
asked, leaning over to nest her fingers in Connie's
permed grey curls.

She rubbed against Trudy's warm fingertips.
Everything about Trudy was right. Even the roguish
twelve-year-old's spirit that often exasperated Connie.
Trudy had asked little enough over a lifetime.

"You were right," said Connie. She'd been about
to blurt the truth of her fear in the light of day, but
she couldn't stand to see the uncertainty in Trudy's
eyes. Instead she said, "It would have been cheating
to make love last night."

Trudy strode in her handsome burgundy pajamas
to the curtains and let in the sunlight. "Our wedding
day," she told the loud streets of the city, her own
voice hushed. She turned. "I've always wanted to
marry you."

"You have?"

"Ring, aisle, rice, the whole shebang, honey. Both of us proud as punch. Let's go for it."

Connie marveled that sixty-eight-and-a-half years had not removed the sparkle from Trudy's eyes.

"What are you wearing today, my love?" Trudy asked just before she disappeared into the shower.

Connie's disquiet found a new focus. She hadn't packed a thing to get married in! She grabbed the March program and frantically searched the schedule. The Wedding was at eleven. No time to shop. Who knew what gay people got married in anyway? Gay people! Her dread returned full force. She wanted to throw up. *I can't get married!* she screamed silently. *Don't make me!*

Trudy was doing bird calls in the shower. This was a wonderful day for her. *I won't spoil it,* Connie promised, rummaging inside herself for strength.

Shaky, sweating, she went to the closet. The closet! Crazy, it was crazy to risk her pension after thirty-three years, two hundred and forty-eight days of caution. She had absolutely no doubt that the three directors and two associate accountants, not to mention seven more junior accountants, would make an example of her. They were crazy on the subject of disease and recruitment and perversion — that's how they talked about gay people.

She heard the shower stop. If Trudy died tomorrow Connie would always regret not doing this. The teariness returned as she chose the pale blue flowered sundress. It smelled of cedar and winter storage. She'd wear her white nylon jacket, though its violet trim would clash. Would there be flower vendors on the way? One for her hair, another —

she'd bring a pin to make a boutonniere for Trudy.
She caught her resolutely knitted brows and big
startled eyes in the mirror — was she still pretty
enough to be a bride, Trudy's bride? The flutter she
felt now was excitement.

At 10:00 A.M. on a windy Saturday, April 25,
1993, Constance Marilyn Kramer and Gertrude
Lynnette Schlegel walked arm in arm under the
uncertain sun, south along 12th Street through the
nation's Capitol to their wedding. One city bird
trilled in a small tree. A few blocks later street
drummers, using plastic boards and orange traffic
cones, serenaded them. Trudy bounded along in
white jeans, navy blazer, white tennis shoes and a
T-shirt she'd picked up the night before that read *I
Can't Even Think Straight!*

Trudy bought a bunch of spicy-smelling white
carnations and wove one into Connie's hair, pinned
one each to their jackets, then gave the rest to
Connie to hold. After that it seemed silly to refuse
to take Trudy's hand. So many from their wedding
party, strangers or not, walked with them, calling,
"Good luck!" and "Congratulations!"

"Where are the crowds?" asked Connie as they
approached the I.R.S. Building. It was too quiet
here. Her insides fluttered. Fears of thirty years ago
came back. Had everyone been arrested and carted
away?

They turned the corner to the Plaza. People filled
the small space. "Thousands," whispered Trudy into
the hush.

It was the muffled sound of reverence that she heard. "This is a real wedding," Connie said. She felt faint and dizzy. In a voice too small to carry over a gust of wind she whispered, "I can't," holding Trudy back while others moved around them.

Trudy's eyes were tender. She hadn't heard. "Aren't we amazing," she told Connie. The crowd folded them inside its celebration despite Connie's reluctance. A couple that had been together thirty-three years, another forty-six, were introduced. "Someday, honey, that'll be us up there."

Connie tried to share Trudy's wonder, but her mouth was dry and her underarms alarmingly wet. Her damp hand had ruined the tissue paper around her bouquet. *Don't make me, don't make me,* she pleaded to the sidewalk, not daring to look up. A shred of resolve kept her upright. All these women and all these men, declaring to the world that they weren't ashamed —

Ashamed? A kind of horror froze her. No. It couldn't be shame that she was feeling underneath everything else.

Ashamed of us? Ashamed of my impish Trudy? Tears crowded her eyes. She squeezed them in yet again. Had it really been the world imprisoning them all these years, or had she and her shame squashed both of them way back in their closet, every twisted opinion the senior accountants could conjure draped suffocatingly around them?

Connie lifted her head and looked at the delighted grins of deliriously glad strangers. Someone announced that fifteen hundred couples had registered as domestic partners. The momentousness of the ceremony moved her outside her worries. She could leave her shame here, where no one would pick it up and carry it home. There ought to be a T-shirt for her: *No More Shame.*

Reverend Perry instructed them to look into their partners' eyes. Trudy looked at her like a teenage groom, face blotchy with nervous color, sweat on her forehead. Connie met her gaze without a flinch. Her back felt straighter and her hands were now dry in Trudy's humid grip. She felt as light as she had at the concert. The Reverend talked, and talked on. He left the subject and rambled into the rights and wrongs of the world. Her arms prickled with sleep from holding the bouquet and both of Trudy's hands, but it was fine. Her eyes stung from locking her gaze with Trudy's, but it was about time. All these years shame had been the third party in a triangle she hadn't realized existed, but today, with thousands of witnesses, she felt awesomely alone with Trudy.

The crowd shuffled, grew restless through the speech, but finally the minister got back on track. He wanted them to say something to their intendeds. What?

"I do," she finally exhaled. Then again, "I do. I do! I do!"

Trudy's voice shook. "Forever."

She heard nothing but the echoes of their pledges until Reverend Perry said, "You may kiss the bride."

Trudy stepped forward, as dashing as she'd been thirty-two years before, and folded her arms around Connie. Her kiss was soft as love. "Married," said Trudy, wonder in her tone, her eyes as light as her kiss.

She leaned her head on Trudy's shoulder, nose in

her spicy carnation, and knew it was finally true. "Married," she agreed.

Her tears didn't come until the trumpeting crowd threw rice.

The Blazes That She
Leaves on Trees

Kathleen Fleming

It is the first day of vacation. I sit reading in the
living room of the rented country house. The
mountains lie blue and purple against the fields and
around the house flowers, yellow, orange, lilac,
purple, blow in the light August wind.

Upstairs she sleeps.

She is extraordinarily beautiful. During our first
months together, when I told her she was beautiful,

she entirely ignored me. Later she would simply look away, lower her eyelids, move on in conversation or in touch. I find the magic of her touch unearthly pure and powerful.

Once she challenged me: "You don't mean physically?"

"Of course I do." She is beautiful. The way translucent agate takes sunlight she takes earth's radiance. Hopkins writes, "The world is charged with the grandeur of God." In such a way her body catches, face conveys the mystery and energy of being. Her intensity is the intensity of the trees in May when every branch, every breathing scrap of leaf, every tiniest probing tendril of darkly hidden root, converts all light and water into vibrant green.

I edge quietly around the room until I am at the stairs. I go carefully up two steps, turn and go down again. I sit on the sofa and begin again to read.

She lives, ear close against the ground, picking up the distant throb of thunder, the close sweet piercing song of larks. She knows the quiet ways of creatures in the night. She knows the flight of hawks. She walks as though in moccasins along ancient mountain paths.

Language is for her translated from the earth. She listens hard before she speaks. It is as though language comes not from the people that she lives among but from the silver veins beneath the earth,

from the deep and caverned rivers underground. As
though the bare footsteps of the past are imprinted
still she scans the ground. She goes alone, a warrior
wearing only a loin cloth, carrying only the slivered
pemmican, a bone knife in her belt. She goes to
reconnoiter, scanning books and languages for wisps
of smoke denoting the presence of our species,
grazing cattle signaling a settlement, drum beats
identifying war.

I wander after, guided by the blazes that she
leaves on trees: these are her poems.

I have come to this place with her to learn my
fate. Seven months now we have written letters
every day. Three months we spent together, talking,
making love. Then she went away to ponder and we
have come together to this place to see if she now
knows.

I've known from the first day she touched my
hand. I would follow her anywhere after that, to see
her eyes darken, lighten in the way she sees, to
hear her voice the way she turns her choice of
words, to know the taste, the touch of loving and
being loved by her.

She, only, has not known. I stand at the foot of
the stairwell. If I tune carefully I can just barely
hear her breathe. She sleeps. I go to read another
story, have another cup of tea.

I close the book mid-sentence. I walk to the
window, walk to the stairs, walk back to the window
again. She may say No. The trees, the fields,
flowers, mountains, sky, at this thought go flat as a
roll of computer paper feeding a word machine,
become nothing more than items on such a page —
unnamed, and listed only, their flat presence slicing

my whole body like a giant paper cut — that neat, that deep, that swift. I stand, hands empty at my sides. I wait.

I was thirteen. It was spring. The war was on.

My older cousin, Sam, was home on leave, shiny and heroic in his uniform. He was taking his new young wife to Orcas Island where our aunt and uncle had a small resort. Who asked him to transport me with them, a dreamy teenage girl, I can't imagine. But I was there. It was a long drive and a ferry ride from home. My mother had no car so on my earlier visits I had taken the Greyhound to the ferry. This time I rode in the back seat of Sam's car, head close to the open window to feel the wind, eyes relentlessly focused on the lovers in the seat ahead.

On the ferry I always rode the prow, letting the wind blast me to the bone. Once on the island I walked the shore, climbing over the rocks, scaling the steep boulders, finding a niche for my foot, a ledge to sit on, half down the cliff, out of sight of shore, alone with the lashing waves and froth on a stormy day or the quiet tides in the sun. I sat with paper and pen writing poems or staring past the great rocks jutting up from the bottom of the Sound, pretending I was staring out to sea.

My aunt and uncle gave a cabin to the newlyweds and kept me in their house. Sam and Susan went to their cabin every afternoon to nap. I shadowed them most of the day, thinking about wartime romance, the rich dark incipient tragedy of it more than anything. I had just found *Wuthering Heights* and the poetry of Wilfred Owen and Sassoon. To the horror of my English class I'd done a project in which I'd read to them the bitterest of each. I'd ended with a perfectly serious poem of my own modeled on "Flanders Field" which started out, "In Flanders Field the poppies grow/ Between the crosses row on row/ But are the men there sleeping?/ Or do they hear the sounds of war/ — The heartbreak and the weeping?"

Somehow Sam and Susan lost their key one afternoon. They sent me from the cabin up the long trail to the house to get another one for them. I hiked up the hill between huckleberries and vine maple, pleased to have purpose to my life, reluctant to leave the couple for so long. My aunt was working in the real estate office at the rear end of the house. I knew she didn't like to be interrupted. But she gave me a key to take to them. "This is the only key I've got for that cabin," she said. "Now don't you lose it."

Aunt May and Aunt Vi were my father's sisters. Aunt Vi taught school for forty years and liked children more than grownups, I thought. Aunt May however always seemed to me not quite certain what children were about and her first thought was that they were somehow up to no good and if she could only guess what it was they had in mind she might head them off at the pass. "Now go straight to Sam and give this to him and tell him it's the only one I've got. My goodness — it's already one o'clock and I have to go all the way across the island to see someone about a lot." Twisting her slender shoulders slightly with her need to hurry, Aunt May was off. I was glad she hadn't asked me to go with her. I wanted to go down by the water. The next morning we were going home.

I walked down the path to Sam and Susan's cabin. They were no longer sitting on the porch where I had left them. They were not anywhere outside. They had crawled in a window, I supposed. Napping already, I thought, envisioning them in bed together. I banged on the door. There was no answer.

I walked around the cabin once. I wanted to climb up a nearby fir to see if I could watch them through the little window but I didn't. I walked around the cabin once again. The key clenched in my fist I knocked again. There was only silence in the cabin.

I walked from the cabin to the beach. It was a windy day and the waves were breaking high against the shore. I climbed over rocks and found a big flat boulder to sit on. The waves pounded against its sides but didn't splash up to its top. I liked to sit on it or stand, staring out into the spray, playing ship or airplane lost in fog on a critical war mission. I stayed there what seemed to me a long time and then I went back to the little cabin.

There were probably fifteen little cabins scattered along the shore. They had shingles nailed to them with names like Dew Drop Inn carved in the wood. Most were rickety. A few were too dilapidated to rent out at all, their plank walls gaping wide, their roofs sagged and split by fallen limbs. The flooring in some had broken through letting brambles and vines take over, twining up the inner walls, closing the windows with a screen of leaves and vines. Aunt May and Uncle Mark repaired the best and rented them during the tourist season.

"My goodness," I'd hear her say, "some of the family just don't realize that it's a business. They expect us to just give them cabins every year. We can't afford to do that for everyone. Of course I don't mean you — I'd be real glad to put you up whenever you can come." My mother always thanked her but she never went. I wasn't ever sure if she didn't want to go or if she couldn't pay and wouldn't stay for free.

I knocked again on the cabin door. By now the key had worn a deep groove in my clenching hand. Again there was that deep silence that was quieter than any empty cabin would have been.

I went back to the shore, to a point of land this time. It was a favorite place of mine. It jutted out above the water between two little inlets lined with rocks. Cedar and magnolia crowded it with their brown and green. There were a few fir and pine. After I had crawled under the lowest branches and surfaced on the point I was alone. No one could see me there unless they came in from the Sound in a small boat. There were hardly ever any boats in the inlet where my aunt and uncle lived so I was safe. I was alone, free to stare at Mt. Constitution rising close enough to see the fir, pine, spruce around its base, high enough, far away enough, to be a mysterious misty blue at its peak.

Sometimes I lay there until I went to sleep. Sometimes I sat there writing poems. Sometimes I remembered the sex scenes from novels I had read and masturbated to such ringing prose as "He pushed her back upon the grass and she looked over him at the sun as their bodies merged."

This day I sat staring out to sea. I hadn't brought paper and pencil as I almost always did. I sat tossing pine cones high and far. Sometimes they were hand grenades and I was the lone American against a German tank convoy. Sometimes they were bombs and I was the lone pilot against the Japanese fleet below.

At last I thought it must be time. They must by now be out of bed, ready to take a walk, play Monopoly up at the house, explore the beach. I stood, started to duck under the magnolia limbs, my hands hanging empty at my side. I turned back to retrieve the key and knew I'd lost it.

I sat again where I'd been sitting and began to search the grass. The bluff was windblown, bare. The soil was sandy and what little grass there was, was short and tough.

I looked underneath my legs and then I stood and scanned the ground. I knelt where the grass was flattened and the sand imprinted where my body'd been. Carefully I searched among the short dry spears of grass, among the little pebbles and the big rocks sunk in earth. I felt with my fingers among the roots of bushes, along the twining, twisting of the surface roots of pine. I stood again and looked grudgingly, slowly out across the closest boulders where the froth licked high to the waters stretching farther out the inlet, to the open space beyond the guarding rise of cliff.

The knowledge came to me fluttering, groping like trapped smoke within my belly that had to rise, its tendrils poking painfully through lung and throat.

I thought that I could vomit but there was no such easy way to ease this nausea.

I knelt again, moving my fingers as though the sloping earth were braille and I could extract its meaning if my fingers stayed sentient long enough. I moved them slowly and then I moved them swiftly, checking each tuft of grass, each underside of stone. Then I stood. My hand closed on a last pine cone and as I cocked my arm and threw it in a high long arc I let myself see the waves, let myself heft the key in memory in my hand, let myself know its weight against the surface of the waves, let myself watch it glide the currents down, passing the lighter pine cones as they swirled and turned, surfaced and sank. The key glided down without that hesitation. It sank to the barnacled rocks on the bottom of the cove. It slid then toward a crack between two sunken boulders and it teetered only a fraction of a second and then it was gone, into that crevasse and below it to another until it came finally to rest forever in the deepest sand and shells, too deep to even catch the sunlight, too deep to cast the tiniest sparkle upward toward the sky.

I turned and walked slowly toward the cabin where the lovers slept. Their cabin was called Wander Inn. The afternoon sun was slanting through the trees. The cabins were all empty because it was early spring. My aunt would soon be back from her business errand.

I had lost the key.

I had lost the only key.

I circled the cabin gingerly this time. I did not pound on the cabin door. I sat down near, under a fir tree, and tossed the cones, one by one, into a nearby thicket. It was not the Japanese. It was not the Germans. It was a tangle of plain underbrush. I tossed fir cones. They were neither grenades nor bombs. They were fir cones. Their pitch stuck to my fingers, their scent stayed in my lungs.

Inside the cabin Sam and Susan slept. They were not Catherine and Heathcliff. They were my cousin Sam who wore a drab khaki uniform and Susan, who worked in the shipyard. They would have babies and eventually he would leave her for another woman and Aunt Vi would say, "There have been men in our family who were foolish and there have been men who made mistakes but there has never been a dishonorable man before."

But that was years ahead. That April afternoon I knew there would be no serious repercussions. No one would lay a hand on me. It would be Aunt May's consternation and her confirmed belief that children would after all inevitably do the wrong thing, with which I'd have to contend.

But I had lost the key. It lay then in deep water past the mossy, barnacled cliffs that I explored. It lay where fish swam in the underwater glow of sunlight streaming through wavering walls of algae, past jungles of kelp and slender strands of radiant sea weed, in the underbelly of the slow dark tide. I myself had thrown the key into the waters' depths where it lay below all the creatures gliding over it, a small still opener of locks, forever and forever irretrievable.

I go again to the stairway in the summer house. I listen to her breathing, in and out, in and out.

I walk to the window and stare across the grass, thick and green around the house. Last year's drought has passed. The open field is lush and green, the trees beyond it quickened with new leaves. Beyond them are the mountains, a misty blue.

It occurs to me that blue is my favorite color because it is the shade of water and of mountains and of sky. I never thought before about the mountains being blue and how when I was very young I looked each morning from the old farmhouse across the valley to the blue Cascades, far in the distance, far beyond the valley where corn and lettuce grew, where the railroad tracks ran their tiny twiglike line, where the train passed twice a day, sending a plume of smoke, mysterious and white into the sky, rising from the green of the valley bottom land up toward the sky, diffusing as it rose, leaving a tiny glistening oddly silent explosion against the blue of the mountainside.

When will she awaken?

I want to go and tug at her arm to ask her if she knows.

Small birds are everywhere I look out there. The thistles blow purple in the breeze. Fence posts lean forlorn, wood without leaf or bark, among the abundant and astonishing green.

I am beyond restraint. Knowing I should let her awaken when she's ready, I ascend the stairs. She hears the squeaking of the wood, its grain polished by bare feet these hundred years. I look to see if she's awake, knowing I've wakened her, knowing I could not wait.

It is later now in that same week. The mountains stretch blue on the horizon, beautiful in the dusk. Above them the sky is streaked purple with sunset. We are lovers now. Her choice is made. We stand together at the window looking out. In the valley one by one the farmers' lights come on. We watch the mountains, their darkening blue and the blue sky above the mountains darkening now, allowing us to see through it, beyond it to the fierce bright stars that have been there all day, shining and unseen. Standing in one another's arms, in a lovers' silence, farther and farther we see, star after lucid star.

Sign Language

Penny Sumner

Roses are red, apples too. This being about True
Love there will, of course, be roses. But the apples
come first: they were my idea.

Red also has a special place in my story because
it was your beret — wool, scarlet — that caught my
eye during that introductory lecture. I doodled, took
in the red beret in the next row and thought to
myself, *Che Guevara.* And then your profile came
into view. *Woops! Red Emma.* That was two, no

three, months before the apples. I know that for
sure because the apples hung on ribbons from the
kissing bough I'd made for Christmas: polished green
leaves, red apples, white berries. Candles too and, in
the middle, mistletoe.

Mulled wine smears my mouth, bleeds into the
silk breast of my shirt. As I pull you forward by the
wrist I can read your sharp surprise. *Here?* you're
thinking. *Here? Now?* And then we both shut our
eyes until we're under the center, safe from the drip
of hot wax. Safe? I look at you again and you glance
at our audience. *Is this safe?* you're asking. *Is this
wise?* And because it isn't — safe, or wise — I give a
low laugh. I laugh even though I know this is to be
a real kiss, not a faint brushing of lips ever so
slightly parted . . .

Stepping back from you amidst more laughter
and even a slow clap, we could be counting. One,
two, three: little finger, index finger, thumb, we
wave at each other, nonchalant. But nonchalant
we're not because what we're saying is *I love you.* In
American, in American sign language. *I love you*
across the center of a crowded room, in front of my
friends, in front of my husband.

I'd watched you after that first lecture and saw
that you always sat next to the same woman. She
was short, pretty, with black, curly hair. You didn't
leave with her, however; you always walked out

alone. My chance came the following week when we both turned up in the wrong room. You walked in ahead and no one else was there, a change in timetable: otherwise known as an opportunity.

"Excuse me," I called, "do you know what's going on?"

No answer.

"Do you..." You turned and your voice was monotone, deep water over a bed of smooth pebbles. "Do you know where we should be? I'm deaf." One of the pebbles fell between us, rolled across the wooden floor. "But I can read your lips."

Read my lips, *I love you!* Said over a dinner table only a month later, said in public.

What? Right index finger across left palm, eyebrows raised in disbelief. *What?* you ask.

I lean forward, reach for a glass of wine. Pissed enough for it to be an excuse, she didn't mean it, she was well away. But not really that pissed at all. Little finger, index finger, thumb; the tip of each spread on the checked cloth. *I love you.*

I hold my breath, two, three. You raise your glass of wine and lean forward not onto fingertips but elbows, your arms casually crossing your chest. Love, the heart zigzagged. Love, the heart enclosed. I breathe again.

In bed you put lights on the tips of your fingers, blue lights, green, that walked my belly. The lights were a joke, left-overs from a psychology experiment, how fast do you sign? How fast can signing be read?

Approaching my breast, blue green, green blue. Christmas lights, your body next to mine a present unwrapped. Blouse first, then the flowered jungle of your skirt. I'd undressed you in the living room, kneeling on the floor.

"Read my lips." Laughter. And then, "Do you like that?"

"What?" Your eyes puzzling down at me, what had I said?

Sitting back on my haunches I fingerspelled the way you'd taught and discovered you were right, the American system, one-handed, is much more convenient.

Do you like that?

Your eyes closed and you nodded. "Yes." Your voice was a drawl, because of the deafness, because you were breathing hard. "Yes, I like that."

Green blue, blue green. These are signs that can be read without light. Blue green, green . . . don't stop, don't stop . . . blue. You laugh, water over pebbles, and roll to the edge of the bed, your hair a mane, fingertips to your lips, a kiss which actually signifies *thank you.*

"Thank *you.*" My gestured reply is exaggerated, my expression designed to be knowing.

Coffee? you ask, two fists grinding. One fist shaken twice means yes. You shrug into a satin gown the color of apricots, and pad towards the kitchen. As you go the phone rings but you can't hear it and I don't answer.

* * * * *

On more than one occasion the doorbell rang too, but there was never the sound of a key although I strained to hear, waited for the step in the hall. It never came and I never had to warn you. Not for us the undignified scramble for clothes, not for us the paraphernalia of actually being caught, and when you finally did leave it was because your year in England was over. And because she was waiting for you.

Beautiful, you sign, your hand a slow crescent across your face, a wing dipping.

Very, I lift my eyes from her photo, my fingers two peace signs moving outward.

She was, too, beautiful, and deaf. And although my marriage had unraveled itself, spilled pearls sitting in my palm, it wasn't her silence that silenced me (I never once asked you to stay, never pleaded "Don't leave!") but her words. "Hi there," she wrote from across the Atlantic, "I'm looking forward to coming over and meeting you!" You'd described me as your married friend, the one you sat with and took notes from in lectures, and in friendship she sent messages, postcards. For my birthday there were earrings of blue and yellow: the color of the sky, the color of the sun. I threaded them through my flesh and let them bounce, cool and smooth, against my skin.

And then it was time for you to go. And the roses? Well you never gave me roses but she did, the morning I drove the two of you to the airport. You both turned at the same time to wave and I waved back *Goodbye!,* which can also mean *Beautiful!* An arc of the hand like the curve of a breast, like a bird's wing. A slow wave which was both an acknowledgment and a letting go.

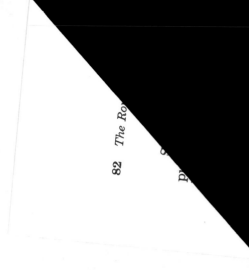

Peaches

Dorothy Tell

I woke up with my face buried in a warm cotton-covered bosom. Strong fat arms cradled me, held my skinny body fast. I opened my eyes a slit and saw a world of blue and white checks. I tried to lift my head but it hurt too bad, so I closed my eyes and tried not to cry at how good it felt to be touched by someone who wasn't red-eyed with anger.

Did my Ma hold me this way when I was a tiny baby, I wondered. Nothing came to mind except the very last time she touched me.

She had stared crazy at me in her fever and pushed away the wet cloth I tried to put on her brow. Her eyes seemed to blame me somehow for still being alive and not being a strong son who could've taken care of her when Pa was called to the Great World War. She turned her face to the wall of our cabin. Her breath came out in a long rattly whisper and she passed dead.

I let comforting arms hold me while I remembered burying Ma and hitching our mule to the wagon that was full of peaches for market. I remembered thinking I could sell some peaches for cash money. It was going to be hard to live elsewise, without the two other sets of hands that kept our scrabbly farm going. And besides, nobody was going to sharecrop with a twelve-year-old girl anyways. Even if I did look like a skinny boy in my Pa's overalls, with my yellow-straw hair, bowl-cut above my ears. I couldn't remember much after getting old Lucky out on the road and pointed toward town. Guess I must've been pretty worn down from nursing Ma and getting the peach crop in.

My memories stopped and I suddenly felt very nervous about being held so quiet and gentle by some stranger. I pulled my face away and opened my mouth to ask where I was. But nothing came out. Not a word. Not even a croak or moan or whisper.

I couldn't talk.

I just looked at the big woman and to my mortified disgust, I felt big tears squeeze from my eyes and splash off onto her blue and white apron bib.

"Bless your heart, child." The woman cooed at me

and patted my backside like I was a tame barn cat. "What's your name? You're dressed like a boy. Are you a boy?" I nodded hard in agreement, prodded to this sinful lie by a spikey little warm spot under my heart that told me it just could be that a boy might get better treatment in this world than a useless girl.

I pressed my lips together and pointed to them, shaking my head.

"Cain't talk, eh?" Her bushy eyebrows rose up a bit and she cocked her head like a hound. "Well . . . how you feeling, son?"

She held me at arm's length, peering close at me. "Where you from? What happen't to you, anyways? Where'd you get that wagonload of peaches? Peaches — that's what we'll call you. Peaches." She rolled the word around on her tongue seeming to see if it tasted just right for a name. She stared at me hard and asked again, "You *sure* you can't talk?"

Overcome with the weight of all these questions, me with answers buzzing in my head like hornets but none of them lighting on my tongue, I felt the tears start again.

"Now, lookit what you done." A soft female voice came from beside me. "If the boy can't talk, he can't talk. Quit your pokin' at him. See iffen he can write."

I sat up then and pulled away from the comfort of the safe round arms and looked sideways at what was most surely the ugliest woman I had ever seen. She was dressed like a man in bib overalls and workshirt and she was big and tall. But her eyes were so blue with the evening sun slanting into them, and so clear and friendly that I stopped noticing the hairy moles on her chin and her big wet lips that shined like ripe plums in the rain.

"You're right, Jessie," my woman in the apron said. "Get that slate from the kitchen up at the house and we'll see what this young feller's all about."

"And mind you," she said as Jessie turned toward the door, "don't you let the boss lady catch on to this *boy* being here. You know how she is."

Jessie turned a thoughtful face toward us. "Yep. I'll take care." She said the words so whisper-soft and tinkly, it made me think of the man at the carnival who threw words to a doll on his knee.

I swallowed as I noticed that she ducked her head so her hat wouldn't scrape off against the top of the doorjamb. She was ever bit as *tall* as she was ugly. I shivered a little and wondered what would come of me now I had got found by these two odd women.

"My name's Cora," the woman in the apron said, as if in answer to my unspoken questions. "I cook up at the main house and Jessie takes care of the stable and the truck garden for the boss lady . . . that's Maude Browney, of course."

I guess I looked like I wanted to know a lot more because she went on. "You've landed yourself at Miz Maude's House of Pleasures. That house up there on the hill," she gestured at the doorway, "is full of whores and high times when the men come out from town."

She looked away from me and seemed to set her eyes on some spot far off.

"I used to work for Maude when I was younger and could cinch my waist into shape. But, I never

had no sense. Never saved a dime...just spent
what Maude gimme on worthless men and gin." Cora
looked back at me with a funny curve to one side of
her mouth. "Until Jessie com along that is, an' I lost
my taste for the life, but...say now son..." Her
eyes softened as she looked me over. "You won't be
sniffin' round women like them for a long time yet."
Her eyes measured my size and height as I sat
beside her. "No sir, Peaches, m'boy." She grinned at
me, her eyebrows lopsided and comical, dog-like.
"You got a might of growin' to do yet, I 'spect."

I will always believe it was God's own grace that
sent Cora and Jessie down that road where they
found me laying across the wagon seat that day. Old
Lucky had just stopped in the middle of the lane,
hung his head and sulled up in the traces until
Jessie got his attention with a big stick across his
nose.

Those women cared for me like I was their own
child. Of course they both knew all the time I was a
girl, but it suited both them and me to let that fact
go unknown by Maude and her girls. Or as Cora
said, Maude would put me to work and I had a
strong feeling I wasn't cut out for *that* kind of toil.

Not even for *money*. Penniless as I was.

I did not regain the power of speaking and for
reasons of better keeping secrets about myself, I
feigned inability to read and write. I soon fell into a
routine of helping Jessie in the fields and barns and
letting myself be bossed around and teased by the
women at the house. As Jessie's newfound "nephew"

I experienced a freedom I never imagined in my past life as a mere girl.

One of my jobs was to tote hot water for baths. It was a time I liked the best, when the men were gone and the women were easy and sleepy and laughed a lot. And I have to say, I secretly liked the way some of the older women treated me. They teased me with their bodies, grabbed their bare breasts and flipped them at me, jaunty as a clothesline in the breeze. Moved their clothing about so I could see their private parts. Trying to get me to blush they said, giggling and teasing me with their made-up lips and eyes.

I reckon it worked, because I seem to be blushing most of the time these days, 'specially when I think of what happened the night I woke up from my sleeping spot in the barn loft and thought the hogs had got loose in the garden. Seems like things I saw that night somehow got painted on the inside of my eyelids.

It started with me going out in the moonlight to check the garden and then coming back past the window of Cora and Jessie's cabin. The night was quiet. Whatever had woke me up was gone. Nothing was wrong in the garden or the hen houses.

The big white August moon hung up in the top of the dark sky like a hole in a window shade. So bright I could see my shadow walking in front of me. I heard low voices as I neared the cabin and slowed my step so I could tell where they were coming from.

Soft light glowed from the open window as I rounded the corner near the porch. I stopped in the shadows trying not to make any noise, so I could eavesdrop of course. I was learning a whole lot because the women just got used to me not talking and I guess they thought I was slow or something because they would go on and say the most curious things, even though I'm sure they knew I wasn't deaf *or* blind . . . just dumb. *Dumb ole Peaches. Don't mind him,* they'd say, *go on girl, tell me more . . .*

Anyways . . . what I saw framed in that window as clear as President Lincoln's picture in Miz Maude's drawing room, was Jessie, naked as a new piglet, with one of Cora's breasts sucked almost all into her mouth. Cora was sitting in a straight-backed chair, facing square toward the window. Her dress was drawn up to her belly and her creamy legs were spread wide. I could clearly see the dark curly hair, even the pink line in the middle where the plump lips came together.

I could not have run away if a snake had crawled up my leg. I creeped up closer to the window to better see what Cora had done with her bosom. She had plopped both breasts out over the top of her apron so they were pushed up like two big pink melons and her nipples stuck up like they were scared of something.

Jessie's back was to me and her bare bottom bounced up and down as she moved her big red lips from one to the other of Cora's wet nipples. I suddenly felt like I had to pee but I didn't want to miss nothing so I just crossed my legs tight and kept on watching.

I realized then that Cora's hand was stuck up between Jessie's legs. I could see it pumping like she was whipping eggs for a cake. Jessie stood up suddenly, so tall her belly-button was even with

Cora's ears. She stepped astride Cora's shoulder and Cora turned her head so she could put her tongue where her fingers had been. Jessie pulled herself wide apart, straining her strong back and pushed close to Cora's tongue. I swear Cora acted like Jessie's big pink twat was better than a bowl of fresh plum jelly.

I could not believe how bad I had to pee. What a time for nature to call. I crossed my legs the opposite way and kept them squeezed tight.

Just about then Jessie bowed her back like a cat on a rail and grabbed her own titties, pinching her nipples and moaning, "Oh Jesus oh sweet Jesus oh oh oh sweet-ee-ee-eet Jee-ee-suh-us." This last coming out like she was riding a wagon down a rutty road.

Jessie slid down Cora's body into kind of a big limp naked puddle at Cora's feet. I jumped when Cora chuckled and said, "You out of oats Jessie, honey? Or can you take care of a little job while you're restin'?"

Jessie looked up at Cora and grinned, her plain face all soft with love and happiness. "What little job you got in mind, darlin'?"

"You know . . . you know the one . . . where you got to get harnessed up to the little helper." Cora had a determined look about her eyes as she got up and climbed onto a low stool and reached high into the cupboard. She pulled out a lumpy pillowcase with a knot tied in one end and slung it at Jessie, who caught it easy and graceful with one big hand. "Go in there and put that on and we'll play Hired Hand and the Lady of the Manor."

I took this moment and sidled into the shadows to squat and pee but nothing came out. I grunted and squeezed but had to pull my overall flap back up without any relief from the pinching that thudded like a fever pulse between my legs. My thoughts were drawn back to what I saw going on inside. Jessie had come back into the room, now dressed in overalls that stuck out in front like the trousers of the fellows who waited about in Miz Maude's drawing room on Saturday nights.

I'm pretty sure I know what happened next, but Cora and Jessie went into their bedroom and out of my sight. I tried to see in the bedroom window but could not, so I just had to be satisfied with what my ears could pick up. Soft laughter and the squeaks of over-burdened furniture, then the murmurs of low voices and after a while just quiet. A warm silence that I carried back to the barn loft and wrapped around me like a quilt as I drifted off to sleep.

I'm not sure if I dreamed that night or just lay in bed and planned the rest of my life, but I thank God for the earthy love of those two good women, and how it prepared me for what would be the most exciting event of my life. The day that Delia arrived at Miz Maude's.

Delia, with delicate violet shadows under saucer-blue eyes. Delia, who outshone either Gish sister on their best day. Delia, my angel-dove. The sun, moon, stars and . . . ah, but I'm getting ahead of myself and lots of other things happened between that August night and my sixteenth birthday. Which was just two days before I first laid eyes on Delia Beausoleil. And that's another story for sure.

The Kiss

Jaye Maiman

I like the way the tight, low grass feels underneath my fingertips. Lying here, on my back, eyes closed, the sun baking my skin, beads of sweat rolling off the sides of my brow, my jean shorts damp from dew, I tickle the grass and suddenly remember the triangle of soft bristles leading to my ex-lover's secret spot. My fingers instantly dig into the dirt.

The break-up occurred almost eight months ago, but the acrid memories still backfire on me at unexpected moments, like now — just an hour before my second date with Deborah. I sit up abruptly and blink into the summer glare. Down the hill, a softball game is in progress. It takes me a minute to recognize some of the players. One of them is a dead ringer for Emily. My stomach kicks rocks into my throat.

Not that I miss her any more, at least not the person she became during the last six months of our relationship. But ten years is a lot of time to lose.

I check my watch and curse. Why did I agree to another date? I'm not ready to get involved again — I'm not even sure if I *can* get involved again. Stretch a rubber band long and hard enough and eventually it'll break.

I stand abruptly and turn my back on the game. The damn video in my head starts again. Emily and Judy. Eating my spinach lasagna. In our kitchen. Laughing. Just friends.

Right.

I spent six months watching Emily fall in love with one of my closest friends. Six, sexless months of seething, fighting, listening to her lies, believing my own lies. Just friends. Close friends. Friends who talked on the phone for two hours straight, seven nights a week. Including holidays. Friends who fell silent whenever I walked into the room. Friends who went out to dinners that somehow lasted until two in the morning.

But Emily kept promising me that nothing was going on, that our relationship was ten years old and still going strong. Tickling my ribs and flashing her too-dimpled smile as she said, "That damn Everready bunny's got nothing on you and me, kid."

Sounding like she meant it. Sounding the way I wanted her to.

I smell smoke and for a split second I'm not sure if it's me or the Hibachi near the overcrowded picnic table. It's a heavy ninety-five degrees and my temper is as hot as the coals searing the franks on the Brady Bunch's grill. Kids scramble past me in a game of tag and I have to bite back the urge to scream.

I climb the hill, enter a patch of shade and pause, my back pressed into the rough bark of an oak tree. I close my eyes, but the video continues. Waking up in bed, Emily curled beside me peacefully. She had come home so late the night before that I wasn't sure if I had dreamt the cursory good-night kiss or if it had been real. I slipped out of bed and headed for the shower. But Emily's jacket was slung over the kitchen chair and I shuffled toward it instinctively. The letter from Judy was folded into the neatest of squares, tucked behind the picture of me that Emily kept in her wallet.

Dearest Em —
Time is on our side. I love you fiercely. As soon as you can break the news . . .

I didn't even bother to read the whole letter.

At first I thought the relationship ended then, the moment I calmly refolded the letter and replaced it neatly behind my stupid, smiling face. Now I know it happened long before then, sometime when neither of us was watching. By the time we looked back, it was too late.

For the past six months, my answering machine has brusquely questioned anyone who dared to call me with Tina Turner's hoarse "What's Love Got To Do With It?" Friends keep telling me that the message may have something to do with the fact that none of my blind dates or personal ad respondents have called back. I'm not sure I care.

I check my watch again. Fifteen minutes left. I heave a sigh and decide it's time.

This is my first second date in almost eleven years. I leave Prospect Park behind me and start walking down Ninth Street. There's a Korean grocery on the corner and I stop to stare at the buckets sprouting flowers. This *is* a date, right? I question myself. Should I bring flowers? The very thought makes me want to kick my too-rounded butt.

A bouquet of irises, a bottle of wine. The accoutrements of fantasies, of dreams that long ago died. Yet somehow I find myself counting out the bills as the clerk rolls the stems into a paper cone. I take them from him, faintly astonished. What the hell am I doing?

I spent less than an hour with Deborah less than a week ago. She had responded to the personal ad I had placed in the *Village Voice* at the prompting of friends who were afraid that certain parts of my anatomy were in imminent danger of shriveling up and dropping like crisp maple leaves in an undeniable autumn. Not that the prospect of sex was unappealing to me. But most days it just didn't seem worth the effort. Or the pain.

I've made it a policy to meet my dates for a quick drink or a cup of coffee. Maybe, if I feel

daring, I'll venture for a moist Tiramisu. But the
bottom line is that I want to be sure that a fast exit
is possible. Even so, I've found it almost impossible
to last an hour with the women I've met. Most of
them were too desperate, too needy, too distant,
too . . . something. In the past month, I've started to
think of my single status as something precious, a
bit of amber that would preserve me for decades.

But when Deborah invited me to a barbecue at
her house, I agreed quickly.

I find myself in a wine store, selecting a chilled
bottle of Beringer's Reserve Chardonnay, remembering our first date. We met at Cousin John's, a
local cafe in Park Slope, Brooklyn. I figured a quick
cafe au lait and I'd be home in time for *Murphy
Brown.* I plopped down in a white resin chair located
outside the cafe and settled in for some serious
people-watching. The homeless guy with the fancy
harmonica was starting on *Amazing Grace* when I
happened to glance up the block. That's when I saw
her. My first thought was, where do I know her
from?

I didn't even realize it was Deborah until she
smiled at me and said my name. I stood up, shook
her hand, instantly reverting to basic business
practice. But all the time I'm saying to myself, who
does she look like? Why is she so damn familiar?

We sat down at the table and made awkward
small talk. I told her right away that I was eight
months out of a ten-year relationship. I like to get
my cards out on the table from the start. She didn't
flinch, so I proceeded to tell her everything about me
that my ex-lovers hated. I'm lazy, possessive,

over-anxious, insecure. I threw in a few extra faults I'm not even sure I have. In a strange way, I had a ball.

The last time I was single, I vaguely remember trying to impress potential lovers. Now I just try to terrify them. It's really quite liberating.

But Deborah met me fault for fault. She even raised me one or two. I was surprised to hear myself laugh. The woman was pleasant, funny, intelligent.

The next day my friend Elaine asked me if she was cute. I wasn't really sure. All I knew was that her eyes were not those of a stranger. Dark brown and expressive, they held my gaze and spoke to a part of me that wouldn't let me eavesdrop. I wanted to ask her, "Where did we meet before?" but I knew we hadn't. So maybe that's why I said yes so fast when she invited me for a Sunday barbecue at her place. It felt less like a second date than the natural progression of a history that had started long before I could recall.

I check the address again, then read the number on the door of the corner brownstone. I tuck the flowers under my arm, shift the bottle of wine to my other hand, and swing the gate open. The hinges squeak and I freeze up. What if she hears me coming? Then I laugh at the absurdity. I'm a thirty-six-year-old dyke with properly wizened romantic notions, and I can't bring myself to ring the damn buzzer. I'm a minute late and I worry that I may seem too interested, which I'm not. I wait four minutes and then start worrying that I may seem rude, so I finally press the button.

She's there before I can lick my dry, chapped lips. It's been fourteen months since I've kissed

anyone — kissed Emily — and my lips are about as
supple as a cement sidewalk. This is what I'm
thinking as Deborah opens the door for me. She's
wearing tight, faded jeans and a crisply ironed white
shirt, the sleeves rolled up to the elbows. I hear
Elaine's question again in my head and I think,
yeah, she's cute. When she turns around, I get a full
view of her butt and I think, no, she's not cute.
She's hot.

Emily was five-three and weighed less than your
average Doberman. She had undefined breasts and
no butt. Now I look at Deborah's back and admire
the way her jeans stretch around her curves.

She takes the wine and flowers from me and
those articulate eyes are having another one of those
hard-to-hear conversations with me. I think she's
pleased and I begin to sweat. As she cuts the stems
and fills a vase, I check out her apartment for
critical clues or, better yet, fatal flaws. I make a
beeline for her music collection. I note a *B-52*
compact disk and almost nod. She's into punk. This
will never work.

Then I notice the Patsy Cline and k.d. lang CDs.
La Traviata. Gershwin. Joni Mitchell. When I see
the Rosemary Clooney tapes, the butterflies in my
stomach start getting unruly.

Her book collection is equally eclectic. Katherine
Forrest. Proust. Shakespeare. Lily Tomlin. Nothing
overtly dangerous. I'm about to analyze the
knickknacks on her shelf when she asks me to join
her in the back yard. I step out into the sunlight
and breathe deeply. It feels safer out here. After all,
the fence is only six feet high. If I had to, I could
take it in one leap.

I watch Deborah dump coal into the Weber grill and realize in a flash that she doesn't know what she's doing. For some bizarre reason, this makes me happy. I offer to start the fire and she willingly surrenders the chore to me with an open smile. As I pile the charcoal into a pyramid, I shiver. This feels so . . . so domestic. With a start, my head snaps in Deborah's direction. She's standing at the top of the stairs, desperately balancing paper plates, plastic cups, ketchup, mustard, and a candle.

She looks unbearably cute.

I rush toward her and take a few items from her arms, and as I do the back of my hand skims the flesh of her forearm and I want to cry out. Youch! My body's talking to me and I'm trying hard to kick it in the teeth. Trouble, I remind myself, that's what this is.

A little while later, the coals and certain long-dormant parts of my body are white-hot. She brings the steaks to me, flashing a smile that is so dazzlingly seductive, I flinch. I glance to my side and realize she's at least a half-inch taller than I. That's when I know for certain that a relationship could never work. Realizing that the worst-case scenario is a night of mindless sex, I feel a lot more relaxed as I fork the meat onto the grill.

I watch the juices bubble and hiss and try to remember if I've ever had mindless sex. Somewhere in the back of my head, I hear my friends laugh. I stab a steak and relent — for me, sex has always been a quixotic prelude and not a simple climax.

For an instant, I panic. Does relinquishing my romantic illusions mean sacrificing sex? I almost moan out load. Just then the grill catches fire and I

quickly smother it with the cover. Deborah is
standing close to me, her silence as thick as the
smoke stinging my eyes. We both step back.

The sun is angling down through the trees and
in the apricot light, Deborah's tan skin seems to
glow. Her smile seems even more engaging. All at
once we both launch into an inquisition. What do
you like to do on vacation? How long have you been
out? The questions grow increasingly personal.

After my breakup with Emily, I teasingly
informed my friends that I wouldn't become involved
with another woman until I obtained solid references
from her parents, friends, last two employers,
previous lovers, and current therapist. As I listen to
myself quizzing Deborah, I start to wonder if I was
joking after all.

We finally sit down to eat. Our chairs are almost
touching and the food is inconsequential. She asks
me what I'm looking for in a relationship. I answer
her, a dull buzz drilling into the back of my skull.
The video is grinding into place again, I note
numbly. As I run through my list of preferred
neuroses and habits, I think of Emily and feel my
eyes burn. I want everything she couldn't give me.
Tenderness. Affection. Honesty.

And I want everything she did give to me. Emily
leading me behind a waterfall in a secluded spot we
discovered on the island of Maui, kissing my cheeks,
licking my mouth playfully, murmuring my name
over and over like a mantra. Emily sneaking a
ribboned box under my pillow, offering me the keys
to her home with a gaze that promised forever.

I look away, not wanting Deborah's eyes to see
how the video wears me out. Just then, she reaches

for my hand and wraps her pinkie around mine. I don't turn around. I ask her what she wants, lob the game back into her court. She starts out by describing something she and her brother have nicknamed "the sweetness factor."

I like the way she responds and hate the fact that I like it all.

My pinkie stays clasped to hers. It's so intimate a contact, and yet it's almost imperceptible. Finally I look at our hands. Then up into her eyes. And I see she knows. *She knows.* My eyes dart to the grill.

"Maybe we should clean up," I say abruptly, the ground unsteady beneath my feet. I can't trust myself, I think as I hastily clear off the table. Her eyes follow me, steady as a deer sipping water from a cool, silent creek. In the kitchen I busy myself washing utensils, but then her hand taps my shoulder. Light. Confident.

"Would you like coffee, tea, or a kiss?" she asks.

One part of my brain is on fire. It's a line. It's a trap. Escape while you can. The other part is reading her eyes. The desire is tender, insistent, and undeniably real. I don't hear myself say yes, don't know how I signal acquiescence, but suddenly her mouth is on mine and I'm an electric hair dryer plunged into a tub of water.

I want to cry, then realize it's too late. I *am* crying. Emily's face rushes toward me and I feel guilty for betraying her. No mouth but hers has touched mine for nearly eleven years, and Deborah's lips are so different — full where Emily's were thin. Moist. I respond to them with an intensity that shakes me. I pull my face away, bury it in her neck, hold still there, tight and horribly afraid. She whispers in my ear, "Shhhh," and a shudder rips through me.

My arms muscle Deborah against me. Her breasts are full, her waist narrow. I can feel her ribs against my stomach. I note these sensations with an odd mixture of excitement, detachment, and grief. I feel like a snake shedding its skin, a shiver of release rattling my spine.

Minutes pass. I press my palms against her shoulders and move away, glancing down at our feet. One of my legs is raised slightly, my foot angled backward. The position is straight out of a forties movie and, despite myself, I laugh. Deborah follows my gaze, sees my errant — and unnervingly femme — foot, and stares at me with surprised amusement.

Maybe, I think, our eyes meeting. Maybe she's real. Maybe *this* is real.

I kiss her again, this time reveling in the difference. Her tongue is silky, insistent. I feel her body press into mine, recognize the rush of my blood, the pounding need her mouth awakens in me. Her knee presses between my thighs and I grasp it greedily, finding a new rhythm, one that drives deep into me. We dance into the living room like that, grinding against each other, our kisses growing sloppier, more abandoned.

We flop onto her couch and I stretch out on top of her. Her fingers dig into my ass, pulling me against her, my thigh tight against her, her moans fluttering over my ears like the wings of a hummingbird.

I suck her tongue slowly, delirious with the knowledge that every inch of her body is responding to my touch. Then, in an instant, the videotape rewinds, clanks, readies itself for play. I lift myself up on my elbows. Deborah's head rests on a pillow, her eyes remain closed, her face flushed and her mouth open. Waiting.

I snap the video off.

The future starts now.

I lower myself to her mouth, finding myself in a kiss that would carry me the long way home.

Love's Own Time

Carol Schmidt

The bishop and Naomi Miller's three brothers decided: Naomi would leave the Lancaster settlement and live with her oldest sister Cora in Shipshewana. Now that Naomi's parents and youngest siblings were dead in a buggy-car collision, she would need a strong and understanding hand through her dangerous teen years, more than her brothers could provide.

Cora had married an older widower who already had two teen-aged daughters. One of the daughters,

Sharon, was also seventeen, the same age as Naomi, another point for the placement. The brothers agreed that Sharon and Naomi were bound to become best friends.

Sharon picked up Naomi at the Greyhound station in the family buggy. They hated each other at first sight.

An outsider, or English as all non-Amish are called, would not have been able to easily tell the two apart, dressed as they were in long, dark-colored dresses, aprons and shawls, their hair parted in the middle and drawn back in low buns under the traditional white organdy prayer coverings.

But instantly Naomi saw that Sharon was a "progressive" — the waistband on her apron was a good four inches wide, showing off too much of her slender figure, her hem was scarcely below her knees, her poor excuse for a shawl was a narrow triangle of material, her prayer covering barely concealed her ears and its narrow straps flopped loose. She didn't even have on her bonnet, and her stockings were flesh-colored and too sheer — and she wore white sneakers!

Sharon drove the buggy by herself. Waving Naomi aboard, she hoisted Naomi's lifetime of possessions in a trunk and two suitcases as if they were pillows. Jerking on the reins like a man, strands of wiry caramel-colored hair flying loose from her bun, she all but sniffed down her nose at Naomi's sturdy black laced shoes and opaque rayon stockings.

Somehow Naomi felt short and dumpy, her ash-brown hair colorless. Her body felt weak just watching Sharon take charge. They exchanged only a few words of conversation in their native Pennsylvania Dutch on the way home; Sharon sprinkled in English slang words that annoyed Naomi.

"Naomi, my darling, my sweet, sweet baby sister, I'm so glad you're here," Cora gushed when they arrived, pulling Naomi to her ample bosom. The hug felt good; Naomi had not yet allowed herself to miss her family.

"We have some news since our last letter inviting you here," Cora said. "Rose left us to marry an English. I'm going to put you in her bed, sharing a room with Sharon. The two of you should be such good friends." The young women stared at the linoleum. "Sharon, show her upstairs and then we can go outside."

Sitting on Rose's bed, Naomi felt like a patch of purple sewn on a brown quilt. As Sharon took her to the bedrooms of the four youngest children and introduced her to the towheaded toddlers, then brought her back downstairs, Naomi couldn't help noticing the well-made wooden furniture in every room. Cora's husband worked as a carpenter for a mobile home factory nearby.

The woodcraft extended into the front yard, which was full of items on sale: patio furniture, picnic tables, porch swings, dog houses. "These are mine," Sharon announced, pointing to rows of lawn and garden ornaments: wooden stakes topped with a painting of a lettuce head, beet or carrot to show what was planted in which row. Sleeping kittens, pups and raccoons that looked so lifelike Naomi was tempted to pick them up.

"You are so talented!" Naomi blurted, before

remembering that no one is supposed to receive praise that might make the person stand out.

"For the greater glory of God alone," Sharon murmured as if saying a rote prayer. Naomi looked at Cora.

"Sharon must always fight the problem of the English customers wanting her to take art classes to do 'real' art — as if taking part in our family livelihood and glorifying God with her handiwork isn't enough," Cora explained. "But soon she will be married and have her own children to provide her with her real life's work."

Sharon walked away. Naomi could only stare at her retreating back. Cora shrugged and showed Naomi the workshop, the saws powered by hydraulics rather than the forbidden electricity. Later, as Cora whisked her from one part of the property to another, Naomi caught a glimpse of Sharon in the workshop, hoisting the heavy saws and lumber with ease, doing her own wood cutting. Somehow Naomi had assumed the men in the family prepared the wood for Sharon's painting. Spellbound, Naomi watched Sharon move, her supple back and long arms reminding Naomi of the smooth powerful grace of a carriage horse effortlessly pulling a wagon.

"Here is the vegetable garden," Cora said, tugging Naomi away to yet another part of the property. "It's first priority for all of us every morning, so get ready to pull weeds tomorrow morning!" That was nothing strange — Naomi had had to pull weeds every morning before the sun got hot at her real home. She wiped back a tear.

"Let's get you into some freer clothes," Cora announced after their tour. "Our bishop must be far more progressive than yours was. Sharon? Come here and help our newest family member with her clothes."

Sharon's reluctance showed as she came in from the workshop, brushing sawdust from her dress at the door. With only the most necessary words, she took Naomi back to their shared room and brought out a pair of tennis shoes. Just as silently Naomi tied on the sneakers, reveling wordlessly in their airiness, wriggling her toes and twisting her ankles to experience their flexibility. Did she detect a grin on Sharon's tanned, freckled face? How dare Sharon laugh at her?

"We're the same shoe size. Probably dress size too, except for lengths. Now your hemlines," Sharon ordered. "Put on each of your dresses and I'll mark them up for you." She retrieved a piece of chalk and some straight pins from her sewing chest. As Naomi stood there in her thin cotton slip, she could feel Sharon's gaze on her body and she felt warm.

"How long is your hair?" Sharon asked suddenly.

"I don't know, I've never noticed. Long. Of course I've never cut it . . ." Naomi was stammering.

"Would you mind if I took it down? You have such lovely smooth hair, and I just want to look."

Naomi let Sharon's fingers find the hairpins keeping her bun in place. The weight of her hair falling in a rush to her hips made her whole body shift in place. She could sense Sharon's frank admiration, though somehow she didn't quite dare meet Sharon's stare.

"Cora's hair is like that, too — it runs in your family. So sleek, so shiny. Mine is like Brillo," Sharon sighed.

"Turnabout's fair play," Naomi said, delighted that Sharon was talking to her. Mischievously she pulled off Sharon's prayer covering and tugged at the thick caramel-colored bun. It was like a Jack-in-the-box springing open, hair flying everywhere, Sharon's mane a wide halo of delicate, fine curls cascading to mid-back. Her head was almost buried in a heap of tiny ringlets that Sharon shook back off her face.

"Well?" Sharon asked with sarcasm. "What a mess, right?"

"You're beautiful!" Naomi whispered. As Sharon's face reddened and her fingers flew to twist the springy curls back under control, Naomi quickly redid her own bun. The organdy prayer covering felt safer somehow. Surely she couldn't have done anything wrong — a woman was only supposed to show her unbound hair to her husband, but the rules collected in the *Ordnung* couldn't apply to stepsisters sharing a room, could they?

Back to maintaining silence, they marked Naomi's hems and got out the foot-treadle sewing machine to shorten all her skirts. By then it was time to do supper chores, peeling potatoes and shredding slaw. Naomi was conscious of Sharon's quick fingers speeding through a dozen potatoes while she was still on her second.

"Our household hosts the church service in just five weeks, so we had better get started with cleaning and cooking," Cora announced at dinner. She outlined chores for everyone in the household, even for her husband's parents who lived in the *dawdyhaus* adjoining the main house.

Naomi was eager to go to church service the next

Sunday at another family's home, to see if the entire
district was as progressive as Cora and Sharon. They
weren't, she found, staring as unobtrusively as
possible at the old women who were even more
covered than she had been her first day in
Shipshewana. A few of them glared at Naomi's
shortened hems.

"Try it, it feels so much better to not have all
that heavy material dragging on your calves," she
wanted to tell them. But of course she didn't say a
word.

After the service and the two meals and the
conversations that went on all day long as part of
church service, the adults and young children went
home, leaving all the teen-agers and young adults
together in the parlor to sing hymns.

Though this was the primary place young people
met their prospective husbands and wives, Naomi
just liked to sing.

She was glad that her religion allowed teen-agers
a few years of relative freedom before they made the
choice to become baptized and adhere to the strict
Ordnung. When the teen-agers at her previous
community had gotten together to sing the old
hymns, they really got moving in high-spirited
rhythm, swaying to the familiar phrases as if they
were in a hypnotic trance, all of them conscious of
each other, of who was looking at which prospective
suitor. This night's hymn-singing in her new
congregation was no different.

The dozen or so young men of the district stared
openly at Naomi as if they couldn't get enough of
her, as if they needed to make up for not having
seen her grow up during the past seventeen years

and could size her up totally in one night. Their
stares made her uncomfortable. For reassurance she
kept looking at Sharon, who seemed to be sending a
protective shield her way by pulling her wooden
chair up close to Naomi's and glaring at the men.

Sharon's voice was deep and resonant; she gave
strong emphasis to the beat of the hymns, moving in
her chair as if she were dancing, her eyes closed
except for occasional glances at Naomi. Naomi felt
her soprano voice meld with Sharon's, echoing the
same beat, emphasizing the same familiar words in
a slightly unexpected way. They could have been
singing alone, as if the rest of the young people
weren't even there.

This is how these hymns should be sung, not the
slow way of the adults during services, Naomi
thought comfortably as the hours went by. The rest
of the household had long ago gone to sleep. Finally,
their own voices grew tired and cracked. The young
men, free to be "wild" for the only time of their lives
— unless they chose to leave their community and
face the "English" world with only an eighth grade
education — raced   to   the   carriages,   hurling
invitations to accompany them to their desired
females over their shoulders.

Several of the men called out Naomi's name. She
looked at Sharon, who was heading to her family's
buggy by herself. "It's up to you," Sharon called
down.

Nervously Naomi scanned the field of men. None
of them appealed to her. "Is it okay if I ride back
with you?" she asked Sharon.

"Certainly," Sharon said, smiling, reaching out to
help Naomi step up into the buggy. Naomi settled

into the hard wooden seat in gratitude. The young
men's hard stares and possessive competition for her
had made her uncomfortable. Sitting next to Sharon,
she felt at home. They drove home together without
a word. None was needed.

As the days passed, Naomi often noticed she was
paying attention to Sharon, watching her, eager to
talk to her.

"It's so nice that the two of you have become
such good friends," Cora said one night over supper.
"I was worried that first day. How are you doing,
Naomi?"

"Just fine," Naomi murmured. She wondered
again if she wasn't too close to Sharon somehow,
though she didn't see what the problem could be.
The *Ordnung* said nothing about this situation; all
the sermons she had ever heard had never touched
upon a woman being attracted to another woman,
though she did remember horror stories about men
being with men in ways they shouldn't, particularly
in the towns of Sodom and Gomorrah. Surely what
she was starting to feel for Sharon had nothing to
do with *that!* She scoured her Bible for answers and
found none.

"I don't want to marry any man," Sharon told
Naomi one night from her bed. "One day I'm going
to walk into church services in a black apron and sit
right down with the married women." Naomi was
scandalized. But the more Sharon talked, the more
she understood.

Many of Sharon's ideas came from her sister

Rose, who kept in close touch with Sharon through letters and occasional visits. Since she hadn't been baptized before she left the community, she wasn't shunned. She now lived in Baltimore with her husband, a genetics researcher at Johns Hopkins University. Rose had met him when he came to Shipshewana to update the heredity charts the university maintained for many Amish families. She had worked with the local midwife and knew much of the information he wanted.

In Baltimore, Rose was taking high school completion classes while also enrolled in a preliminary class at a community college. She hoped to be a social worker one day and at the same time raise a family. Naomi didn't see how that could be possible.

Rose encouraged Sharon to go to art school and kept mailing her information. "She sends me stuff you wouldn't believe," Sharon revealed. She shared it with Naomi. When Cora was out of the house, Sharon even dared to begin using her acrylics on canvases Rose mailed to her.

Naomi, meanwhile, learned how to make fancy breads and cakes to sell at the stand in front of the house, as her contribution to the family's income. "You could work in a bakery to make some money till you got some schooling, if you ever wanted to leave," Sharon hinted.

Naomi was scandalized. "I'm never going to leave my faith," she said with intense determination.

"Never?"

"Never," Naomi insisted. Sharon sighed.

As time passed, Naomi settled into her new life.

Her nineteenth birthday approached; others her age were starting classes to prepare for baptism. Naomi signed up for instruction. But Sharon was having second thoughts. "I can't stop painting, I want to be a real artist," she insisted to Naomi.

The idea shocked and scared Naomi — she couldn't bear to lose another person who had become so entwined in her life. They had finally become the best friends her brothers had predicted. Naomi had never felt so close to another human being, closer than she'd thought possible. Sharon wouldn't leave, she just couldn't.

Sometimes they cuddled in bed together and talked late into the night under the covers so that the household wouldn't hear. One night when Naomi was feeling particularly needy of Sharon, she dared to ask about the facts of life. "Your mother never told you anything either?" Sharon said. "Rose sent me some books on sex." They crawled into bed together to read *The Joy of Sex* by moonlight. Sharon took her nightgown off. Naomi did as well.

Naomi stared frankly at Sharon's body silhouetted in the moonlight and wondered at the strange feelings low in her stomach.

"I wish you could see your breasts the way *I* see them, the way I would like to paint them," Sharon said.

"How do you see them?"

"Oh, Naomi . . ." Sharon seemed speechless for a change. "Naomi . . . your breasts are so beautiful." She reached out and cupped them. Naomi drew back for a second, then let Sharon's hands stay. The thought occurred to her that she could also touch

Sharon's breasts, to see how they felt. Her mind recoiled. Her hands reached out. So soft. The place below her stomach wrenched.

"Mine are so little compared to yours," Sharon said, letting her fingers roam over Naomi's body. "Yours are . . ."

"*Your breasts are like twin fawns, the young of a gazelle that browses among the lilies until the day breathes cool and the shadows lengthen,*" Naomi said, remembering the poetry of *Song of Songs* from the apocryphal books of the Bible. "*I will go to the mountain of myrrh, to the hill of incense. You are all beautiful, my beloved, and there is no blemish in you.*"

"*I am a flower of Sharon, a lily of the valley,*" Sharon continued from a few verses later, her voice lowered. "*As a lily among thorns, so is my beloved among women . . .*"

"*I adjure you, daughters of Jerusalem, do not arouse, do not stir up love before its own time,*" Naomi whispered. But it was too late, or perhaps it was love's own time, for she leaned forward and kissed Sharon's sweet mouth.

What Sharon had told her, now she was shown. Naomi felt hands gently knead her breasts, her nipples; lips took them in, kissed them, suckled on them. Sharon's mouth kissed every inch of Naomi's body, and Naomi responded in kind. Shifting in the small bed, Sharon touched down there, kissed down there, opened her lips with her fingers and her tongue, sought out the small button that had the strange name of clitoris and rested there, licking at the center of all feelings radiating through her until Naomi exploded and Sharon put her hand over

Naomi's mouth so that she would not cry out and bring parents and younger children into their room. Naomi let herself writhe in Sharon's arms, knowing Sharon would take care of her, knowing Sharon was in control.

Sharon kept on, drawing more and more feelings out of the button, sucking every last ripple of feelings from her breasts, her lips, her neck, her ears, and again to her vulva, bringing up more and more pulsating rhythms until she was too dizzy to even know where she was. Naomi lay back, exhausted, drained, in love.

Momentarily she remembered past sermons, old warnings. She groaned. And Sharon's lips covered hers, and she was lost again, swimming in wonderment. This time she repeated the movements Sharon had done to her on Sharon's lean, strong body, diving deep into Sharon's golden mound of thick hair and finding the clitoris, tasting it, working it, loving it.

Sharon put her arm in her own mouth to keep from making a sound, trying to keep her body rigid and soundless. I love this woman! Naomi said to herself. She said it aloud: "I love you!"

"That's what I've been longing to hear," Sharon said in delight. "Naomi, I love you. I've grown to love you. Come away with me. Rose will put us both up for a while, until we can get jobs. She's showing my paintings around the art department at the university, and she's sure I'll be able to get in on a scholarship and really learn how to paint. You'll find there's all sorts of things you're good at, I know, because you're so bright. You're so beautiful, I love you, I love you, I love you . . ."

The words spun in Naomi's head, they grew in volume until her head could have exploded. The good feelings were so powerful, yet the teachings against them came roaring back like a tidal wave to smother them.

She buried her face in her pillow and sobbed. This is wrong, this is very, very wrong, voices inside said. You have got to get out of here. And she grabbed her nightgown and ran from Sharon down to the bathroom and poured cool water over her face and washed her body and sat on the toilet until her breathing slowed.

When she dared to return to the bedroom Sharon lay in her own bed, worry in her eyes. "I won't go with you, Sharon," Naomi said. "I can't love you. This is wrong. It won't happen again." And she turned away from Sharon and stared into the plaster wall all night.

"You know that I'm going to have to leave," Sharon whispered from across the room. Naomi heard, with tears in her eyes. "But I'll come back for you. Somehow. Some day. If you won't leave, then I'll have to come back. You're going to be under a lot of pressure to marry once you're baptized. I'll understand if you give in. I just ask one thing: Don't marry anyone you don't really, truly love. I'll be back. Do you hear me?" Naomi nodded, her face buried in her pillow in silent sobs.

The next morning she and Sharon were strangers. At lunch Sharon was gone. Her family looked everywhere for her, questioned Naomi on what could have gone wrong, drove the cart to every place she might be. A letter from Rose told them that Sharon was safe. Naomi felt as much grief as she had when her parents were killed. Somehow she felt that the grieving Cora blamed her, and somehow she felt guilty.

Though Sharon could have kept in contact with her family, she didn't, especially after Naomi wouldn't answer her letters. Naomi's salvation lay in submission to the Amish community. Her baptismal instruction reinforced her beliefs. She would not dwell on the past. On Sharon.

On the day she was baptized at Sunday service, the deacon poured water into the bishop's hands so that it dribbled on her head as she repeated the vows. It felt right, but not as fulfilling, as overpowering, as she had expected. As cool air dried her hair and skin, she wondered if that was all there was, all there would be.

Now that she was an adult, the men who had been looking at her at the Sunday night hymn fests started showing up Sunday nights at the household's "boyfriend door" that led directly into the formal parlor, wanting to court her.

They bored her silly. Despite her intentions, she could only think of Sharon. But there was no way for Sharon to ever come back, despite her promise.

When the letter came to the bishop from a new settlement in Marling, Michigan, asking for any single women who might be interested in moving there because they had a surplus of unmarried men, Naomi took sorrowful leave of Cora and the adopted family that had been so kind to her. But anything had to be better than waiting for who knew what. No men in Shipshewana interested her.

Unfortunately, Marling was only a smaller version of Shipshewana and Lancaster. Hans and

Ella Bieler, who took her under their wing in return for help with household chores, were kindly but busy. None of the new men attracted her, which irritated the Marling community and her adopted family, but she couldn't help it.

Until the day she was sitting in church with the other white-aproned single women and she felt the hairs rise on the back of her neck. Someone was watching her. Her breath caught. She was not afraid, but she didn't dare turn around.

She was not at all surprised that night when Ella Bieler called up to her room that she had a visitor in the parlor. She smoothed her dress and hair, threw back her shoulders, and went forward to she knew not what.

"This is Aaron Yoder, and he has just joined our congregation," Hans Bieler introduced her. "He just moved here from Florida because his sinuses can't take the intense heat and humidity. Our bishop has a letter of introduction from his bishop." Naomi's heart leapt for joy — could it be?

"He makes custom stained glass windows for kitchen cabinets and private homes, and he is renting an English house until he can find a suitable home here. He saw you in church today and wanted to make your acquaintance."

"Pleased to meet you, Mr. Yoder," Naomi said, hiding a smile that threatened to explode all over her face.

"Call me Aaron," Sharon said, her voice low and level. Her wiry hair was cut straight back from her earlobes and her wispy bangs fell to mid-forehead, the fine short curls shooting upright all over her head like a dandelion gone to seed. Her collarless white shirt, black vest and navy broad-fall trousers were freshly ironed, the black shoes polished. Yes, she could pass for a young man easily, handsome if fine-featured. No one would ever know.

"He has brought our family a fine gift, this stained glass display case for our Bible," Hans Bieler said. "I will leave you two alone now."

It took everything in her not to run forward and hug Sharon, to hang on her, to take her back to bed, to kiss her forever. But small eyes were everywhere in an Amish house. The two women beamed at each other, letting their love show only in their gaze.

"I've arranged my life so that I can marry you and be with you here if you still want to stay," Sharon finally said. "Or if someday you want to leave, we can make a life anywhere now. I told you I'd come back."

"How . . ." Naomi was overwhelmed with questions.

"Rose and her husband have been busy. First, from his research he knew of someone who had left Florida with a letter of introduction from a bishop who keeps lousy records."

"Somebody with a sinus problem," Naomi giggled.

"Right. Then the guy moved someplace else, so that will confuse the records. Besides, do you know how many Aaron Yoders there are? Sixteen in the Ohio settlement alone!" Naomi remembered at least three or four in Shipshewana.

"Next, when I have to start growing a beard after we're married, I have enough artificial beard of different lengths to last several years, thanks to the Johns Hopkins theater department," Sharon explained. "The only way we could get in trouble is if Cora ever comes here to visit and sees me, so you'll have to visit there a lot. The other thing is if I ever need to go to a hospital, we'll have to make sure it's not one around here."

Naomi's head whirled with all the information pouring from Sharon. Naomi was an empty pitcher being filled with fresh warm milk.

"We won't be able to have children, but Rose's husband says there's even some ways to go about that. I think this can work. Naomi, is it love's own time? Will you marry me?"

"Oh yes, yes, yes." Naomi dared not move or she would be in Sharon's arms, they would be on the floor peeling off their clothes, no matter what spies were afoot. It was the hardest thing she had ever done, to stand there as if they had just met. She devoured Sharon's face with her eyes.

"We'd better sit down," Naomi said. "We have a lot to talk about. You'd better take the chair over there and I'll sit here." Safe distance between them, she felt the flush in her cheeks. "How did you come up with the idea of posing as a man?"

"Women have done it throughout history," Sharon said. "Wait till you read some of the books I've got. I'll see if I can sneak them to you tomorrow so that you can be thinking of me until next Sunday. Women have loved women all through history. Just as I love you."

She'd read the books tomorrow. For the first time in her life, Naomi looked forward to tomorrow.

Boundary Lines

Anita Skeen

The Paula Austen that I remember wears a V-neck sweater more gold than the leaves which curl inward and drop from the trees bordering the school yard. She stands with the other cheerleaders and her friends on the corner of Jefferson and Lee while the boys from the high school drive by in their fathers' new 1959 Ford Galaxies and Chevrolet Impalas. The boys drive by slowly and the ones in convertibles encourage the girls to ride with them. The girls pretend not to be interested.

In the center of Paula's sweater is a letter like the ones given to the boys who hurl their bodies to victory every Friday night at Shanklin Field. The letter is the first letter of the last name of the man for whom our school is named. Paula's skirt drapes in pleats, that same gold hidden behind royal blue. When she leaps into the air during a cheer, the blue pleats part and the gold inside glows like treasure. I watch the letter rise and fall on her chest. I can't keep my eyes on the ball.

I go to the girl's gym sometimes over the noon hour to watch the intramural games. On Wednesdays there are the Noonday Dances, but I don't go to them. Instead, I work on my Algebra in the study hall above the gym. I hear the music climb out of the gym's gut, loll in the first floor hallway, then snake up the steps to tease the few of us working in Room 210. "Hey, Paul . . . Hey, Paula," the voice croons. I try to solve for X, but the letter perfectly stitched to Paula's sweater is the only one I can see.

All but two homerooms have been eliminated, and those two are playing for the championship of the eighth grade. Not many students are in the gym watching because it is only the girls who are playing. The boys' tournament was last month. The gym was hot and tight. Then, I stood with my friends near the back doors where we felt the air from the hallway, sweet and cool as the concrete, not

like the smell of sweat and overripe fruit that
follows boys and sports. The boys' game was close,
and balls spun on the metal rims at both ends,
sometimes caressed by the nets they dropped
through, sometimes swishing through as though no
net were there. When the favorite team won, the boy
who scored the winning basket pulled off his dark,
soaked shirt and threw it to a girl in the balcony.
She hugged it to her chest. Her girlfriends clutched
her, encircling her in their arms. Later, I notice the
boy and that girl holding hands outside 106.
Someone tells me he was expelled for three days for
violating the school dress code.

The girls' Kick-Pin-Ball game is almost over. I
am sitting on the front row of the balcony, my bare
arms resting on the top metal railing, my chin on
my hands. Paula is pitching for her homeroom. She
is wearing a faded gym suit, as are all the girls on
the gym floor, as all girls must who participate in
Physical Education or any intramural activity. I
notice how well her gym suit fits, unlike my own,
which was given to me by my next-door-neighbor
when she moved up this fall to the high school.

The gym suits are all nondescript blue cotton. No
personal clothing is allowed past the locker room. If
a girl forgets her gym suit on Monday because she
is late for the bus or because her mother has
forgotten to wash it, that is no excuse. She receives
an "F" for the day and sits upstairs in the balcony
while the rest of us smash dodge balls against the
walls or perform exercises to "Chicken Fat."

Some girls, it appears, like to sit in the balcony. They have their periods every week, and that *is* an excuse. But most of us appear on the gym floor with our gym suits dutifully washed (and ironed), gripper snaps snapped and bloomer legs properly bloomed. It is an offense to tuck too much of the pant leg into the bloomer so that one appears to be wearing short shorts. This can result in a trip to the balcony. I notice Paula has tucked up her pant legs and I see how long and strong her legs are. She is the prettiest girl on the floor, taller than most, and her cornsilk hair bounces in a pony tail. I watch her hands curl around the ball, watch her roll it across the floor to the girl who kicks it into the air, watch her stretch into the air for a catch. The girl is out, the game over. Paula's team wins, and the girls from her homeroom swell around her, their shouts ricocheting off the walls, off my heart.

My friends decide to migrate to a new spot for our after lunch gatherings. I bring my lunch and eat in the study hall, but most of them go to The Sweet Shoppe, Woolworth's or Valley Bell Dairy for lunch, or over to the high school cafeteria. Then we congregate for the twenty minutes or so we have left before the bell rings for fifth period. We have been hanging out on the front steps of the school, but a group of town boys who smoke cigarettes and say rude things has begun to collect there. They never speak directly to me, but Joanne and Cheryl have been singled out for their whistles and insinuations. I'm not sure what some of the things they say mean, but Cheryl blushes and Joanne tells them to do it to themselves.

We move up the sidewalk about halfway to the corner, as far as we can go without encroaching upon eighth grade territory. There are no lines or fences, but there are boundaries. To the north of us are the girls in our class who always go to the Noonday Dances, and who get asked to dance, and to the south are the eighth grade cheerleaders and their friends. I stand on the south end, and sometimes, if the traffic isn't too heavy or the wind too loud, I can hear some of the eighth grade conversations. I learn how to listen out of both ears at once so my friends won't know that I am listening for Paula.

Paula does not seem to talk as much as her friends. Sometimes, during the whole noon hour, I can catch only a sentence or two, and then, because her voice is low, sometimes I don't quite understand what she says. Once, I hear her talk about her dog, Yippie, and another time about a girl in her Sunday School class. The cheerleaders talk about the eighth grade teachers, whom they don't like, and the eighth grade boys, whom they do. Two of the three cheerleaders are going with a boy. Paula is not. I don't know why, because I've heard her say how cute Timmy Simms is, how neat the Adams twins are, how stupid Terry O'Connor is. That could mean anything. Terry O'Connor is not stupid, at least, my friends don't think so. I wonder if those boys know that girls are talking about them. I wonder if something tickles inside their ears when Paula says "Timmy Simms" or "Walker Adams" or "Terry O'Connor." I wonder what it would be like to have my name held on someone's tongue, in that way.

That night, when I turn out my light and lie under the covers I say, "Paula Austen. Paula Austen. Paula Austen."

Soon, I say to my friends while we eat Eskimo Pies, "What's the main character's name in Austen's book we're reading? Is it something like Ann? or Paula? or . . . that's not right. I know that'll be on the test."

"Elizabeth," Beverly says. "How could you forget 'Elizabeth'? Paula's not even close."

I smile. For some reason, I feel power.

I read the headlines from the student paper to my friend Barbara who is trying to write her theme for English.

"Trojans Defeat Patriots in Last Minute Rally. Teacher Involved in Auto Accident. New Hours for the Candy Store. Paula Austen Elected Student of the Week."

Barbara keeps writing.

"Do you think you'll ever be Student of the Week?" I ask.

"Get serious," she replies without even looking
up.

I try to find the chance to say Paula's name at
least once every day. I need an audience. It's no
good anymore if I say it alone in a dark room. As I
approach the first syllable, I feel my breath catch,
my body heat up. No one seems to notice this at all.
I'm very careful to watch. I don't want to take too
many risks, get too reckless with my secret. I can't
afford to get caught.

In my government class each Friday the Student
of the Week comes to tell us what he thinks it
means to be a good citizen. On Wednesday, I start
making a list of questions in my spiral notebook to
ask Paula:
1. Do you like the Everly Brothers?
I write slowly and in the proper cursive style I was
taught in second grade, careful with the loops in the
capital "d" and "e," not in the half-print-half-straight-
up-and-down scratch I have adopted in rebellion.
There is something delicious in the flow, the curves.
As I write, the strains of "To know, know, know
him, Is to love, love, love him" play in some
basement of my brain.
2. Do you like to play in the woods?
My pen takes a long time on the word "you" and the
word "play." I think of the woods behind my house,
the leaves now warm and wrinkled when I lie

among them, the path only I know to the old sawmill. I see the shafts of light lancing through the slanted trunks that have been fashioned into the frames for teepees, though no skin or fabric now covers them. I love to sit under those poles in the late afternoon, to think about how I could live my whole life there.

3. What do you

I hear my name spoken in the front of the room. It seems unrelated to me.

I memorize Paula's telephone number. It occurs to me that if I call, she may answer the phone. Or someone else in her family. If I hang up on them, they will think I am a wrong number. If Paula answers, she will say "Hello" specifically to me. I will need a response. There is nothing I can say. I can't say what I want.

On Friday, ten minutes before the bell, Paula walks into my government class. Because it is Friday, she is dressed in her cheerleading uniform. Because my last name starts with "A," I sit on the front row only a few feet from where she stands. She looks directly at me when Mrs. Crockett asks her why good citizenship is important. Her eyes are so blue I see nothing else. Blue moon. Blue gill. Blue jay. Blue pencil. Blue ribbon. Blue racer. Blue sky. Blue grass. Blue jeans. Blue ridge. I say all these words to myself, and finally, Sharp Blue, because what I feel is a knife.

The bell rings. This is the last period of the day so everyone is halfway to the door as Mrs. Crockett thanks Paula for coming to our class. I am still bolted to my seat. As Paula turns to leave, she looks my way again. I look down.

I dial 555-1206 and hang up before anyone can answer. I am breathing as hard as if I had just escaped with life.

I will be late to English class again, I know it. I'm on the third floor, the final bell rings, and I have to get to the basement in two seconds. I've been watching for Paula, but I've missed her somehow. I've discovered that her third period class meets in room 306, the art room, so every day I plan my trek from Algebra, in 206 to English in 101 by way of 306. This is not easy as the school is overcrowded, there are only three minutes between classes, and students stuff the stairwells like too many crayons in a box. I am small for my age, so often I slither through quickly. Unnoticed in the crowded hallway, I wait for Paula to pass. Sometimes I brush my arm against her books or dip my shoulder against hers. Then I am blessed for the day.

But today, there is no Paula, and I have to turn

back toward the stairs. I've already been late to
English class twice this month. I say that I have to
stay late in Algebra to ask Mr. Whitney about
values I don't understand. Mrs. Diebolt, my English
teacher, tells me words are as important as numbers
and just because I'm advanced (which she says in an
odd way) in mathematics doesn't mean I can ignore
the English language. "To know how to speak
correctly what others only think is what makes men
poets," she instructs me, looking toward something
on the ceiling. "Now, sit down, young lady."

I think about all this as I head toward the
stairwell looking down at the grey tile floor, noticing
how some squares have been worn almost white by
years of students dragging to English class. I begin
to feel the swelling in my throat that comes before
tears and I swallow hard to hold back some part of
me that wants to scream but has no words.

Now I am aware that someone is standing beside
me, has come up in front of me, and is placing a
hand on my arm. The hand is slim and delicate, and
there is a ring with a blue stone on the fourth
finger. The hand is a girl's hand and the pressure
light, hesitant and steady at the same time. When I
look up, Paula Austen stands beside me, her hand
on my arm.

"Are you okay?" she says. "Is something wrong?
Has something happened?" Blue light, blue light
everywhere.

I can say nothing, and I feel her grip tighten,
her other hand move to my shoulder.

"I'm late for my class," I say. "I keep getting
there late."

She takes her hand from my shoulder, but I feel its ghost weight.

"Is that all? You look like you're about to throw up. Are you sure you're not sick?" She pauses, squinting my way. "What class are you going to?" Her hand still rests on my arm; inside my body, things explode.

I tell her about who I have for English and she tells me Mrs. Diebolt is all words and no action. She tells me she had Mrs Diebolt for English 7, and one time when Mrs. D. went into her book closet, her "inner sanctum," as she calls it, someone got up and locked her in. Then the whole class left the room so no one person would be blamed.

I laugh so hard the tears come.

I don't know how long we stand in the hall, but it is quiet and the drones of adult voices slip out under nearby doors.

"Uh oh," I say, "now you'll be late, too."

"Don't worry," she grins and taps my shoulder. "It won't be the first time. Besides, it's only Dopey Dobson's drawing class." She winks, turns, and ducks inside an open doorway.

I look at my arm where Paula's hand lay, surprised to see nothing. No trace, no sign, no badge to show I'm singled out, that we've exchanged words and touching. I spin down past her gestures, her words. Her eyes light my passage. My nerves buzz sharp blue.

The Poet's Descendant

Lori A. Paige

The late afternoon shadows were slanting across the long walnut table where I was working, and I was wishing I'd written the purchase of a laptop computer into my grant proposal the previous semester. On second thought, though, I was glad I hadn't. My dissertation committee had looked skeptical enough when I had proposed the topic to be funded: Lady Julia Stanmore, a virtually unknown eighteenth-century poet I'd discovered in a little-read volume in the rare book room. They had been almost as surprised as I was when I'd managed to make contact with some of her descendants, who still resided in the family home just outside London. The grant I had obtained had enabled me to travel to England, rent a room in a nearby village and spend my whole July in the Reynards' antique library taking notes from Lady Julia's own collection. Far from being jealous of their privacy, the family was thrilled that someone might make them famous via an illustrious ancestor, and had given me free range of the library while all of them except their oldest daughter went off on holiday to Greece.

This daughter was, I presumed, supposed to keep an eye on me and the rest of the place during my last week. Claudia Reynard was about my age and had just finished reading Economics at the University of London. On the whole, I found her unpretentious and beautiful, with her short light hair and tweed coats which put a pleasantly feminine twist on the typical "country squire" look. Occasionally she'd stop in and ask about my progress, and if I ever unintentionally bored her she was too gracious to let it show.

On that day I'd been working with particular diligence, since I had only five days left before I was to go to London for the rest of my summer, where I'd use up my grant on museum visits and maybe a couple of trips to the women's pubs, then fly home and attempt to arrange my boxes of notes into something resembling a coherent Ph.D. dissertation. I was trying to visualize some compelling London adventures when Claudia walked up to my chair.

"How's it going?" she asked, and I was amused to see her wearing a raincoat and those big waterproof boots the British call Wellies. Underneath, she wore a dove-grey sweater with a high neck, and I couldn't help noticing how perfectly its color matched her eyes. "I was out walking but the rain got so bad I had to come back. Too much mud."

Claudia was so charming, I thought. As she stood there, the wet threads of grass plastered to the toes of her boots, I felt a jealous stab because the whole rest of England got to stay here with her, while I had to go back to grad school and the usual isolation, drudgery, and frustration.

"You know," I blurted out rather recklessly, "I'll miss your conversation once I leave here."

To my relief, Claudia didn't appear threatened at all. "I feel the same way," she admitted, the tips of her ears reddening slightly, "though I couldn't bring myself to say it." I had no idea how to respond. Maybe she hadn't meant it in quite the way I hoped. The tiny, knowing smile she flashed me, however, suggested that she did. She started poking her mud-stained toe against the protruding edge of a floorboard. "Can you stay to dinner tonight, then? Or did you need to be back to your room at any certain time?"

"Actually, I don't have plans. And I'd love to have dinner."

"Well, that's set. It should be ready in about an hour. I'll see you at the table after you're finished here." With a rattled haste I found promising, Claudia left the library and strode quickly down the hall. Alone again, I tried not to concoct too elaborate a fantasy regarding that dinner, well aware that disappointment would then almost inevitably follow. Still, perhaps Claudia would wear that brocaded, sapphire blue dinner jacket with silk lapels that I'd seen her wear a few times. More than once I'd imagined running my palms down its front and then slipping it off Claudia's shoulders, planting moist kisses along her bared neck as I did so ... I was sweating a few moments later as I hastily piled up my notes. Well, never mind passion, I thought. I'd be content to get through dinner without spilling anything!

As it turned out, my composure returned admirably once we were facing each other across a tastefully arranged dinner table, perhaps because she had not, after all, put on the blue jacket. Since her parents had left her to fend for herself, we feasted on Indian take-away which she had gone to town to pick up before changing out of her rain gear. We conversed easily, mainly the relative merits of British and American television programs. She preferred my country's selections, I hers. I felt encouraged by the fact that most of her favorite shows featured strong female characters and that she had taken a course on feminist media studies in college.

When the last of the cardboard cartons was empty, she suggested coffee in the sitting room. I offered to make it, since she'd gone for the food and we were both content with instant anyway. She went into the next room to wait, and when I finally blundered in balancing the tray, I couldn't help stopping dead to stare at her.

Only the hall light was on, and she was standing in front of the French window, a beautiful shadow against the dim outline of the hedges outside. Had Lady Julia taken that same pose, looking out at the muted starlight and breathing in its quiet, while thinking out her newest poem? I wished I hadn't made so much noise, because she immediately turned to me and fidgeted self-consciously. "I thought it would be nicer without all that harsh light," she apologized, and I could see the outline of her shoulders move in a shrug. "I guess I forgot that you might spill the coffee. Sorry."

I could see well enough to detect an end table just to my left, so I safely deposited the tray. She was coming towards me as if to reach for the light switch, but I intercepted her and touched her wrist. "No, don't," I said, and laced my fingers through hers. "I can see well enough."

She responded by hooking her free hand around my neck and pulling my face down to meet hers. I felt oddly conscious of the little hairs on my arms standing up the way they were supposed to at scary movies. Since I never went to scary movies, I wasn't sure this had ever happened to me before.

Her kiss was hard, much more urgent than I had expected. After all the guilt I had experienced, she had ended up starting things! Her teeth grazed my lower lip and then my cheek. I pulled her even closer against me, until I could feel her belt buckle press against the fly on my jeans. "Do you want me?" she whispered against my skin.

"Yes, of course — I always have. I felt foolish for thinking you'd be interested."

"And do you feel foolish now?"

"Certainly not!" In truth, I was glad the light was so dim, because it concealed the warm blush on my cheeks.

"Come over to the sofa, then," Claudia urged, and guided me through the near-darkness to the couch in the corner. As we lay across the soft cushions, our kisses became even less inhibited, and her fingers brushed along my shirt buttons. She moved her lips to the swell of my breast and again applied the gentle pressure of her teeth to the cotton veiling it. My breath caught and I slipped my fingers into her hair, rubbing the nape of her neck. This seemed to please her, for soon she was also rocking her body back and forth against me. The whole thing seemed so well orchestrated and coordinated that I was genuinely startled when the couch seemed to pull away under us and we tumbled to the floor, Claudia shrieking with laughter.

"So, the earth did move," I said, sharing her amusement once I realized what had happened — the sofa cushions had moved off their mooring — and wishing once again that my comic repartee was more highly developed. We sat up together on the rug, and Claudia leaned against me with her head on my shoulder.

"Are there lots of women like us in America?" she asked me after we had giggled together for some time, the incident providing a welcome release for a variety of tensions.

"I don't have much trouble finding them, though that hasn't always been a good thing. London?"

"Oh, yes, same thing. They always seem to take up with me for the wrong reasons. Then when the fun part is over they can't be bothered any longer."

"Ah, college relationships," I said with mock wistfulness.

She took my chin in insistent fingers. "I never doubted there'd be something better eventually, though," she said, and kissed me hard. "I always did fancy Americans. Something about the accents. I've been planning a trip there for some time, you know. My only problem was that I didn't know where I should stay."

"Somehow," I kissed the bridge of her nose, "I don't think that will be any problem."

"And I understand that once you reach a certain stage in your program, you can mail in bits of your dissertation from anywhere in the world, really, so long as you can find a computer to put things on."

"Yes, that's certainly possible. Some say it's even possible without a computer, though I must say I can't imagine how."

She wriggled out of my arms and crawled over to the coffee tray I'd so happily abandoned, then scuttled back and set it down on the rug between us.

"Well, now that we've settled that, perhaps we ought to have a toast. Not a proper one, of course, but I don't really want to go look for anything else, do you?"

"Certainly not," I agreed, and we clicked coffee cups and drank from them together. The coffee had gone lukewarm and really tasted pretty foul.

"Coo," Claudia exclaimed in a broad London drawl, holding the cup out in front of her critically, "but if this won't keep me up all night long!"

"That," I said as I pried it gently from her fingers, "is probably inevitable."

A Lustful Feast

Jackie Calhoun

I focused on Joanne's tongue, flickering out to catch the juice escaping down her chin, and caught a glimpse of white teeth behind sensual lips. Never missing a beat in the conversation, she wiped her face with the heel of her hand. Mesmerized, I forgot my own food.

"I know this is interesting, but not enough to hang on every word," she said suddenly. "Aren't you hungry?"

And I had thought she was too wrapped up in

talking to notice me. Clearing my throat, I glanced indifferently at my plate. "I was just thinking..." I began. What was I thinking? That I'd like to taste the juice on her lips? I couldn't tell her that. Neither one of us was free to sample the other.

"Earth to Abby. Are you there?" Her eyes narrowed and my heart involuntarily bumped into high gear.

I laughed. "I'm just not hungry, Jo."

She leaned forward and her blouse gaped wider, revealing a white undershirt and the clear delineation of breasts. "How do you want to spend the afternoon?"

Choking down a provocative reply, I shrugged instead. We were artists — struggling, little known. Perhaps that was why I had never tried to move beyond friendship with her. Believing that competition and jealousy might be byproducts, I didn't think it wise for two artists to become lovers.

"The art museum? The lake shore?" Her soft brown eyes widened with the questions. "You certainly are acting strange."

"The lake. What a good idea. I'll catch this." I grabbed the bill and went to pay. Drying sweaty palms on my jeans, I told myself to get a grip. This was just Jo, after all, whom I had known for years. We sometimes exhibited at the same shows. Her medium was watercolor, mine steel. I made strange concoctions out of bolts and nuts and springs and angle iron — anything that could be welded together. She used vivid colors to paint the images around her.

* * * * *

Throwing my head back to the April sunlight, I sniffed the air as we scrambled among the rocks along Lake Michigan. Inland it had to be fifteen degrees warmer, and the cooling effect of the lake on air temperature kept us moving. Memories flooded back with the odor of water and weeds and fish. The wind tore at my hair and would have whipped my jacket open had I not held it tightly wrapped. Gulls called as they swooped around us and over the lake.

"Are you cold?" she asked, standing next to me. Her eyes, shaded by dark lashes, dominated her face. She had broad cheek bones made ruddy by the wind. Her hair, the same dark brown as her eyes, curled in an unruly mass around her face. We stood about the same height.

I was shivering. "A little."

"Why don't we go to my place. It's nearby."

I looked at her, trying to read her thoughts, and she smiled disarmingly. "That'd be nice," I said.

She shared the apartment with a woman named Gerry, whom I had met twice before. I stood just inside the door, getting a feel for the place, thinking they either didn't believe in furniture or couldn't afford it. The walls vibrated with Joanne's watercolors. Then I noticed the painting in progress on a table across the room. The light from the window next to it gave life to its colors.

"Did I ever tell you how much I admire your paintings?" I wasn't trying to snow her with compliments. The bright colors she used shimmered with energy.

Standing behind me with her hands resting on her hips, she leaned forward until I felt her warmth through my shirt. "Thanks," she said, her breath against my ear.

I turned and straightened to put some distance between us. I wasn't going to get caught by a jealous lover in her own apartment.

"Want something to drink?" she asked, a quizzical smile stretching that sensual mouth.

I licked my lips, which suddenly felt parched. "Water. Please."

After handing me a glass of ice water, she sat down on a futon and patted the space next to her. "Let's talk art."

I hesitated. "Where's Gerry today?"

"She works at a mortgage company. It's a week day, Abby. Remember?"

"When does she get home?"

"She bowls tonight. She won't be coming home until late. Why?" A teasing grin lit her face. "We're safe."

Blood thumped through me as I scoffed, "We're not doing anything."

"Not yet," she agreed. Then said, "I love your work. All those wonderfully imaginative creations made out of discarded odds and ends."

I flushed with pleasure and sat at the far end of the couch. "Thanks."

"I can't weld."

Shrugging, I said, "So? I don't paint."

"I saw some paintings you did several years ago."

"I should have said I don't paint anymore. Your paintings are much better than anything I ever did." I felt sure she was edging toward me, and I couldn't retreat any further without falling onto the floor. But why did I want to get away from her now when just this afternoon I had been lusting after her? Coward, I told myself. When the act became a possibility, I backed off. All of a sudden I had to pee. "May I use the john?"

She gave me a crooked smile. "It's down the hall."

I peeked into rooms as I made my way past the kitchen and bedroom. They were as uncluttered as the living room, except for the walls which glowed with Jo's art work.

"I have to go," I said, returning to the living room. "I just remembered I promised to meet Meredith after work."

"See you next week." She walked me to the door without protest. Perhaps she felt relieved, too.

Outside, I filled my lungs with as fresh air as Milwaukee provides before I climbed into my beater of a car — a 1986 Ford Thunderbird with 117,560 miles on the odometer. The driver's door sagged on its hinges, rust spots freckled its dark gray exterior, but it ran too well to justify parting with it. Besides, I couldn't afford anything better.

My meeting Meredith had been an excuse, of course. It had freed me from a situation which had been spiraling out of control. Looking across the table at my lover that evening, I wondered what had caused me to even consider infidelity. Her gray-green eyes glowed in the candlelight, her high cheek bones created shadows, wisps of nearly black hair framed her face.

"Feeling romantic tonight, darling?"

Nodding, I smiled nervously.

"I thought maybe you were getting a little tired of me." Meredith's teasing too often verged on truth.

"That'll never happen," I promised with crossed fingers. Then I noticed her mouth, still unwiped after a bite of stir fry. Her teeth gleamed in the flickering flame and she licked her lips. "Come on," I said, throwing my napkin on the table. "I can't wait." At least I didn't have to quell my impatience. We knew each other well.

"But Abby, I'm hungry."

"So am I. Please," I urged, taking her hand and leading her toward the bedroom. I saw Joanne's apartment, nearly devoid of furnishings but bright with the life of her paintings, and shook myself a little to escape the image.

"Are you not feeling well?" Meredith asked solicitously.

"I'm desperate for you." We had reached the neatly made bed. Facing her, I began unbuttoning her blouse. Meredith, who worked as a paralegal in a law office, dressed up for her job. She had seven suits in the closet and at least four times as many skirts and blouses and dresses.

Taking my face between her hands, she kissed me. "If we're going to do it, let's do it right."

We, too, were of like height. I gazed into her eyes, which appeared more gray in the darkening room, and said, "Is there a right or wrong way?"

"Let's not be in such a hurry." She kissed me again, her lips softly pulling on mine, her tongue outlining the inside of my mouth. She took over the job of loosening her cuff buttons and shrugged out of the blouse. Her skin appeared dark and smooth against the white of her camisole and I kissed her shoulder while tucking a finger in her cleavage. The sight of her in bra and slip always excited me.

I often released her hair at night, which in the morning she invariably pulled back and curled into a loose bun. I did this now and ran my fingers through its thickness until the tangles dissolved into silken strands. Then I undid the clasp on her skirt and let it fall around her ankles. After lifting her camisole over her head and sliding her half slip down over her hips, I gently lowered her onto the comforter. Unsnapping her bra, I gazed hungrily at the fullness of her breasts — the milky white skin with its delicate tracery of veins. Softly moaning, I leaned over and took the pale, pink nipples to suckle.

I only wear hose when forced to do so and now, as I began removing her pantyhose, I resisted the temptation to jerk and tug. Carefully, I worked the nylons over her hips and thighs and rolled them off her feet. She never wore panties under them and I bent to kiss the black curls between her legs. Going further, I tongued the tiny, pink clitoris protruding from the thick triangle. Meredith groaned and took my head between her hands, holding it there. And dropping to my knees, I coaxed us both into a froth.

"Come here," she urged huskily. "I want to taste you, too."

I tore off my clothes and crawled up next to her. Drawing her close, I whispered, "Not yet. You said you wanted to go slow."

She arched her upper body, and I nibbled her exposed neck. During lovemaking she often reminded me of an ecstatic feline, stretching her body with languid pleasure. Her hands moved over me with strong, sure strokes — the caresses of a confident lover.

Slowly I lowered the length of my body onto hers — breasts to breasts, belly to belly, pelvis to pelvis. Sighing with pleasure, I felt her skin and flesh molding to mine — smooth, soft, warm. We kissed — tasting lips, touching tongues. As the kisses grew more passionate and our tongues plunged deeper, we began a slow pelvic thrust.

Shifting my weight a little to one side, I cupped her breast and flattened my hand over her ribs and taut belly to the joining of her legs. Covering the wiry mound, I slid first one then two fingers into the damp curls.

Meredith rose to meet my touch, a soft moan again escaping her. As I thrust inside, feeling the textured, pliant walls tightening around my fingers, she groaned louder. "Feels good," she said, breaking into my concentration with a voice thickened by desire. When I withdrew to caress the swollen lips with long, slow strokes, she gasped.

Working her way out from underneath, she wrapped an arm around me as I did her, and we stroked each other until we lay on the edge of orgasm in a sea of desire.

I struggled to my knees, staving off climax by temporarily pulling away from her touch. Leaning over, I took her nipple in my mouth while my fingers moved within her to the pace of her rhythm. Before taking her other breast to taste, I murmured, "Don't come."

I strung kisses down her ribcage and belly to her thighs, which she spread for me — a feast for the lustful soul. And I gave tongue to the leaves and folds, loving the taste of her, gorging on it.

Moving against the sheets, letting her excitement meld with my own, I barely heard her voice importuning me: "Come here. I want you." She attempted to lift my hips off the mattress where I lay, belly down.

Rising once again to my knees, I felt her shifting toward me, knew she was putting a pillow under her head. I straddled her face then and she pulled me down before I could lower myself to the warm wetness of her mouth. When her fingers entered me and joined the pulse of her tongue, I felt the moans rise deep in my throat, heard them become sound and blend with hers. We moved frantically now, all semblance of control gone.

Climax burst over me — a huge wave of pleasure rising and crashing upon itself, shuddering and breaking into wavelets of gratification that radiated throughout my body.

Meredith still quivered in orgasm under me, and I again pulled away from her and lowered my belly to the sheet. She closed her thighs together then, shutting me out. I sighed and clasped my arms around her legs.

"Come up here. I want to hold you," she said.

We fell asleep wrapped around each other, our skins drying and cooling until I reached down to pull the covers over our nakedness.

It should have been enough, I thought the next morning after Meredith left for work and I threw out yesterday's unfinished meal. Eager to use the renewed energy pouring through me, the result of released desire, I put on my welding clothes. The phone rang.

"How about lunch?" Joanne said.

"We had lunch yesterday," I replied, dismayed by my quickening interest.

"We didn't finish our conversation."

"I thought we could continue it next week, same time, same place."

"I'm going to be in your neighborhood around noon, delivering a painting."

"Then stop by."

I met her at the door of the garage with my welding helmet in hand, my jeans and shirt shot through with tiny holes burned by the cutting torch. I ran work gloved fingers through my hair and thought it didn't matter, since it was dishwater blonde anyway.

She came in and sat on a stool near the welder. "You have the prettiest eyes. Do you know that?"

I knew they were my best feature, large and hazel and slightly slanted, shaded by long, curly lashes. I had admired them just that morning in the mirror, but I frowned for effect and said nothing.

"Brought my lunch." She pulled an orange out of a bag and peeled it. "What are you working on?"

I had been welding what I call animal art, something that resembled a cross between a Komodo dragon and an armadillo. I gestured at it and watched her bring a slice of orange to her mouth.

"Looks like what I'd want on my front lawn."

I couldn't tell whether she was teasing and didn't

care. I caught a glimpse of tongue and teeth as she ate the orange.

Somehow we became pressed against the closed garage door. I guess I had backed her there, because I was leaning into her, kissing the juice off her lips. She kissed differently than Meredith, more open mouthed. I felt dizzy, unable to catch my breath.

She turned me, imprinting my back against the overhead door, and her hands roamed over me. "You have a nice body."

My work kept me in shape — all that bending and kneeling and lifting. If I spoke, I'd have to stop and I didn't want to do that yet — not while she was unzipping my jeans and reaching inside my bikinis. Tilting my pelvis toward her, I gasped at the feel of her inside me.

And then I was opening her shirt, undoing her slacks. She was a sea of passion, and my fingers slid easily in and out of her. Matching my rhythm to hers, I picked up the tempo as she did. Her breathing sounded loud in my ears, as did my own. We held to each other with locked arms and urgent kisses.

Afterward, she backed off and looked away from me. The strength had gone out of my legs when she had reached for me and returned slowly as I buttoned my shirt and zipped my pants. "I don't know where that came from," I said, seeing that she had also fastened her clothing.

"Neither do I," she replied, finally meeting my eyes. "You're an exciting woman."

I laughed. "Oh yeah, especially in my work clothes."

"I better go."

My legs still shook. I clasped myself in a solitary hug. "Good idea."

She turned at the door and gave me a dazzling smile. Her eyes danced mischievously. "Lunch next week?"

I picked my welding helmet off the floor and stared at her for a moment. "We can't do this again," I said.

"I know," she replied.

"Okay," I agreed, too readily. "Next week."

Juanita Is Flying

Lauren Wright Douglas

Today is the last day of February. I am already so sick of 10 D that unemployment seems attractive. It is on days like this that I wish I had taken the offer to play semi-pro basketball with the Moose Jaw Brewers instead of this job teaching physical education to the daughters of the ultra rich. Rose Hall Academy. I have yet to find one rose in this briar patch.

Toni, Kiri, Suzi, and Debbi are best friends. They are blonde, wear braces, and have decided that the

proper diminutive for their names must end in "i."
They sit on a bench against the wall in a sullen line
as I give them hell. They are soooo, I mean, bored.
Censure is *trop déclassé*.

"Funny, ladies," I tell them. "Tying Juanita's
clothes in knots is very amusing. Too bad it didn't
amuse me, kids. I'm the one who counts here."

Suzi gives me a vapid blue-eyed stare of ennui. I
bare my teeth at her and the look trickles away.
She may belong to the upper class but she doesn't
know a thing about the world. Fighting for rebounds
under the basket is a skill she'll never master. Too
bad. It has plenty of carry-over value.

"You're not getting away with this," I tell them.
"I just need time to think up a truly creative
punishment. Something memorable."

Toni sighs audibly, the remarks she would like to
make locked behind her almost-perfect teeth. When
the seventeen pounds of aluminum braces come off,
she will be quite pretty. No, scratch that. She will
be extremely pretty. She will not be beautiful. She
and her friends are predators. This is not a quartet
of young debutantes. This is the Gang of Four. A
hunting pack. With mindless jackal cruelty, they
have banded together to cut their prey out of the
herd. Their prey is Jaunita. They are determined to
have her. I am just as determined that they will
not.

Physical education has been hell for Juanita. Her
mind doesn't yet know that her feet belong to her.
She could trip over the lines painted on the floor.
The Gang of Four, realizing this to be Juanita's
Achilles Heel, so to speak, have hounded her
unmercifully. For six months, she has endured being

called "Bigfoot," "Flipper," "Elephant Toes" and other not very clever names. They haven't been able to break Juanita, however. Until today.

Juanita is waiting for me in my office, under the harsh, fluorescent lights. She sits rigid on a straight-backed chair. Dressed in the red nylon windsuit I have loaned her, she is trying to untie the knots in her clothes. She is not succeeding. Tall and slender, with long straight hair as black as a starling's wing and eyes like anthracite, she will someday be heartbreakingly beautiful. Right now, though, she is a gangly sixteen-year-old. I have read her file. She is a scholarship student. Her brains, not her father's money, got her into Rose Hall.

I know something else about Juanita — something that isn't in her file and will never be. Unless she commits some awful indiscretion. I know that she is a lesbian. How do I know? I know because she has told me so. She has telegraphed her messages in a code as sophisticated as any cryptographer's — a code to which I hold the key. Like calls to like, as my Scottish grandmother always said.

I know what is happening to Juanita. For years she imagined herself to be singular, an exile, the only inhabitant of a country whose name cannot be spoken aloud, yet whose language she knows as well as she knows the rhythms of her blood. But years of loneliness have made her prescient. She has discovered a sister exile. She has discovered me.

She is sixteen. I am twenty-four. The difference is insignificant.

I close the door and lean against it. Juanita raises her head and looks at me. She has been crying. The Gang of Four have reduced her to this.

"Why can't they just leave me alone?" she bursts out. "I know I'm not pretty like them and I'm a klutz but why do they care? Why can't they leave me *alone*?"

Time ripples and a moment of *déjà vu* claims me. In another gymnasium, in another lifetime, in my own crisis of passion and prescience I, too, had appealed to a sister exile. My basketball coach. "Why aren't I like them?" I had asked. "Why am I different? It's not fair."

Then, seven years ago, what I received was what I thought I wanted. Her hands were as strong as I had dreamed, and she peeled me out of my shorts and T-shirt as fast as I had hoped. Yes, she knew the places to touch me. But when it was over I felt ... cheated. *Put your clothes on, honey. And hurry up, okay? Oh, and you do know enough to keep your mouth shut, don't you? I could lose my credential for this.* Later that night, lying on my bed at home, I realized that what she had given me was not a memory I could cherish. It was not something with bright feathers which would soar for me whenever I called it out. What was the lesson here? Was this all I could expect from other women? Women like me?

I look at Juanita and see myself. When I had come to another woman in pain, loneliness, and confusion, I had been given something ... flawed. And now it is my turn to give. I can lock the door, rid Juanita of her borrowed windsuit, and teach her the lesson she thinks she wants to learn. My palms already know what her body will feel like. But tonight, lying in her bed at home, what will Juanita feel? And later, when she needs a memory that shines, that soars — what then?

"Listen to me. You're going to meet Tonis and Kiris and Debbis all your life. People like them look for victims. Don't be their victim."

Her lips compress into a thin line. "How? They're right, you know. I am a klutz. I'm uncoordinated. I have big feet. I mess up. I just wish I were . . . invisible."

"Well, you can't be. And if invisibility isn't possible, maybe you should go to the other extreme."

She shakes her head. "What do you mean?"

"You're vulnerable because you're a klutz. What if you weren't?"

"But I *am*," she wails.

"So fool them into thinking you're not."

"Fool them? Fool them how?" In spite of herself, she's interested.

"With a lot of hard work, a little luck, and a dose of *legerdemain*." Seeing her blank look, I sigh. "What do you kids learn in French class, anyhow — how to read menus? Sleight of hand, Juanita. Deception. Magic." *My gift to you, Juanita. A gift I wish I had received. A gift I can receive, now, finally, by giving it away.*

She looks at me appraisingly. Should she trust this crazy lady?

"What about it? I'm game if you are."

"Well . . . all right," she says.

We have now finished gymnastics. The Gang of Four has been quiescent. Perhaps it is the chastening effect of five solid days of detentions spent scrubbing gym equipment with toothbrushes and Comet. Today I am marking their gymnastics routines. In theory they should be more skilled than when gymnastics began. In actuality, they aren't. They are lazy cowards. The balance beam and parallel bars terrify them. Apart from the few basic skills they have had to learn in class, they avoid that equipment. They have elected to do tumbling routines. Something close to the ground. Something safe. None of them wants to soar.

Toni and Debbi do exactly the same routine: three forward rolls, a backward roll, and a split jump. I am not impressed. I have seen more adventurous routines from performing circus dogs. These are skills the girls brought to my class. They have learned nothing in four weeks of gymnastics. I give them each a "D."

Suzi is a little more daring. She, too, does a tumbling routine, but tries some of the skills I taught them — a handstand and a cartwheel. Practice would have helped. I give her a "C."

Kiri surprises me. She is going to try a vault. I instruct two other students to spot her. She takes a long run up, punches the board with her feet for takeoff, then loses her nerve in mid-air. She ends up sitting on the horse with an embarrassed grin on her face. I fail her.

The rest of the class presents their routines and then it is Juanita's turn. The students help her move the parallel bars out into the middle of the floor, and a buzz of excitement begins. Juanita takes a yardstick and measures carefully, making certain the bars are the correct distance apart. Satisfied, she chalks her hands and the backs of her knees and

approaches the low bar. I stand between the bars to
spot her. Just in case.

Juanita's back is to the class. She has already
forgotten them. And me. Concentrating hard on the
low bar, she takes two running steps. *Don't trip,* I
pray. She doesn't.

She grasps the low bar, pikes her body, swings
underneath, then simply uses her momentum to kip
herself up onto the bar. Now she is resting on her
hipbones. She snaps her legs forward, then back, and
somersaults around the low bar. A pretty move. Not
difficult, but showy. Swinging her legs up to sit on
the low bar, she transfers her grip to the high bar
and swings out into space. At the apex of her swing,
she releases one hand, turns her body, and regrasps
the high bar. Somebody gasps behind me — Kiri, I
think. She's right. This takes guts.

Juanita kicks herself over the high bar with
perfect form, never pausing to rest. *Careful now,* I
say to myself. The hardest part is just ahead. She
turns her body, circles the high bar, and hooks the
backs of her knees on the low bar. Then, drawing
herself up to the high bar as close as she can, she
simply releases her hands.

In the silence, Juanita lets herself fall. Physics
takes her and her body describes a perfect circle
with her knees the center. As her upper body passes
beneath the low bar, her hair brushes the gym mats
with a heavy silken sound like a sigh.

Now the circle is half closed. Now comes the
magic, the gift I can give Juanita.

As her body passes underneath the low bar,
Juanita swings her arms forward, increasing her

momentum, defeating the force that would drag her to earth. She reaches with her arms . . . and releases her knees' grasp. In an instant she comes off the bar like a spring uncoiled, like a bright bird seeking the sun. For one impossible moment, she is in flight.

The moment bisects itself into two moments, then four, then sixteen, then an infinity of moments. No one speaks or moves or even breathes.

Below Juanita, the class is rapt. Beauty as unexpected as lightning on a clear day has struck their souls and for a moment, they render it its due — silence. Because forever, caught in the net of their memories, Juanita is flying.

Crawl

Amanda Kyle Williams

I sensed it the way an animal knows fear —
immediate, unmistakable danger.

It was in her clothes — button-fly Levi's, faded
and paper thin at the knees. Boots, black, western,
tipped with silver. The sunglasses that hadn't been
touched since she'd stepped into the room. *Careful.*

Someone said her name was Taylor. *Taylor.
Taylor. Taylor's here.* The name swept through the
room in reverent undertones as the faithful

whispered her praises and I, the uninitiated, got my first look at perfection.

I watched her, watched the long fingers that moved like liquid, the tilt of her head when she talked, the *fuck you* walk — a woman fully aware of her own power. She flirted easily, almost intuitively. I watched in utter fascination. I watched because I could not take my eyes off her. I watched and an eerie sense of predestination took hold of me. I knew I could love her. Perhaps I loved her already.

I was looking at her back. She's thin, wide shoulders. *Great ass.* I see her turn, see her reach for the sunglasses, slide them to the tip of her nose. Her eyes fix on me, drop, scan the edges of my shirt collar, my jeans. She runs a hand over the dark hair, nods. I feel a stab between my legs. Someone is talking to her but she's not listening. She's coming towards me. Long, slow strides. *Keep coming, baby. Keep coming.*

"Name's Taylor." Her voice is deep, softer than I'd imagined.

I take her hand, hold it a moment too long. "Kendall," I answer, but my voice is nearly gone.

She smiles. She knows she has me. "Parties are a drag, aren't they?"

I'm watching her eyes over the tinted glasses — steady, clear, grey. Dark lashes. She moves a step closer. I feel weak, fragile. "Want to go somewhere?" she asks.

Oh yeah, somewhere in your mouth, somewhere between your legs. "I came with friends. It would be —"

She takes my hand, pulls me behind her up a flight of stairs, propels me through an open bedroom door, locks it behind us. I can't see her eyes behind the glasses when she turns.

"I saw you watching me." She leans against the bedroom door. That brilliant smile again — dazzling, slightly superior.

She unbuttons her fly and shows me a patch of thick curly hair. "Is this what you want?" I start towards her but she holds up a hand. "Crawl."

Crawl? Jesus. I'm stunned, frozen there in the center of the bedroom. My feet are cement.

She laughs. "Poor baby girl hasn't learned to crawl yet?" There's an edge to the soft voice I hadn't heard before. She moves towards me, grabs my hair, forces me to my knees. She yanks my head back. I see her looking down at me, see the smile as she opens the last button on her fly.

I feel her hands in my hair. She presses herself into my mouth. She's salty and strong. I take her greedily, hear myself moan at the first taste.

"Yeah, you like it don't you, baby," she whispers. "I bet your little pussy is all wet for me. You're all wet, aren't you? Fucking slut."

I'm insulted. I'm confused. I'm hot. So hot, so hungry. She's rough. She's a bad girl, a dirty talker. I like it.

Yes. Yes. Yes, I want to say, want to tell her I'm wet for her, that I'm a slut, her slut, that I just want to please her, feel her come in my mouth. But I can't say the words, can barely think the words.

She tightens her grip around the back of my head and pumps harder. "Can't talk with your mouth full?" Her tone is condescending, dead calm. I run my teeth over her clit, put my lips around it, suck lightly. "Oh, yeah. You like getting your mouth fucked, don't you, baby?" She grinds into me. My teeth are pressing so hard that I think my lips might bleed. I feel her body tense, her hips rock against me, her legs tremble, feel her come, feel it dripping down my chin, see it glistening on her thighs, milky and white. She holds my head while I lick it off, praises me, tells me I'm a good girl, then pushes me backwards until my back is on the floor and presses a boot between my legs, gently at first, then more pressure.

I'm so wet. I feel it running down my ass, soaking into my jeans. I raise my hips to her. I want more, want her mouth on me, her hands, her fingers — those beautiful long fingers — inside me.

"You're not going to come all over your jeans, are you, baby?" She takes a step back, looking down at me lying on the floor, legs spread. "You can't come before you learn to crawl," she says, bending, opening my jeans. She touches me, brings the moisture to her mouth, runs it over her lips, then mine, teases me with it, watches my desperate tongue lap at her fingers.

"Tell me you're wet," she whispers, lowering herself to me. "Tell me you'll crawl for it. Tell me you're mine."

Her voice is deep, steady. I feel the weight of her long body on top of me, feel her hot breath against my neck, smell cologne and cigarettes on her shirt collar, taste the beer she's been drinking when she clutches my jaw and forces her tongue into my mouth. I feel my clit swelling, pounding against her.

"Yes." I hear the words, realize they are mine. "Yes. I'm wet. I'm yours. Yes. Oh God. Yes, I'll crawl for you."

When Stars Collide

Robbi Sommers

She said she'd meet me in her car at a fast food
parking lot.

I drive to her, debating what I'll say. Can lace
words break through steel walls? I want in. She is a
collage burnt into my heart. Fragmented desires drift
before me like a thin mural on the windshield. The
setting sun, bursting with red-oranges, amazes me.
Darkness is near yet the sky is a brilliant
kaleidoscope. I head for the promise of color.

Will she be there first? When I pull in, will she

be sitting on her car hood? In her car listening to music? A nervous beat spins my heart. Apprehension and desire twist tightly in my belly. She waits for me — I can feel her — and the compulsion to speed ahead struggles with an anxiety-induced bid to slam on the brakes. The pedal is pressed to the floorboard, involuntarily or not, and I soar toward the sunset — thinking of her sweet words. If only I had captured them in a tiny golden vial, I would still have them. I hurry toward the sunset — thinking of her shy kisses. If only I could have pressed them like flower petals between thickly bound books.

From the freeway, the restaurant becomes a bright beacon in the darkening sky. Even so, I can barely decipher the parking lot. I can't see her, but she is everywhere, all over me — I'm filled with her, soaked with her.

I exit the freeway.

She's on the hood of her car, waiting for me. She slides from her car, runs a hand through her short dark hair and slowly walks toward my approaching car. In the headlights, she is spotlighted destiny.

From my car, I stumble. Like a falling star, I spill into her arms. The warm night enfolds a streaking star as she reaches for me. I am a simple wish waiting to happen.

She says hello and kisses me lightly. In a vision, I capture her words in a glittering net and tie them to my belt. The imprint from her kiss, I peel from my cheek and slip into my pocket. I must remember to be careful with these treasures until I get them safely home.

"Did you see the sunset?" She smiles and I wonder how I ever lived without her.

I nod and glance as the retreating daylight is courted by the rising full moon.

"I thought we could walk through the park to the lake." She points to a haven of trees across the street.

Lovers stroll through parks at night and are bewitched by the fragrance of night-folded roses. Books I've read — the very volumes I will soon fill with her pressed kisses — have taught me this. We'll hike to the lake and wander in mists of lilac and gardenia. I'll gently corral the scents in the palm of my hand and carry them home to weave. Tomorrow morning, I'll leave a braided garland of perfumed memories on her doorstep. I want her. I want her so much, I would string the stars into a necklace for her, if I could only reach that high.

Surrounded by soft-breathing flowers, we walk arm-in-arm. Water splashes from a marble fountain into a paved pond. I fish for a penny in my pocket, careful not to crush the saved kiss.

"Make a wish," I say as I offer her the coin.

"I wish . . . I wish . . ." She closes her eyes and tosses the coin into the water. Like a small girl guarding a secret, she purses her lips flirtatiously. "Do you have a wish?"

Her genie eyes offer to grant me anything but I say nothing. Instead, I watch a shimmering silhouette of myself cartwheel across the lawn. Hundreds of cartwheels later, I glance back to her. She smiles, as though she saw the apparition too, and slowly moves closer. Her lips inch toward mine.

Her alluring perfume holds me spellbound. She is seconds away, millimeters away — a mere breath, a quick heartbeat. Her hands cup my face and then push through my hair. Her lips steal across my cheek to my ear and a tiny heated breeze escapes from her mouth.

"I've missed you," she whispers.

I gather her words in dreamlike mesh knowing that later, I'll sprinkle them across my pillow. There's so much I want to say to her, so much that can't be put into words.

There is a moment in time, an instant, when you look at a woman and suddenly love her. I am suspended in that moment. One second I am me, the next, I am us.

Completely seduced by her, I pull her toward me, impatient for her plush lips to touch mine, her soft mouth to yield to my warm tongue. Her dewy lips tease. She is the oasis and I am suddenly parched. I would traverse a waterless desert for one nectarous kiss. She moves closer. Her breath becomes mine, my breath is hers. The grass somersaults toward the sky. The awakening stars swirl toward the ground. Everything seems to revolve, although nothing has moved.

I tenderly touch my lips to hers and free-fall into purple heat. Deeper and deeper, I descend into honey-cream sensations. I don't stop. Won't stop. Consumed with passion, I grab her, then press my mouth against hers. Desire spins like a rumbling cyclone. She is luscious. She is sensuous. I feel her heartbeat. I hear her quickened breath. She will be mine, I know that now.

I kiss her, again and again, as I unclasp the

buttons on her shirt. My fingers flirt against her warm smooth skin and I hunger for more. I step back to admire her. The dusk has curtained the sun, yet I can see how my rough kisses have darkened her lips. Her unbuttoned shirt tempts me and I pull it completely open. Her areolas are pale pink. I imagine dipping a thin brush into the bruised-red color of her lips and painting her nipples with that same hue. Instead, I cup her small breasts in my hands.

"Oh, yes," she moans.

"Yes," I whisper.

I pinch her nipples between my fingers and they harden to cherry-red. The abrupt transformation from flat, pink circles to stark, claret points ignites a blaze of desire within me. Suddenly off-balance and weak-kneed, I grab her to avoid certain capsize. Doesn't matter, we tumble to the grass and roll down a slight slope, ending our journey, hidden in a thickening of bushes.

Evening has chased twilight and the full moon climbs the sky. Silver light bathes her in a haze of sterling beauty. I waste no time. Her skirt lifts easily. Her panties come off quickly. She spreads her legs. She is asking to be mine.

Into her musky darkness, I dive. She is moist and slick. She is sweet and sultry. She is creamy and delicious and mine, mine, mine. I lick her. I lap her. I open her with my fingers and suck her into my mouth. She whispers my name. She pleads my name. She begs and promises and whimpers my name.

My breath is her sex. Her sex is my breath. The moon and stars are no longer above. Nothing exists

— not the sky, not the trees, not the night-closed roses. The entire universe, everything there is, begins on the tip of my tongue. Where I am now, I create the world. I am music, poetry, art and dance. I am passion, power, strength and love. I am her, she is me.

I tongue her and nibble her and flatten her and pierce into her. I sink into her and have her, over and over. I want to see her face. Her moisture covers my mouth, my cheeks, my nose. I am saturated with her. And dear God, she is so beautiful.

With two fingers, I thrust into her. Then again, hard. Then three, then four, again and again.

She arches in pleasure — and the earth is ours.

She grabs my hair in ecstasy — and the sky is ours.

She scrapes her nails against my flesh — and the universe is ours.

As she soars to the height of release, I follow her. We ride a wild roller coaster across the sky. High up, then crashing down, we turn and swoop. My stomach plunges, my heart pounds.

A meteor storm dazzles the sky or so it seems. And I love her, she knows it. She loves me, I can see it. And there is nothing, but us, as the stars collide.

Strawberry-Blonde

Nicole Conn

I awake to see you backlit in your closet; the
perfect image of WOMAN,

> Cream of your skin, haloed in light
> Skirt simply fastened as you move slowly
> To put your heels on, and in that gesture
> the sanguine grace of your long limbed
> loveliness, you are
> > the woman of my dreams ...
> > ... the vision will caress and torment me

I wrote that deep in the bubble of love. I meant every word of it.

I met her in San Francisco. Coincidence. Fate. Timing. We discussed everything as our bodies lay sweetly, softly, our skin enveloped in what she referred to as "osmossisy..." I completed for her simply, "stuff." I had spent the last year mending a ravaged heart, hidden deep in work. She had been in a loveless secure two-year partnership. I was a romantic. She was a pragmatist. A double Scorpio and double Capricorn. I could be our kite, she would be our anchor. Oh. Did I forget to mention. She was twenty-five. I, thirty-three.

Her strawberry-blonde hair glittered in the candlelight. We were having dinner at Louisa's. All six of us. My ex and I had come to visit Tracey and Vicky. She and her lover were mutual friends of Tracey's. It was all very innocent and coincidental. Within twenty minutes our eyes had sparked small brush fires. I was bitten. I was the arched pale neck begging for the love that never dies. I couldn't keep my eyes off her. And, I didn't dare let them run into hers. I spent the entire weekend pretending she didn't exist. The nine hours it took to drive back to Portland I fantasized about having babies with her.

> I guess you'd call it an irony
> or twist of fate, though many have
> crooned the very same ... It wasn't lost ...
> I *found* my heart in San Francisco

> The bewitching smile of a strawberry-blonde
> on a trolley car bearing Garland's name
> could not make a heart lunge deeper
> than this newer 1992 version of
> 'somewhere over the rainbow'

It washed over me like a fever. After all, what's romance without terrible poetry. I was a sucker for sap. I wailed out of tune in the shower, all the wrong lyrics . . .

Monday I called Tracey. "I've got to tell you something."

"No you don't." Tracey's voice purred smugly. "She feels the same way."

We endured a month of sheer delicious AT&T torment, endless interwoven conversations about our pasts, our abuse issues, how we survived it all, what we didn't want, how we were both fiercely independent, how we had both been searching all our lives for this thing . . . this thing . . . we had no words for. We submitted our resumes for love. We sounded like the perfect applicants for each other.

She lived in North Hollywood. Her apartment was generic; faded brown carpet, brown appliances, beige walls. She spiffed it up with colorful prints and two-tone towels. It reminded me of my faded brown drinking days. I didn't tell her this until much later, of course. I let it slip from my mind as we spent the next ten days we had, night after night listening to OUR music with the candles framing the highlights of her creamy skin, the texture of our lust and love as we tore into the very core of each other.

We were the gooney-pie queens. The Bobbsy Queers. Every bad love song, a saccharine movie montage. We were beyond in love. And, yes, completely disgusting.

It was simple. I would move to LA. She'd move out of her apartment, move in with me. After all, we had just spent Christmas with my sister and her lover. Beaner (she hates it when I call her that) and Kate were the perfect guppy marriage. They had my beautiful insemination-created niece, another munchkin on the way, a home they were remodeling, a gargantuan Christmas tree and k.d. lang crooning in the background as they squirted red-dye #2 for the infamous coconut ball roll. As we were shrouded in the mist of this Waltonesque homecoming, I gave her my most romantic possession: the small hand-carved wooden heart my real father had made my mother. And yes, she wanted my baby.

We traveled back to LA via Route 101 along the majestic coastlines of Oregon and Northern California, our love bubble ever deepening. Wasn't my sister's life everything we'd ever wanted? Our own lives had no real meaning. We were both traveling the Type-A train, hurry up and wait, fast track to the slow no. Forget that days earlier we were rabid about our personal philosophy; monogamy was a parameter set by the insecure. We fell into each other's arms, gasping, raw and spent. Yes. Freedom was the ultimate in erotic.

Making love with her was what I always dreamed being a lesbian was about. When I called her the woman of my dreams it was true. Every taste, smell, and texture was the conjuring of a mind that had gone drunk with lust. But it was more than that. Her soul danced with mine.

I told her one night, as we were listening to our music, that the escalation of the higher octave piano notes were like a bird unwrapping the layer upon layer of scarred bondage that had banded my heart in protection. And she finished for me, yes, the bird gets to the end and your heart is set free . . . see where the violins swell like that. We spent the next hour telling the tale of each note of music that followed. Life was sublime.

She moved in several weeks later. I couldn't help her. I had a deadline. I think she sort of resented that I wasn't participating in the start of our lives. I rushed out and got chicken Santa Fe and nachos to go from the Good Earth, a split of champagne and roses. We made up. We played our music. We made love. I hadn't wanted to and I don't think she did either. I just wanted to hold her and run my hands through her silk strawberry-blonde hair. It comforted me more than it did her.

It was only weeks before our days took on a familiar pattern. I'd work at home and she'd come home from work, both of us exhausted. We'd lie on the borrowed futon in the living room, build a Dura-Flame fire, and have a bed picnic. Neither of us had the energy or inclination to do anything else. We'd either pass out or finally talk ourselves into making love.

One night she came home in a funk. She didn't know what she was doing with her life. She hated her job. It was then that I was introduced to the Persnickety Thing, a term we endearingly labeled her inner child. How progressive. We were having a relationship with it. At first I indulged her. She could be quite adorable. And it was a treat to be able to see the part of her that helped pull her out of her heinous childhood. But I wanted the woman I had fallen in love with, and the more absent she became, the more I retreated into my work.

She started calling in sick. I was pressing to meet another script deadline. She walked around in a daze. The pervasiveness of her ennui and indecision sliced right through me until I began to feel de-motivated. We'd drive to the Bourgeois Pig and have double lattes. The best in town. We'd discuss our aspirations, our plans, how we should move to Portland. She didn't know if she could do the commute one more day; an hour and a half in the endless smog-baked traffic. Quit. I encouraged it. I didn't care to know what generated any of this. I just wanted it fixed. I had too much on my plate to deal with the meanderings of her twenty-five-year-old mind. She could go to school in Portland, she calculated excitedly, find out what she really wanted to do. Sure, I smiled. Gee, I was in a good mood. Or maybe it was the coffee.

She gave notice, started selling some of her larger pieces of furniture. We hadn't made love in a week. I was either having a flu bug or a nervous breakdown. I think it depended on what she wanted from me: "I quit my job, moved in here with you, am relocating to Portland. What are you giving up for this relationship!?"

It got down to that. The score card for Things We Were Giving Up. The column for Things We Were Putting In became smaller and smaller. Our white picket fence had been girded by a steel-plated gate the size of King Kong.

Over the Dinah Shore Palm Springs weekend the Persnickety Thing shifted gears and became her it's either-you-or-me survivor. Never much good with nuance, she barked in both of our faces. I think she hated her tough little warrior as much as I did that weekend. But we were both grateful for her consummate and bravura performance. It shook me. The next morning I wandered out to the pool. It was early morning. Everyone was still nursing hangovers so I was the only one there. As I looked at my reflection, I realized that I had completely lost myself. It wasn't her fault. I had been as lost in my work as she was in her identity. Work had taken over me a long time ago. I guess I thought somehow she was going to lead me back from it.

So, lost in our own personal miasmas and versions of hell, we broke up. The night before I was to leave for New York we decided to try again. But we broke up again via AT&T. Feeling grimly masochistic, I thought it held some poetic justice.

I returned to Portland. Oh, we called a few times, and even got back together in a variation of a theme called No Parameters but then enlisted our boundaryless situation to buffer our insecurities. The last time we "spoke", which I suppose would have to be a euphemism for how uncivilized we actually became, we screamed all the things broken people unleash when threatened with extinction.

I spent the next few months despondently experiencing I don't give a shit to the second power; that charming state of existence where you don't give a shit that you don't give a shit. I did the

things, you know, that absolutely defy explanation.
Took her pictures out. Put them away again. Played
our music until I could listen no more, wondering
where she spent her time, how her day was filled,
whether her heart was empty, was it broken like
mine? Did she long for me as I longed for her? And
the endless droning of what had happened beat
through my mind. This was supposed to be the Ayn
Rand of relationships. Now it was just a torn thing
we had battered by the sharpened hatchets of
expectation. Two wandering minstrel romantics who
belonged together but couldn't quite find our way.
Come to me in another form . . . come to me I beg
you.

And then even I would falter at my self-imposed
angst, run on the beach like I was Rocky going to
finally conquer Bonnie Raitt's "Thang Called Love" at
pitch levels on my headset.

With the absoluteness of being alone and the
absoluteness of having myself to myself, I got
stronger. I finally arrived at the simple I don't give
a shit stage and mustered enough self-care to begin
socializing again. Spent time with friends. Read a
lot. Occasionally went to a movie and worked. Found
a therapist.

A year later I was on a trip to LA, on business,
having lunch at Butterfield's. I was blithering
aimlessly, schmoozing with intent, when I almost
choked on my curried chicken salad. She was there.
Five tables away she sat with a group of women.
The conversation floated around me as I watched her
strawberry-blonde head turn to me. I saw the slight
catch she controlled, wonderfully contained. The

anchor. I smiled. She returned it and excused herself
from her friends.

We met somewhere in the middle of a hundred
people doing lunch, caught in a time warp. "Hi
there," she said. We awkwardly moved to each other
in an uncertain embrace. Her China Rain shot
through my olfactory senses and every fiber of my
unendurably nerve-wracked being. We parted, both
more than a little shaken.

We did the catch-up thing. She'd found a new job
that gave her a lot more freedom to go to school
part-time. She was leaning toward psychology. Good,
you can fuck up the rest of the planet, I didn't say.
How was my work. Oh, you know, pretty much the
same. Trying to put deals together in this town was
like trying to defy the chaos theory. How you doing?
Which could cover an enormous amount of territory
but we both answered with sort of wistful conviction.
Pretty good, I think. Yeah. Me too. I was sweating.
My heart was screaming. My jaws clenched until I
thought they'd drive root canal to China. She was
completely cool. We said goodbye without touching
one another.

OK. So I was still affected. OK. So I was
extremely unhinged.

A month later I sat in my favorite cafe in
Portland, with my usual double mocha, writing notes
for my next story meeting. Wendy, a cute
half-shaved headed teeny-bopper dyke came by and
refilled my cup. But she stood there too long and I
finally looked up. She smiled and placed a bread
plate with a crudely wrapped object on the table.
Oh, shit, she has a crush on me I thought. I

couldn't be rude. I opened it. Out tumbled the wooden-carved heart, with a piece of paper that said, "I think you lost this in San Francisco." I looked up.

Strawberry-blonde. There she was. She smiled. Uncertain. I went up to her.

"Hi there." Her voice cracked.

I simply stared, then "I love you" involuntarily escaped from under my breath.

A tear slid from her brimming eyes. I led her back to the table.

"What are you doing here?"

She regained some of her Capricorn composure. She exhaled slowly and said, "What do you think."

I waved for another mocha. I ordered the All-You-Can-Eat Special and proceeded to have breakfast with the woman of my dreams.

Lesbian Cartoons

Rhonda Dicksion

Love Amongst the
Horseradishes

Anita Cornwell

Dennison snuggled down in her bachelorette quarters in the new, half-filled apartment complex for new faculty and grad students, just off the main campus of Centron U, and prepared to teach summer school English Comp as her very first project.

Her second project would be learning to live with her aborted love affair with one Matilda Jones, whom Randi would always think of as The One

Great Love Of Her Life. As a matter of fact, Randi was seriously thinking of becoming a sort of new-age nun. She'd have loads of friends, but no love affairs until . . . Until . . .

Randi shuddered even though she had her windows open as the air conditioning hadn't completely been de-bugged yet, and the temperature was at least 88, and climbing.

Although Randi had reached the ripe old age of twenty-four and most of the friends she had left behind in Bleeker Falls were either married or engaged or had escaped to San Francisco where they freely participated in all of the Gay Pride Marches under the sun, she was sadly and deeply undecided what she wanted to do with her life.

Randi gave a deep sigh as she tried to figure out how she had come to be a Ph.D. candidate in English Lit and Black Studies at non-prestigious Centron U in tacky little Old Centron City, perched unhappily between New York and Baltimore. And she would bet her last five dollars that most folks in Centron City thought a Gay Pride Parade was something given by the Vets of Foreign Wars.

"Oh, nuts!" Randi exclaimed as she finally hopped up from the sofa and slammed out of her apartment.

"Friday afternoon in mid-August, and no one to tell my troubles to," Randi mumbled as she entered the A&P in the tiny shopping center down from her apartment. But already she felt she was gaining strength from her new resolve to become a new-age nun.

After all, if more people would stop racing around trying to find someone to hop into bed with them, they would have more time to enjoy the finer things of life such as ... Well, such as joining Gay Pride Marches for one thing, Randi decided as she started past the long line of cashiers.

Then — WHAM! Right between the eyes! Randi felt as though someone had dropped the entire store down on her head as her eyes landed on Cashier Number Three.

Randi stood rooted to the floor as she stared at the cashier, who surely must have descended from the heavens that very moment with her two long, silken, jet-black braids that hung nearly to her waist, and her beautiful bronze complexion that seemed to sparkle like ... like ... Randi searched frantically for the right word. Jesus, she was a Ph.D. in English, couldn't she even think any more?

Suddenly, Cashier Number Three looked up and caught Randi staring at her. She gave Randi a dazzling smile that blinded Randi far more than the mid-August sun ever could. Did *she* really mean to smile at me that way? Randi pondered in profound confusion.

Randi wandered around the store, pushing her food cart in absent-minded-professor fashion until she ran into a distracted housewife. "Watch where you're going, girlie!" the woman snapped.

Finally, Randi abandoned the cart somewhere between cereals and canned fish, then stuck her hands in her pockets and wandered over to the meat department. Where on earth has *she* been all my life? Randi wondered as she stared vacantly down at a prime rib of beef.

Was it possible that she had seen *her* before, that in fact she may have even been in *her* very line and was so lost in the intricacies of Freshman Comp that she'd failed to note that the woman of her life stood at the tip of her undiscerning nose?

A swift pain shot through Randi's heart, and she turned, lurching away from the meat counter into the path of three more scornful shoppers. Then, finding herself backed up against the lunchmeats, she decided to get something for dinner.

Clutching a package of sliced cheese and another of chopped ham, Randi moved around the corner toward the front of the store. As she passed the huge array of sodas, she snatched two cans of grape and charged up toward Cashier Number Three.

Randi stood in the short line staring at *her*, open-mouthed, transfixed.

Finally, as though she felt Randi's eyes burning holes in her face, Number Three looked up and stared at Randi, who promptly dropped all of her groceries.

Flushed, breathing hard, and trembling like a clumsy school girl, Randi finally managed to gather her items, and she scooted back around the corner, barely missing several startled shoppers, down past the lunchmeats and frozen fowl, on around another corner past the cantaloupes, bananas and apples, then up another aisle past the canned soups and vegetables until she came out into the line of Cashier Number Six.

"I mustn't stare," Randi told herself as she shot furtive glances down at Cashier Number Three. But she immediately forgot and stared with such intensity that once again Number Three looked up and fastened her deep, bewitching brown eyes on Randi. Down went her groceries once more while she stood limp and helpless under Number Three's compelling gaze. Finally, with a faint smile on her lips, Number Three turned back to her work, and Randi bent down and retrieved her mangled food items.

Back home at last in her tiny apartment, Randi paced endlessly. Why hadn't she acted with some spunk and stayed in Number Three's line? "Perhaps I ought to go back down there now," she mumbled and actually started toward the door before remembering that she'd left her wallet on the dining table.

She plopped down on the sofa and began to reflect more calmly. Tomorrow morning would be a much better time to try to find out Number Three's name. There was usually a different brand of customer in most supermarkets on Saturday morning when everybody seemed a little bit nutty, so who would give a damn about her ogling the cashier?

As distant church bells began striking the ten o'clock hour, Randi took several deep breaths, straightened her shoulders and marched into the

A&P. Then — WHAM! There *she* was! Randi eased on into the store without her New Love seeing her and fled into the rear as though pursued by hungry tigers.

"Perhaps I should see an analyst?" Randi mused as she moved toward the fresh vegetables. Why hadn't she prepared some strategy last night? she fretted, gnawing absent-mindedly on two raw string beans.

The clerk in charge of the department approached Randi. "Can I help you, Ma'am?" he inquired in a doubtful tone.

Randi gave a violent start, stared blankly at the half-eaten string beans clutched in her left hand. "I ... I don't think so," she mumbled then sauntered off toward the cantaloupes.

Clutching a cantaloupe in each hand, Randi eased her way up toward the front. Finally, there *she* was, almost within reach of her itchy little fingers.

When Randi's turn came, Number Three gave her that dazzling smile again. "And how're you this morning?" she asked in the most melodious voice Randi had ever heard.

Randi opened her mouth. "I ..." She only managed to get that one word out, and it was somewhere far beyond high C.

The cashier glanced away, and Randi realized her New Love was trying not to crack up laughing. Her ears burned while she fumbled for her wallet. Oh, lord, she had left it home! Finally, she found a crumpled five spot in her back pocket. When the cashier gave Randi her change, she grabbed her

cantaloupes and dashed out of the store like someone
practicing for the Penn Relays.

After classes on Monday, Randi scooted home for
a quick shower then ventured forth once more for
the A&P. She sailed into the supermarket, and lo
and behold! Number Three was not there. *Not there?*
Perhaps she was out on break, Randi decided as she
latched onto a food cart and started pushing it
around the store like someone stuck in a funeral
procession.

The following day, Randi left her last class and
rushed down to the store. There *she* was again!
Vivacious, smiling, unattainable!

Wednesday, Thursday, Friday, and Saturday,
Randi virtually bought out the store. But still she
did not learn the name of her New Love. Next week,
she vowed firmly, things would be different!

Things were different. The next week, Cashier
Number Three was not in one single day. Nor did
she return the following week. Randi practically
went out of her mind. *She* was gone forever! Randi
screamed in silent agony as she paced back and
forth in her tiny apartment that now resembled a
junior A&P.

Finally, the fall semester began. And Number
Three did not return. Then one day, driven beyond
all reason, Randi approached another cashier. "The
tall girl with the long black braids, when is she
coming back?"

The cashier, a short, stocky fellow with wiry red hair, gave Randi a sullen look. "You mean Licia? Naw, lady, she's gone for good. She was a student, see? In chemistry or something, so she's gone back out to her University in Illinois, see? And the manager says the next idiot who asks . . ."

Randi turned and fled the store.

When she reached her building, numb and heartbroken, Randi saw that the apartment across from hers was now occupied. As she stood there gaping, the door suddenly opened and a woman and her small daughter nearly ran into her.

Randi smiled, a vague expression in her eyes as she said, "I'm Randi Dennison. Did you just move in?"

"Last month," the woman said. "I'm Edna Williams and this is my daughter, Penny."

Edna Williams worked as a freelance editor for several medical publishers in the city. Her Significant Other, Lee Wentworth, taught math at the University. In no time at all, Randi, Edna, and Lee were fast friends. And Penny, the little brown, freckled-faced imp, claimed Randi as her very own true love.

One Saturday afternoon when Randi was babysitting with Penny, she got down to the nitty-gritty. "Well, Aunt Randi, if you can't marry me, why don't you marry my girlfriend up on the third floor. She used to play shortstop for the Upper Darby Wildcats!"

Randi shuddered.

"Aunt Randi, are you cold?"

"No," Randi said wearily, "I'm hungry. Aren't you?"

"Oh, yes! Let's go down to the Hot Shoppe. They have the best burgers in the whole wide world!"

As they approached the restaurant, Penny suddenly pulled away from Randi. "There goes Al!" she cried, dashing down toward the women's shoe store.

Randi took off after the flying Penny.

"Hey, Al! Al! Wait!" Penny called.

Then, Al stopped and whirled around. And Randi, reaching out for the excited Penny, froze in mid-grab.

My God! It was *her! Cashier Number Three!*

Penny raced up to Alicia. "Come, I want you to meet Randi!"

Alicia scooped Penny up in her arms. "I was looking for you. I just baked a pan of your favorite brownies. And we can have some baked beans and hot dogs!"

"Can Randi come up, too?"

"Any friend of yours is a friend of mine," Alicia said.

Randi barely uttered three words as she grudgingly followed Penny and Alicia back to their apartment complex. One part of her mind told her she was acting like a jerk. After all, was it Alicia's fault that she, Randi, had made an ass of herself this summer?

On the other hand, she was ticked because Alicia

hadn't given her some kind of signal. After all, in a sticky little old town like Centron, you couldn't afford to be too indiscreet.

"Make yourselves comfortable," Alicia said as they entered her colorful beige and yellow living room.

"I have to go to the restroom," Penny said, giving them a toothy smile before she took off.

Randi slumped down on the beige leather couch. "You're *supposed* to be in Illinois," she muttered.

"I finished my undergrad work there last spring," Alicia said. "I'm doing advance work in math and chemistry here at the University now."

"Big deal," Randi said under her breath as she stared down at her sandal-clad feet.

Alicia sat down beside Randi and took her hand in a warm, firm grip. "I don't blame you for being ticked with me, Randi. But you see, I thought you were just a kid. Then the other day I saw you with Lee and Edna and realized you were the new young graduate assistant they had told me about."

"So what did they say, that I'm some kinda nut?" she demanded as she retrieved her hand.

"You're something else," Alicia said, her large brown eyes smiling warmly at the sullen Randi. "They think you're somebody I would be delighted to know."

Penny came racing back into the living room. "Are you two getting it on?" she demanded in all innocence.

Randi and Alicia looked at one another, and suddenly all three of them collapsed in laughter.

Near to Me

Catherine Ennis

We had been long hours on the interstate. When we started this morning, my smile had stretched from one horizon to the other, and I had to take deep breaths to keep from screeching aloud my pleasure in this wondrous day. Eva, my darling Eva, was sitting in the passenger seat, one slim leg curled beneath her, the other stretched straight ahead like an arrow pointing our way. I am not the world's most comfortable driver, but I'm adequate, and my car was new. Each passing mile brought us nearer to the entire summer we were to spend together . . . or so I thought.

She had to know what this trip meant to me. It had been her idea, after all. "I'm coming home for the summer," she'd said. "We'll spend it together, just the two of us. We'll go wherever you like."

The grownup in me said to the child in her, "Are you sure you can take the summer off? Aren't you supposed to be teaching or taking some sort of class?" I was remembering the content of her letters, filled with her plans, more activity than one short summer could hold. "I wouldn't want you to miss something important on my account," I said. I would stop breathing if she asked it of me, but she didn't know that. "If this won't put a hitch in your career, my dear, I'd love for you to come home. We'll spend the time together, and I'll have Cousin Alice bake a cherry pie for you every day."

She had laughed at that, but Alice had laughed the loudest. "Last time Eva was home she told me she was getting too fat and cherry pies were off her list." Alice shook her head sadly, remembering the reason for Eva taking leave from her job last year. "I don't know what she calls fat," Alice mumbled, "She can't weigh more than a kitten." She avoided my eyes then, fearful that her words had triggered memories.

Memories were all I had now. It is said that time heals all wounds. This is not true. Time can also allow the hurt to fester, to seek deeper levels of flesh, to numb the brain so that healing cannot take place. And, I could not seem to heal. Margaret's death had caused within me a slowing down, a central weakness that drained strength faster than energy could be replaced.

After the funeral, Alice had taken over in the kitchen, providing mountains of food that I couldn't eat. Her busy presence continued even after Eva had gone back to her commitments at the university. But I began sinking into a depression that lifted only momentarily when Eva's letters were delivered, or when her cheery voice reached over the miles to say "Hi, Aunt Willie! Guess who!"

Alice and I were at the airport to meet Eva's plane. The three of us hugged and cried and laughed through our tears, and I kept Eva's hand in mine on the drive home.

A whole summer, she promised. An entire summer to spend together. My loneliness evaporated, replaced by a surge of happiness.

Eva had a bundle of unopened mail and memos which she'd brought with her. "I didn't have time for these before I left," she said. "I'll read them on the way."

When I stopped for our second refill she began opening the memos first. "Oh, no!" I heard her exclaim, "No, no, no!"

"What is it? Is there some problem?"

"The class I was to teach didn't make, so I was to be off the whole summer. Now they want me back ... and by Monday!" She turned to me, her face beginning to crumple with tears. "We won't have our summer after all. I have to go back."

And so my happiness vanished, replaced by a disappointment deeper than pain. "It's probably just as well," I said, trying to keep my voice steady, as if it didn't really matter to me all that much. "We'd probably be at each other's throat before a week ended. Don't give it another thought."

And so I turned around at the next exit, my eyes burning with unshed tears, neither of us speaking. Exhaustion prompted me to swerve off the interstate, pull into a motel driveway. "Might as well stay the night here if they have room, it's getting late and I'm tired. We'll head home in the morning and you can leave for your job whenever you like."

An antique car auction had filled the motel with out-of-state guests, but there was a single available. "We'll have to share a bed, Eva, is that okay?"

She shrugged, disinterested.

We had to park some distance from our room. I carried my small overnight case to the door, noticing that Eva hauled all three of her bags. "Why don't you leave a couple of those in the trunk, honey. They'll be safe."

She shook her head, not speaking, not looking at me either.

We dumped our cases on the floor, then I touched her arm. "What is it?" I asked. "What's wrong?"

She turned to face me. And what did I see in those icy clear eyes that glared at me. Pain? Was there something in the mail she had been reading to cause the hurt that I saw? Who would hurt Eva, the gentlest, most giving of us all?

"What's wrong?" I asked again.

"Nothing, there's nothing wrong. Not any more."

"Then let's go to the dining room and get something to eat."

"You go. I'm not hungry."

"And when have you not been hungry?" I smiled at her, but she turned her head away. "Then I guess I'm not hungry, either. But I am tired, so maybe I'll just get ready for bed. You want to shower first?"

She shook her head. I sighed, wondering what had caused her to change so quickly. There would be time after bathing to discuss whatever it was that was bothering her.

When I came out of the bath, more tired than I had realized, I sat on the edge of the mattress. More than simple fatigue, this tiredness, this despair, slowed my mind, made me take huge, deep breaths in between the regular ones, made my arms leaden, my heart ache dully. I lay back on top of the spread to wait for her to shower, and fell asleep.

How much later did I awaken? Hours? Minutes? No matter. I opened my eyes to see Eva sitting at the table, her head bowed, arms crossed, a picture of dejection, of hurt. No one, no one on this earth had the right to make her bend that bright head. Whatever the cause, I would soothe her. I would clasp her to me as I had done for so many years. I would hold her as I'd done when she'd throw her skinny arms tight around me, sobbing at some pain, some injustice, knowing that I would make it right.

"Eva, come to bed, child." I held my hand to her.

"I'm not a child!" She did not look up. Her words were a soft, low growl. "I'm NOT a child!"

I reacted with astonishment. "Well of course not. I only meant . . ."

"You meant what you said . . . Eva, child! Child! That's all I've ever been, all I'll ever be, isn't it?" Her voice trembled, "Have you looked at me in the last few years? Have you?"

Was it possible that I was the one causing her pain? But pain over what? How? "Eva ..." I began.

"No, let me tell you." She moved to the bed, sat at the foot, huddled, not touching me, her voice so low I thought for a minute she didn't intend for me to hear, but then, as I listened, I knew that her throat was constricted by pain. She was forcing sounds, trying to make them into words. Tears had caused her nose to close, and she didn't have a tissue. I resisted the impulse to hand her my handkerchief, I needed it for myself, for the tears that started as she poured out her heart in halting, broken words.

"I thought if time passed it would change things but time hasn't done a damn thing! To you I'm still only a child. You'll never see me any other way, I know that now. You've made it perfectly clear." Her voice picked up strength. "So, in the morning I'm leaving. I can get a bus or the train from here. I'm going back. I can't spend my life tagging behind you, thinking about you. You don't even want me to."

She had talked herself past anger and into hopelessness. But hopeless about what? Did I know? How could I not? And what could I say to her?

"Eva," I began.

But she went on, not hearing me, her voice deep with pain. "I have loved you for so long." She may even have been talking to herself, her voice was so heavy.

I poked her thigh with my foot, to get her attention. I had a starting place. "I love you too, Eva." I spoke the truth, there had never been a day that I had not loved her.

"Yeah," she said. "Yeah, I know." Then she was

silent. When she began speaking again, I had to strain to hear.

"I know you care for me, even love me . . . but I'm *in* love with you. There's a difference, I think. No, I don't really know what I think any more. It was because I knew how lonely you were after Aunt Margaret died, how much you loved and missed her, that I thought a summer with me would help . . . getting away from the memories. I hoped you'd find that you could love me as much, too. You'd see that you could be happy again. I thought if we were together you'd find that you needed me, wanted me." She was squeezing her hands so hard I could hear the knuckles crack. Her sigh was deep. "In the morning I'll go. And as far from you as I can get!"

Her words triggered a memory. Years ago, probably jealous of the closeness Margaret and I shared, Eva had run away. "No Eva, you can't run off like that again."

"Oh, I'm not too young this time." She laughed. "I may be a child, but I'm a twenty-three-year-old child. I'm old enough." She stood and looked down at me. "I wanted you, long before I even knew what it meant to want someone that way. Aunt Margaret told me I'd grow out of it." She laughed again, an ugly sound. "She also told me there'd be no crumbs for me from your table. It was a long time before I knew what that meant. Or how true it was."

Margaret? Margaret had known all this? How could she have known what Eva was feeling? "Eva —" I began again.

"You don't have to say anything," she broke in. "It's over. Not that anything was ever started, but I'm over my mad, and I still love you for all you've done for me over the years. You can go on living with your memories of Aunt Margaret, I won't bother you again."

There had to be a way to stop all this pain. Hers and mine. I held out my arms. "Sit here by me, Eva, please."

"Am I going to get a crumb after all?" Her words were bitter. She was sitting so very straight, her slim shoulders stiff as a ramrod, her body tense, I could almost hear her heart thudding, her pride crackling.

"Eva, don't." My arms were still reaching.

Then slowly, so slowly, she moved to sit at my side and looked down at me. I looked up into her woman's eyes. Gone was the huge, freckle-nosed grin that had almost always split her laughing face. I saw a countenance refined by time; serious, not laughing, but fine and slender, with clean lines, a high, smooth forehead, generous lips. I touched her tangled, unruly curls, let my trembling hand brush her cheek.

"Eva, there's a truth here, and you shall have it." She waited, still leaning slightly, her face white in the dimness of the room. I paused, needing time to compose my thoughts, perhaps invent a truth for her. But I knew that she deserved to hear, honestly, what I had long held. What, to my detriment, I had long held in my heart. So I spoke the words plainly.

"When your Aunt Margaret and I took you into our home, our love for each other was new and precious. We were together, body and soul, and neither of us wanted, or needed, anyone else. But, Eva, we gave you what love we could share. I think I knew when your childlike feeling for me deepened

into something more, but I had no way to handle
that emotion so I ignored it. Perhaps I, too, thought
you'd outgrow what you felt. I wasn't that
experienced, you know. I was only nine years older,
remember."

Sighing, I reached for her hand, wanting to clasp
her warmth to my breast, but she pulled her hand
away. In despair, I continued, "You're right, I've
always treated you like a little girl who had an
affection for an older woman. It became a habit for
me to see you that way. It was easier than facing
what I knew. But, Eva, even though my heart and
my life was full, I enjoyed your adoration. I
understand that through my selfishness, my
cowardice, I've cheated you, and now it's too late to
change a thing. I love you, Eva, I love you fully, in
every sense of the word, but in finding you I've lost
you!"

My tears were streaming, unchecked. I was
choking on them. She would be gone in the morning,
and I knew now that it was I who had sent her
away. Between great sobs, I managed to say, "Get
on with your life, my dearest, you deserve all of the
happiness there is."

Two soft hands touched my face, and I heard,
"You are my life. You have always been my life. I
have never, ever, wanted any other."

She leaned and gently, gently, touched her lips to
mine. My heart almost stopped when I felt her
breath caress my face, the pressure of her mouth.
Ahhh, her lips were closed, the kiss was that of a
child!

It took much of my strength to keep my own lips
tight together. I wanted to open my mouth under

hers, to take her into me, but no, I must not take advantage of this woman who loved me. That could not be my intent. I must not take of her goodness, her innocence. Then, what was it that I intended? Was I simply giving out a free sample? A drop of sweetness to tantalize? Ah, no. In fairness, I should move her away from me.

Eva raised her face an inch or two, then brought her mouth to mine again. I held my lips together, chaste and pure, so as not to frighten . . . and felt her tongue at the corner of my mouth. It was seeking entrance! It moved slowly to the other side, gently inserting itself. Then, as my lips and teeth moved apart, her tongue slipped into the cavern of my mouth.

I groaned, and my hands closed on her shoulders. Whether to pull her to me or push her away, I'll never know. I simply clung to her as she withdrew her tongue, lifted her face for a moment, then brought her lips back to mine. And my mouth opened to receive her.

How long was it until I felt her hands on my breasts? And, when had I caught fire? Desire raged within me. Was it abstinence that caused me to kindle and burn so quickly? Should I curb arousal so as not to frighten her? Could I do that? No, I could not do that. Not when her hands were warm on my naked flesh, her fingers a feather touch against my skin.

Her mouth was lightly touching mine, and our tongues moved together, slow, wet, soft. Eva set the pace and I followed so as not to . . . to what? I could not remember what it was that I intended not to do.

Ah! I gasped when her mouth touched my breast. A piercing sweetness almost more than I could bear. And how did she come to lie between my thighs, between my parted knees? My heels dug hard into the mattress, and I sobbed aloud when her fingers slipped through wetness and into me. She held my hips on her broad hands, pulling me to her in little jerking movements so that her lips could catch my private, tender flesh, rocking me away as her lips gently held what they had caught, stretching that part of me, her hands cupping, squeezing.

Eva had made me ready, and now she would spend my passion in her own good time. Her fingers entered me again, sliding easily on the mixture of my moisture and the water from her mouth. Her tongue touched and moved in lazy circles, teasing. But, slow was not enough! "Eva," I whispered. "Eva!" I did not want to rouse every other guest in the motel, but . . . "EVA!" My need communicated itself to her when I caught a handful of curls and pulled her face against me. I heard her grunt and the cadence quickened. This was no butterfly touch! She moved me at a gallop and, breathless, I surged against her, faster and faster until I soared like a kite on a string, flying high past the blue dot of earth, embracing the sun as it entered and exploded within me.

Much later, I gathered Eva in my arms, feeling against my breast the wild fluttering of her heart. My own breath, still harsh, matched hers. I lay in blissful silence until some quick movement of hers startled me. I raised to touch her eyelids with a kiss, and found that she was crying! Her face was wet with silent tears. I wiped her cheeks with the edge of the sheet, then wiped the sweet wetness of her body from my lips with that same damp spot. I tightened my arms, "What is it, darling?" I kissed her ear. "Are you unhappy?" She could not be. We had loved each other deeply, passionately, completely, again and again. We were resting at the moment, but I knew that our bodies would join again before morning.

"No," she answered dreamily, "I have never been happier, not in my entire life. How many people have their dream come true?"

"Well, not many, I guess." I could not resist asking, "Have you realized your dream?"

"You have been my dream since the day I first saw you." She sighed and snuggled closer. "I think all I'll want to do from now on is hold you and make love."

"Then why were you crying?"

"My dearest, dearest, darling. Don't you know me yet? I cry when I'm happy, I do."

I laughed at her words, stroked her strong woman's body, and whispered that I loved her. But, know her? I'm not sure I do know you, Eva, I thought. Where did you learn to make love like that? You were no fumbling innocent . . . you seduced me. I smiled, remembering my fear of leading her down the garden path. Someday, perhaps, I would ask her. Maybe when we were both very old.

Eva fell asleep in my arms much later that night. She breathed softly against me, her generous, warm heart drummed next to mine, and my own heart was, finally, at peace.

Curiosities and Surprises

Nancy Tyler Glenn

I looked at my watch. I wanted the Franklin proposal to look over during the weekend and I had an appointment to drop off my Jaguar for servicing. I pressed the intercom button. "Is the proposal typed yet?"

"Yes." The voice sounded relieved. "I was about to bring it in to you, Ms. Michael."

It had been a hell of a week. My secretary, Georgia, had retired two weeks ago. The woman they'd sent up from the pool was competent, but she was afraid of me. Not that anyone could blame her. In the fifteen years I'd been with the company I'd gotten a reputation for my management style — kick ass and take names. I grabbed the stack of resumes on my desk and stuffed them into my attaché case. So far the applicants to replace Georgia had been under-qualified but maybe there had been one I missed.

I hadn't planned on being an executive. I'd taken a job the summer before grad school at an ad agency and found that I liked the corporate world so much I changed my major from art to business administration.

The climb up the ladder had been easy and I was way beyond the glass ceiling before I even knew there was one. I wasn't that ambitious but those who tried to hinder me seemed to fall by the wayside. Jill had said I advanced by the seat of my naivete.

Why was I thinking about Jill again? She'd been on my mind lately. Dead ten years, she still came back to taunt me. My perfect relationship. Damn her for being born with a weak heart. There had been others but. . . .

Evelyn came into the office and placed a folder on my desk. She looked down, then said, "I . . . they've reassigned me . . . I. . . ."

I looked at her. I wanted to tell her to be more direct, to find her power, to. . . . "Thanks for being here. You've done a good job. I hope you enjoy your next assignment."

The elevator was empty except for my CEO, Ann Lord, a tall, elegant looking woman with grey eyes that could command a board room, but now they were soft and warm. I smiled.

She smiled in return. "Sneaking away early, Sharon?"

I nodded and glanced at her attaché case. "You too."

"Guilty as charged." She grinned.

The door opened at the parking garage and I waited for her to exit and then followed her into the structure. She turned and waited for me. "Can you do lunch on Wednesday?"

I looked at her. Lunch with the boss, something must be up. "Yes, I can," I said.

"Good. I'll see you then."

I watched her walk away. She was the woman I most admired. Ann had always stood behind me, supporting my decisions, defending my positions. I was lucky to work for her.

I drove my Jaguar to the shop and handed Walter my keys. "I'll need it by Monday."

"No problem Ms. Michael. I'll get Sam to drive you home."

"No, thanks. I'd rather walk," I told him.

I took a shortcut. I'd never come this way before and the stores were unfamiliar. Then one particular shop caught my eye. The sign above it with peeling paint, said CURIOSITIES AND SURPRISES. I was hooked. One of my weakness was junk stores.

A bell tinkled when I opened the door and an older woman seated behind an antique desk looked up, smiled, then went back to the book she was reading. I suppressed a sneeze. Dust covered everything. I glanced casually at the assortment of bottles and flasks, old clocks, dolls, antique toys — and then I saw it. *It* was an old brass oil lamp. It would make a wonderful planter.

When I paid for it the woman hardly looked up from her book, but curiously enough I felt her eyes on me as I left the store.

At home I changed into jeans and a T-shirt. I was excited about my new lamp. I found some brass polish and applied it liberally and began buffing it with a soft cloth. Then I noticed smoke coming out of it. Alarmed, I quickly set it down and stared. A form began to appear. Then I was facing a total stranger.

"At your service," she said, and smiled, eyes twinkling.

Not wanting to believe what I had just seen, I answered in my coolest board room voice, "I didn't call the agency."

She laughed. "You know who I am, and where I came from."

Anyone who has moved in the corporate world, or even seen movies of it — knows that I have faced, in my career, some of the coldest, toughest people in the world. But I was scared.

"What can I do to put you more at ease?" she asked.

"Go away." My voice was shaky.

As quickly as she had appeared, she spun until there was only smoke and it drifted back into the lamp.

I'd never been one to run from challenges and I had questions. I tentatively rubbed the lamp again.

A little wisp of smoke began emanating from the mouth, and then she was in front of me. She was smiling again. "I thought you might change your mind. I'm glad you did."

I felt foolish but asked, "Who are you?"

"I'm Gina and your wish is my command, Mistress."

"If that's so," I said, "my first wish is that you call me Sharon. I don't like being called *Mistress.*"

"As you wish . . . Sharon. I've always been pleased to grant the wishes of my . . . masters."

"And if they didn't have wishes?" I questioned.

"That's never happened," Gina responded.

I hesitated. "What if I asked you for something and then changed my mind."

Gina laughed. "I'd disappear whatever you didn't want."

I'd skipped lunch. "May I have something to eat?" I asked.

I followed her gaze to the dining room table. It was brimming with the most exquisite foods I'd ever seen. The delicate aromas filled my senses. "It's too much food," I said.

She smiled, following me around the table tasting the delicacies. "Don't worry. I always recycle anything that isn't used." She seemed to enjoy the meal as much as I did and it gave me a chance to look at her. "How old are you?" I wanted to know.

She looked at me. "Older than time as you know it."

"How did you get into the lamp?"

"I chose it. I have always worked in the capacity of making wishes come true, but most people just forget to ask for what they want. This method seems to be the most efficient."

"What if you got into the wrong hands, some. . . ."

"I wouldn't work for a bad person," she beamed.

I was surprised. "Are you saying you chose me?"

"Yes, Sharon."

"But, why?" I was incredulous.

"Because you need . . . things."

"You're wrong," I said. "I have a terrific job, stocks, stock options, I own my own home and have good health."

She nodded. "I've seen your portfolio. You certainly have done well, but you still don't feel complete."

It was true. For all my material assets and success in business, I still felt futile at times. "What do you suggest?"

"That's not my job." Gina put down her fork. "My task is to give you whatever would fulfil your dreams."

"The only thing missing in my life is a lover," I said.

Gina looked around the room. "Is there space in your life for a lover? All I see here is Jill."

I was startled. "You know about her."

Gina looked into my eyes. "How could I not?"

"What would it look like without her things?" I grumbled.

In a flash all of Jill's things disappeared. I started to cry. "Put them back. I can't bear it."

Immediately the room was restored but I was left with a feeling I didn't understand. It was an agonizing emptiness, but also a stronger sense of myself than I'd ever experienced.

"Now then." Gina looked pleased. "We'll take a look at the eligible lesbians in town." She turned toward the television and with a flick of a finger an image filled the screen.

It was Lynn Obregon. I'd known her for years. "Lynn is very attractive, but she has a reputation for playing around."

Gina nodded and the image changed. Sally Kass.

I shook my head. "She uses drugs. What a waste."

The image changed and I started. It was Ann Lord, my boss. I felt an excitement looking at her but shook my head. "Part of my success in business is my policy of not dating colleagues."

Gina flashed face after face. Some of them I knew and some I didn't, but none of them fit my picture of a perfect partner. Finally she said, "You're exhausted and frankly, so am I, if you don't mind I. . . ." She slowly dissolved into smoke and poured herself back into the lamp.

When I awakened I was clutching the lamp in one hand and the polishing cloth in the other. I laughed and gave the lamp a final rub. Nothing happened. After putting away the polish and cloth, I walked around the house taking stock. I *had* been hanging on to Jill's things. I looked in her closet and everything was the same as it had been for the last ten years. "What am I going to do with all this stuff?" I mumbled.

My musings were interrupted by the telephone. It was the Women's Shelter. The voice at the other end said, "We're having a garage sale next weekend to raise money for the house. Since you're one of our supporters we . . ."

"Can you bring a truck over tomorrow?" I asked.

"Four o'clock okay?"

I spent the next few hours folding Jill's clothes and carefully packing them in the sturdy trash bags I usually reserved for yard cleaning.

I woke up the next morning feeling better than I expected and decided to go through the things in the garage. I was moving Jill's weight-lifting equipment when I saw my easel. When Jill was alive I loved to spend my leisure time painting. I found my paint box. The tubes of oils were dried hard. I took the easel into the house and put it into Jill's room which had the best light. I'd go shopping for oils and maybe stretch a couple of canvases.

At four o'clock the truck from the Center pulled into the driveway. In a few minutes everything was loaded and I was alone. When I went back into the house I again experienced the devastating emptiness but also a feeling of wholeness and completeness I had when Gina.... I smiled. Part of me still believed Gina was real. I went over to the brass lamp and gave it a little rub and said, "Thanks."

By late Sunday afternoon I'd done all I could do. I took a shower and got into my PJs and robe, made a sandwich and sat down to look at the Franklin proposal. I was disappointed. The Franklin account was important and the ideas for their next ad campaign struck me as being pretty stale. I sighed and put the folder on the desk. "I wish I had something fresher," I muttered. Suddenly I had an idea. I grabbed a stack of paper and started making sketches. I made notes in the margins of the original proposal and deleted whole sections. Finally satisfied, I opened my attaché case and took out the stack of resumes. "I hope the secretarial pool sends me someone who can read my writing." I sighed. A folder slipped out of the pile. I looked at the name, Maggie Stark. I glanced at it and realized she was already working in the secretarial pool and she was very qualified. I'd call Monday.

The next morning I started to walk toward the garage when I remembered the Jag was still with the mechanic. "Damn! I wish. . ."

Just then Sam pulled into the driveway with the car. "Walt told me you'd probably want this early. Hope I'm not late."

I started to laugh and got in. I was still chuckling when I dropped him off at the shop.

Evelyn's replacement was already at her desk when I got to my office. "Hi," I said. "I'm Sharon Michael."

The plump, redheaded young woman got up and extended her hand. "I'm Maggie Stark. The pool assigned me to you."

"Come on in, I'd like to talk to you."

When she was sitting across from me I said, "I was looking at your application. I think you're qualified for this slot. What would you think about a permanent assignment with me?"

"I want to be honest with you, Ms. Michael."

"Call me Sharon," I requested.

"Sharon, I'm not sure I'd be permanent. I've been thinking about going to grad school and . . ."

"Your first assignment is to retype this proposal if you can read my margin notes, and get the sketches to the art department. Your second assignment —" I handed her the stack of resumes, "is to notify these applicants that the position has been filled and thank them for applying."

Wednesday morning I was feeling quite ruffled. I tried on three different outfits before I felt dressed.

The morning went slowly. I was sharp with Maggie once and had to apologize.

Ann had made reservations at Dorothy's, a restaurant patronized by businesswomen. When I got there she was already waiting. A quick glance at my watch told me I wasn't late.

She smiled when I sat down. "The Franklin proposal came across my desk this morning. It was brilliant."

"Thanks . . . I —"

The waitress came and we both ordered the special. The food was delicious but I was nervous.

Finally, over coffee, Ann said, "I wanted you to be the first to know, I'm leaving the company."

I was astounded. "Where are you going? I can't imagine working for anyone else . . ."

"I was thinking about proposing you for my replacement." She put down her cup. "You're probably the best *man* for the job, but we'll have to work out a strategy."

I shook my head. "Where are you going?"

"I'm retiring," she stated. "I'd planned to work a couple more years but I don't know if the company will last that long."

I was shocked. "There have been rumbles about a merger."

She shook her head. "I've been slowly unloading my company stock, and today I made a sweet deal for my stock options."

I believed Ann, but was too stunned to speak.

She glanced at her watch. "I have to get back.

Look, I'd planned to take my mother to Santa
Barbara for her birthday, but this morning she
canceled. I still have reservations. Why not drive up
with me this weekend and we'll work out a
strategy."

"I don't know if I could do your job. I'm still . . ."

She reached across the table and touched my
hand. "Then we'll just do a *what if*. Is it a date?"

Ann was a different person in casual clothes. She
wore white jeans and jacket with a soft pale pink
shirt. The white set off her tan, and her wavy dark
hair, streaked with grey, was brushed back. She was
a gorgeous dyke. She threw my bag into the trunk
of her convertible and then moved around to open
the door for me. I was wearing shorts and a tank
top, and I felt her eyes on me when I slid into the
passenger seat.

The coastline was magnificent. "You still haven't
told me what you plan to do with your retirement."
I felt relaxed and chatty.

Ann glanced at me. "Maybe I'll sit in a
wheelbarrow for a year. I've thought about doing
some writing."

We talked about our lives. I told her about Jill
and she told me about Joan, a woman she'd been
with for fifteen years who suddenly left five years
before. By the time we'd reached the small Inn in
Santa Barbara, we knew many of the intimate
details of each other's lives. I felt easy and happy.

Ann had made reservations for adjoining rooms.

We quickly unpacked and got into our suits. When I saw her long straight tanned legs, and the fullness of her breasts, my breath caught in my throat.

She brought a notebook and pen with her to the pool, and between sunning and swimming, mapped out a strategy for moving me up to her job — who would have to be lobbied, and how I could be made more visible. Once in a while I'd look up and catch her staring at me and a couple of times she caught me looking at her.

By dinner time the tension between us was almost unbearable. Neither of us spoke much and when we did speak we were both tense. She suggested a walk after dinner.

Ann was a power walker and it was all I could do to keep up with her. She didn't hold back for me and sometimes when I fell behind I watched her stride. The strength and agility of her body enticed me. I wanted her. I wanted to be in her arms. Rules be damned — my body ached for her touch.

Back at the inn we took a quick plunge in the pool and then sat wrapped in our towels and watched the night sky. Then Ann reached over and touched my hand. "I think it's time to go in."

Excitement coursed through me. *At last,* I thought. I could feel my heart pounding as we walked down the hallway. At my door Ann stopped, put her hands on my shoulders, and kissed my forehead. "See you in the morning." Her voice was husky.

Disbelief washed through me as I saw her walk away. Angry — no — furious, I let myself into my room. I took a quick shower and rinsed out my bathing suit. I was so disappointed I wanted to cry, but I wouldn't do it. I wouldn't let her get to me in that way.

I got into bed but I knew I wouldn't be able to sleep. Finally I switched on the bedside lamp and picked up the book I'd brought with me. It was no use. I wouldn't be able to read. I put the book down and stared at the ceiling. Why had I come with her? What a fool I was. Frustrated I said, "I wish . . ."

Just then the phone rang.

Her husky voice caressed my ear. "I couldn't sleep, then I saw the light under your door. I've made a pot of herb tea if you'd like to join me."

I smiled. "I'll be there in a minute."

I felt spent, but I had to see her. I ran a comb through my hair and went to the door joining our rooms. It was unlocked.

Ann was sitting on the bed. When I came in she stood and her robe fell open. The sight of her full breasts, her muscular abdomen, and her tightly curled pubic hairs sent a shock of desire through me. I lifted my eyes to her face and saw passion.

Her arms opened and I went to her, letting my own robe fall open. When our skin touched I began trembling. She held me tightly in her strong arms and rocked me. "I didn't know it would go so fast," she groaned. "Me and my strategy! I planned to court you, to win you. Sharon, I've wanted you for so long."

I raised my face to hers and our lips came together. We sank down onto the bed. Our hands now kneading, now caressing, our breasts pressed together. I was out of my head trying to keep up with the sensations in my body. Every touch drove me deeper into senselessness. I couldn't speak. I heard myself moan and when she reached her fingers into me I let out a gasp that caught in my throat. The power of *her* inside of *me*. Then I felt the softness of her mouth engulf me. She hadn't withdrawn her fingers. I wept tears as she propelled me higher into ecstasy and when I orgasmed I bawled. She wrapped me in her arms and we pitched and rolled all over the bed. My hungry hands sought her breasts and belly and the wetness of her. As her wetness engulfed my fingers, swallowing them into her hot opening I laughed with joy.

She thrust against my fingers hungrily, passionately until her powerful orgasm left her damp and passive on the drenched sheets. I didn't let her go and I rested my cheek against the dark, damp, curly hairs of her mons, caressing her with my face and then turned so my mouth could envelop her and sucked gently. She protested, but so defenselessly — I didn't stop and felt her clitoris become hard and push against my tongue. I licked and grazed until I felt her begin to move with me and to thrust and twist with desire. She caressed my hair and groaned, sometimes curling her body upward, saying things so softly I couldn't hear and then she came with such power it almost pushed me from her.

I released her and climbed up her body, inch by inch, until our mouths were together. Our legs wound around each other pulling us closer. Her arms surrounded me again and I clung to her.

As sleep overtook us our bodies began to relax away from each other. Our hands found each other and we clasped fingers, not wanting to let go.

Almost asleep, I felt her raise up and embrace

me again. "I'm buying a ranch here in Santa Barbara," she said. "I'll show it to you tomorrow. We could live there or we could live in town and come out for the weekends. I want you. I never want to lose you."

I opened my eyes a little and looked toward the window. It seemed that a wisp of curling smoke was being swallowed by the night sky. "It's gonna work out," I murmured. "You'll see."

Chinese Dinner

Penny Hayes

From across the Formica-top table, Sherene sat completely enchanted by June.

"We could go to the Italian restaurant," June said, picking up her thick coffee mug with slender, tiny-boned hands. She brought the cup to her lightly lipsticked lips.

Sherene looked away. It wouldn't be cool to

blatantly stare at June, to watch those lips gently kiss the rim of that cup.

"Or perhaps you would like to suggest a place to dine?"

What finesse. Sherene would have said, "Hey, June where do ya wanna eat tonight?" "Let me think," she said. Something Sherene hadn't been able to do since this apparition from heaven had suggested three days ago that they do coffee. She took a polite bite of her sugared cream puff. Thoughts of June in an intimate position leaped to her mind: legs spread, soft, soft inner lips laid against the tender outer ones, the glistening pink skin just begging for a mouth to be pressed against it.

She inhaled quickly. The cream puff still to her lips, sugar was sucked into her nostrils, tickling her violently. She grabbed her napkin, pressed it to her nose and sneezed her composure away. "Pardon me. A slight allergy." She tipped her head slightly. She could look as haughty as June, too. If she didn't tip her head back so far that she was looking at the ceiling . . .

"Is your neck all right?" June asked.

Sherene straightened. "Just a catch. It's nothing."

She studied June's eyes, two dangerous pools of indigo. June's cheeks were covered with oh, so silky skin, fine high cheekbones lying just beneath the surface. Sherene longed to touch June's salt and pepper hair, short enough so that if Sherene ran her fingers through it, punk spikes would stick up between her fingers.

June ran her hand down her rich tan silk blouse. "We could do the Chinese buffet on South Street. I

like variety. Lots of variety." She looked dead-on into
Sherene's eyes.

Sherene swallowed. No one had dated this
woman since she'd come to town six months ago. Not
a man, not a woman. Sherene had kept track.
Closely. "When would you like to go?" she asked.
She would keep it light, not push, not leap across
the table and hysterically grab June. Just casually
allow her to make the decision so that June wouldn't
feel manipulated — like Sherene was being
manipulated — and she couldn't stop June, and
what's more, didn't *want* to stop June.

Sherene hoped they'd meet within the next week
or so. And it would allow her time to get her act
together, to buy some new clothes, do a little reading
on what was going on in the world so she didn't
seem too dull; research a few Chinese cookbooks so
she could speak intelligently on how delicious the
bamboo shoots were because of this or that cooking
process, or how tasty the green beans were because
of such-and-such spices added during preparation.

June checked her watch. "Would seven suit you?"

"That'd be fine," Sherene answered nonchalantly.
She wondered if June could see the vein protruding
along her right temple, pounding at a hundred-sixty
beats per minute.

She looked at her watch. Not a delicate piece of
jewelry like June's, but a big sucker like a racetrack
driver might wear. She dropped her arm below the
table thinking she had from twelve-fifty to six PM to
change her life and find something decent to wear.
There was no way on Earth she'd ever get to look at
a Chinese cookbook. And to hell with world events.

At seven sharp, she waited shaking in the

parking lot of Wong's Buffet. Odors of exotic foods leached from the building, wafting to her car where she sat with the window wide open in the thirty-five degree temperature just to keep herself cool. She had showered and washed her shining black hair twice, insisting her housemate, a beautician, style it for her. Thirty dollars hadn't seemed too steep a price to pay.

She wore silver earrings, a small silver labrys, a white turtleneck and black wool slacks. No makeup. At five-eight and no fat on her runner's body, she looked good. And she was hungry. Hungry for food, hungrier for June.

She got out of her car as June joined her. Even in the heavy tweed coat, June looked tiny, standing not more than five-four or so. "Hi," she said. Her eyes appeared soft, doe-like.

Sherene wanted to pick her up and carry her away to a safe place. She seemed that vulnerable. *You make my breath catch every time I look at you,* Sherene silently told her as they walked inside.

They shed their coats. June was dressed in black, the blouse pleated, the slacks set off with a wide patent-leather belt. She wore dangling gold earrings and a black onyx ring. Sherene wanted to shout, "MY GOD, YOU'RE BEAUTIFUL!" She managed to say, "You look lovely."

"So do you," June replied. "You should wear slacks more often. They show off your nice long legs."

Sherene blushed.

They ate and chatted and tried everything offered at the buffet table. As it turned out, neither knew a great deal about Chinese food other than it was very good. Through the course of the evening, they sampled thirty dishes or so.

Then the dinner, the laughs and the talk stopped. Without preamble, June said, "Come home with me, Sherene."

A woman who came straight to the point. Sherene's head pounded like a kettle drum.

In a bedroom full of lacy curtains with a lavender bedspread, they undressed each other and stared at one another. And then they danced belly to belly to the sounds of an electric violin and k.d. lang's golden voice.

Their lips drew close without ever making contact. Their breathing caressed each other's ears. Their hands floated across soft curves. The sensations were electrifying.

Sherene could almost encircle June's waist with her large hands. She slid her palms over June's charmingly small breasts, her heart shuddering as she cupped them both.

She picked up June and carried her to the bed, then lay full length alongside her. Slowly Sherene kissed her. Never before had she kissed lips like these. Never!

She snuggled against June and began to caress her, running her hand over June's breasts and down her sides, feeling June's ribs beneath her long fingers.

Air expelled from June's lungs in a wild gasp when Sherene pushed a finger through the curly triangle of hair between June's thighs. She was as damp as a London fog. Sherene knew that very soon June would come.

She did, gasping, her chest rising and falling

rapidly as Sherene drew slow, tantalizing circles around June's clitoris.

Then June lay still, staring at the ceiling. "That was nice," she said.

Sherene felt herself deflate. Nice? Only nice? She wanted to get dressed and go home. She'd done everything perfectly: picked up the dinner tab, danced with June, caressed her, even carried her to bed. Pretty damn romantic, she thought. And to June, it was only *nice*?

June sat up. She put a hand on Sherene's chest. Sherene started to protest. She was never comfortable when her lovers came on to her, but before she could speak, June slid her hand to Sherene's face, across her wide forehead, along the bridge of her crooked nose where she'd broken it twice in fights, and over her narrow lips making them tickle until Sherene had to lick them to make the tickle go away.

June leaned over and blew into Sherene's ear. Nobody was allowed to do that to Sherene, but Sherene let it go, let June move her tongue around Sherene's ear and dart the tip in and out. It wasn't so bad after all. Kind of like eating some of those tiny tastes of Chinese food they'd had tonight. Not much of any one thing, but all very delicious.

Then June did something Sherene had never experienced before; had never even imagined. June sat cross-legged between Sherene's thighs and just — looked!

Sherene fought the desire to clamp her legs shut. To have someone deliberately *stare* at her . . .

June touched her and Sherene leaped. A jolt of desire flooded her. She could feel wetness surge from her and roll down her ass.

Slowly, and breathing with small mewing sounds, June pressed her palm against Sherene, then inserted her finger inside and at the same time pressed her thumb against Sherene's clitoris. Sherene arched her back. She clenched her teeth and grabbed the bedspread with both hands.

June removed her hand and leaned forward, placing her cheek against Sherene's belly. She blew warm breaths against Sherene's skin and licked her abdomen several times. She reached up and took Sherene's nipples in both hands. Gently, she pinched the hardened brown flesh between her fingers and rubbed her palms across them and circled them with light touches. She placed her lips on top of Sherene's coarse, black hair while still caressing her nipples.

"No more," Sherene whispered. Her assertive nature was crumbling like limestone. She was no longer in control. She was no longer Sherene.

June asked, "How do you feel?"

Sherene mumbled something and felt June smile against her. June pressed with her tongue.

Sherene groaned and again clenched her teeth. She put her hands on June's head wanting to tear her mouth away, yet wanting to push her face through the bones of her pelvis.

With the tip of her tongue, June pressed against Sherene's clitoris. Sherene felt warm fluid run down her bottom again. She had been holding her legs rigidly straight. Now they bent of their own accord drawing up alongside her without her having had a say in their positioning. She grabbed her knees and held them. She felt completely exposed — and giving.

Again June stopped.

"What . . ." Sherene glanced at her. She couldn't stop now.

June hadn't. She straightened and lay completely on top of Sherene, her legs between Sherene's. Sherene had never been at ease this way. *She'd* always been on top. But this was wonderful!

June began to grind against her; Sherene matched her rhythm. They swayed for several moments. Two more seconds and Sherene would come. Now she knew what being hot meant. It literally meant *heat*. Real heat. Fire. She breathed deeply and allowed the climactic sensation to hit her.

And then June moved again.

"Damn, June. What'er ya doing?" Sherene was going to explode pretty soon if this kept up.

"I'm taking my time. Don't you like time taken with you?"

The low light from the bedside lamp made June's skin glow, as though she had been created from pastels. And she was muscular, yet so completely feminine. Sherene wondered how June balanced her strength and her beauty with such perfect precision.

"Take time?" Sherene asked through numbed lips.

June smiled and sat up.

"Are you getting up?" Sherene asked. June couldn't leave!

"Just getting ready for the next course," June whispered in Sherene's ear. "There is nothing so lovely as being able to do many different things in order to please each other beyond sanity, don't you think? Variety."

Like their dinner tonight. Thirty choices, all great, and in the end, satisfying Sherene's hunger. She let her muscles go slack.

June rested on top of Sherene, this time facing Sherene's thighs while her legs straddled Sherene's head.

Sherene's mind filled with thick heavy sensations. She could barely breathe, yet June didn't weigh a hundred and ten pounds.

June clamped her mouth upon Sherene.

Sherene heard herself moan repeatedly as she moved her lips and tongue against Sherene. Sherene took June into her mouth.

They moved as one. Whatever Sherene did, June duplicated. Whatever June did, Sherene repeated. They spoke through their bodies, each telling the other precise moves to make, exact strokes to perform with willing lips and tongues. They wrapped their arms around each other's strong thighs.

Sherene had become a continuous titanic climax as it simultaneously hit June. They clutched each other, their tongues pulsating against clitorises, undulating, swollen, wet, grasping.

Flashes of June's medley of lovemaking tore through Sherene's mind with conspicuous clarity. June was on her, in her, part of her. They melded together in coalescent heat that threatened to consume Sherene.

Then ever so slowly the tornado receded. June lifted her face from Sherene as Sherene released her. June shifted and moved alongside her. Sherene wanted to snatch June to her breast and never let her go.

June lay in Sherene's arms, hers draped across Sherene's chest. "You're a beautiful lover, Sherene. Lots of things to do with you."

Sherene shook her head at her own ineptness as a lover. "I never knew. I'm so ridiculously basic."

"Variety," June whispered.

"Yes," Sherene agreed. She thought of their dinner.

Summer in the Cold Time

Mary J. Jones

The rain began just as I pulled into the street that ran alongside Turner Park. I glanced at the crowd in front of the bandstand and thought that with the temperature already in the thirties and now this rain, sane people would go home. But there they were, sixty or so of them, waving their placards and chanting their sad slogans. The thing I hate worst about covering an anti-abortion rally is that I've got to talk to those people: the men with their mad monk eyes and the women looking like they accept David Koresh as their Savior.

Of course, I didn't really have to come myself. My business card reads, *Kit Connolly, Editor-in-Chief, Larousse County Journal.* I could have sent one of the reporters. But I've always covered our little city's political demonstrations — what few there've ever been. More important, though, it would keep my mind off Pam. I hoped.

Two months ago, Pam, my partner of more years than I care to say, came home one afternoon and announced she was leaving me to join a women's commune in New Mexico. "I need the high desert now," she said. As if she'd ever seen a desert, high or otherwise. What she needed was the red-headed charge nurse who'd been strutting her ass past the door of the hospital administration office for the last year. Pam was the assistant administrator.

I'd spent this morning trying to call her at the commune, with the usual poor luck, so I was late getting to the rally. The parking lot was already jammed, but I finally found a space and nosed into it. Then I grabbed notebook and umbrella and hustled into the park, passing another latecomer, a tall woman hunched in a sheepskin coat.

Turner Park lies on the edge of our business district, tucked among handsome Victorian buildings somehow left behind by urban renewal. It consists of no more than the bandstand, a lot of grass, and one shake-roofed picnic shelter — under which was now huddled the Channel 5 crew, camera trained on the Reverend Mr. Heil, the rally's organizer, up on the bandstand already delivering his speech via bullhorn.

He sternly warned his listeners that though there might not be an abortion clinic within a hundred miles, Larousse County could any moment fall to the godless enemy.

As for the crowd itself, there were an amazing number of full-length fur coats, as well as the usual signs — from the sentimental bullshit of *Everyone Deserves a Birthday* to the kind that condemned anyone practicing her constitutional rights to eternal damnation. Around the crowd's edges prowled a half-dozen cops, cold, wet, and bored. Across the street a counter-demonstration braved the rain.

And the rain was getting worse, the temperature lower. Nevertheless, by now Mr. Heil had some of the anti-choice people praying and weeping; mostly, though, they listened in solemn silence. I recognized a number of them, people who seemed quite normal when they brought in their relatives' obituaries or called asking me to send a photographer to their church bazaars. And I'd gone to school with some — Trish Arnold and Rose Biegenwald, for instance, hotshot softball players when we were at St. Pat's. There they stood now, slavering over the speech like a pair of starved rottweilers. The rest I didn't know, though the woman in sheepskin seemed familiar.

When Mr. Heil finally wound down, a woman wearing a tight polyester raincoat led the crowd in what I suppose was a hymn. I couldn't catch the words, but the tune sounded suspiciously like "Deutschland, Deutschland Uber Alles." As they sang, a man slowly and ominously swung a plastic bag full of red fluid, pig's blood perhaps or maybe just cherry Kool-Aid. A little distance behind the main group, a gray-haired woman in a mink stole explained to a young boy that abortion was murder. When the child made no response, the woman grabbed his shoulders and swiveled him toward the counter-demonstrators across the street. "They oughtta be hung," she said.

The pro-choicers were a much smaller group, hardly more than a thin line of college kids shored up by some out-of-towners and the local radicals — three female professors, a fifty-year-old hippie who peddled New Age artifacts out of his '73 Volvo, and my aunt Colleen, late of the Little Sisters of the Precious Blood. Ten or fifteen, at the most. Ours is a city not precisely set on the cutting edge of the twentieth century.

A priest was speaking now, in a much more impassioned tone than Mr. Heil could ever muster, and, in response, the crowd surged crazily toward the bandstand. Pretty soon, they'd be in full cry, with screams and curses spewing out of those holier-than-thou mouths. It's hard to tell what a mob might do, even in a cold rain. So I positioned myself in the relative safety of the picnic shelter, just behind Channel 5. I'd do my interviews later. Meantime, let TV get the view — and the pig blood, if it came to that.

But the crowd stayed quiet after all — perhaps because the rain had by now turned to sleet. Or maybe because Channel 5 was beginning to pack up its equipment. Anyway, they sang another hymn, then shuffled their wet feet uncertainly. At last, after a war council by the event's organizers, the Reverend Mr. Heil squeezed the trigger of his bullhorn and told everyone to go home. They beat a hasty retreat to the parking lot, humming "Onward Christian Soldiers" as they fled.

The woman in the sheepskin coat didn't move as quickly as the rest. The wind whipped through her dark hair, cut in a smooth, timeless page boy, and a sudden blast of icy rain made her turn her head in my direction. In that moment I recognized her. My breath stopped. It was Ann.

Ann Sommers, my first, my best love, lost to me long years ago. Except at her father's funeral, I hadn't seen her since I was twenty-one years old, in her parents' backyard, through a shell-burst of anger and tears.

I wanted to call out to her, but I could make no sound, no move, though I didn't for a moment doubt that it was Ann — she still had the listing gait that was the legacy of a childhood bout with polio. When we were young, she'd been tall and blade-thin with black hair and generous big breasts; and skin of a sweet smell that lingers high up in my nose even now. Her slanting eyes could brood darkly or flash bright as a lake in the summer sun. I don't say she was beautiful, perhaps not even very pretty. But she radiated a crackling kind of energy that was part sexual, part spiritual, and for me, at least, absolutely irresistible.

This woman was older, heavier, but definitely Ann. Nor did I wonder what she was doing in town. I knew very well that she lived — had lived all these years — not more than two hours away, in the state capitol; that she was an English teacher; that she had a daughter named Katherine and a husband reputedly devoted to them both. Yes, it was Ann — running past me again.

Our city is home to a small college, which Ann and I attended. We'd been born and raised locally, but before college we barely knew each other; she'd gone through the public schools while I endured the nuns at St. Pat's. But at college, we found we had much in common, both town students, both the eldest children of working people — her father was a police sergeant, her mother a housewife; my father was a pressman for the *Journal,* my mother worked in a laundry. We were the first of our families to go to college and though our families were inordinately proud of us, they were also fiercely demanding. We were expected to work hard not only to keep our scholarships but to pay for our keep at home. Ann clerked in the dime store and I took classified ads at the *Journal.* Even so, we found time, lots of time, for each other. I filled myself up with her laughter and her eloquence. With her.

I had not spoken to Ann since a week after graduation, when she told me she would marry Joseph Goring. Of course, I knew she went out with him sometimes, just as I occasionally saw Ron Nixon. But when she said they were getting married, I'd been hurled far past fury, toward some distant crater of hell. We both thought I might kill her there and then. Instead, I ripped off the silver triskele pendant she'd given me for my twenty-first birthday and threw it at her feet. For a long moment, we stared down at that ancient Irish symbol of destiny, then she turned and walked away.

Later, when she was truly gone, the pain came. I've never known such anguish, neither before nor since, and there was nothing in this world or any other to quench its flames — and, believe me, I tried enough liquor to know.

Somehow, though, I survived her — the booze, too, in the end — went on to love again. Not with the same intensity, of course; that never came again and I've long since quit looking for it. Life with Pam was good, comfortable, sweet, even if what I felt for her could never adorn the spires of heaven as had my love for Ann.

"Go after her, you fool," I said to myself there in the park. But still I could not find the courage to move. Just then, Ann changed direction, the force of the storm driving her to the shelter where I stood.

I shivered as I watched her run across the grass, shivered with cold and anticipation, just as I used to long ago when I waited for her to join me under the covers in a dark bedroom.

When we were young, people saw no reason to put twin beds in their daughters' rooms. And so on the many nights we spent staying over with each other, we slept in big, sexy double beds, next to her brothers' room or across the hall from my parents.

Sunday mornings were the best. Our families were regular church goers who let their almost-grown daughters sleep in, confident that I would go to late mass, Ann to Wednesday night services. And sometimes we did. But what we did on Sundays, in her sagging Sears, Roebuck bed or under my high pine backboard, was celebrate the miracle of our bodies. And the fear of a door suddenly opened only added to the thrill.

There was a certain amount of guilt, of course, given the times and our upbringing. Less on my part than Ann's — I always was a creature of the flesh. But, really, she suffered not so much from the fact that this was lesbian love than that it was sex in any form. Her people were of a Moravian sect, only two generations removed from communal life and still strict as to the pleasures of the world. I think she was surprised, shocked, at how much she liked sex.

And, oh my, she did like it. It didn't take much experience on my part to tell that. How many Sunday mornings I would wake to find her naked body pressed against my back, hands covering my breasts, warm breath on my neck.

"I love you, Kit," she'd say and then in a cold room under three quilts, we'd tend the fire of our desire with tongue and teeth, lips and fingers. I remember she liked to take the triskele's chain and then the nape of my neck in her teeth. When I groaned with the pleasure of it and fell back against her, she'd straddle me and stroke my clitoris hot and hard. And as I came, so did she, with a sharp little scream and her heart pounding against my ribs. Then, while the sun warmed the room, our tongues would be on each other till we were both ravished.

Finally, we would lie in my pine bed and I would recite an old Irish love lyric — "She's my pulse, my secret, the scented flower of the apple. She's summer in the cold time. . . . " We'd laugh then and, arms tight around each other, fall asleep.

By the time Ann got to the picnic shelter, we were alone in it. I watched as she ran an elegantly gloved hand through her hair, then took off the sheepskin coat and shook it to rid it of the icy water.

Against her black turtleneck sweater, at the end of a thin chain, there lay a silver triskele pendant.

As she put her coat back on, she glanced around. And saw me. A strange look passed over her face — a mingling of fear and joy.

"Hello, Ann," I said. I didn't move from where I stood.

For a moment the fear and the joy fought each other. Then, without a word, Ann walked across the shelter floor and took me in her arms. She folded the sheepskin coat around me. Once again, it was summer in the cold time.

Heading Home

Marion L. Head

Restlessly, Troy scanned the highway stretching before her. It had been some time since she had seen another car; the monotony of cracked, black asphalt, broken white lines and rolling prairie was taking its toll on her patience. Several hours before, she had lost interest in her long drive. It was now a matter of toughing out the last fifty or sixty miles and she would be home.

The sun was low enough in the sky that she removed her sunglasses, laying them on the dashboard. She stretched, resting one arm on the back of the bench seat of the truck, and shifted about in search of a more comfortable position for her tired back. She made a quick check of the instrument panel; all the gauges were fine, the speedometer held steady at a mere five miles an hour over the posted speed limit. She frowned at the radio, irritated with herself for never having had it repaired. Any distraction, even a local farm report, would help her boredom.

Troy looked in the rearview mirror and grinned at the sight of a car coming up behind her. It was moving fast and Troy attempted to accelerate to match the speed. Her truck grumbled at the exertion and, frustrated, Troy backed off the pedal. The car raced past her and disappeared over the next rise. Her only diversion gone, Troy resigned herself to another hour of tedium.

Troy squinted into the distance, thinking she saw a person standing by the side of the road. Her foot lightened on the gas pedal as she tried to make out any details of the apparition. The figure took a step to the edge of the highway and extended a thumb.

As Troy passed, her foot was already pressing against the brake. Grabbing the steering wheel with both hands, she brought the truck to a bouncing stop on the gravel shoulder.

Troy watched out the back window as a woman sauntered up to the passenger side of the truck. One hand on the window frame, she leaned forward and smiled at Troy.

"Where you headed?" Troy asked.

"Where you going?"

Troy grinned. "Aberdeen."

The woman shrugged. "That'll do." She yanked open the truck door and climbed in.

Troy studied her for a moment, the grin still on her lips. The woman was slim, a little on the short side, her black hair curling haphazardly around her shoulders. She was dressed in a pair of carefully ripped jeans, a cutoff sleeveless T-shirt and a pair of loosely tied white high-tops. She watched Troy taking her in and then turned indifferently toward the windshield.

Troy put the truck in gear and pulled back on to the highway. "I'm Troy," she offered, turning to look at her passenger.

"Rosie," the woman answered, her eyes still on the road.

Leveling out at her accustomed speed, Troy relaxed into the normal rhythm of the truck. She leaned one elbow out the open window, her hand loosely on the wheel.

"Do you mind?" Rosie said.

Troy looked at Rosie, who held a thin joint between her lips, a lighter poised beneath the tip. "Not if you share," Troy said.

Rosie flicked the lighter, took a deep drag and held it in her lungs for several seconds. As she exhaled she smiled at Troy. "Sorry, you're driving."

"It's only illegal if you get caught."

Rosie shook her head. "It's also illegal to get in an accident." She took another puff and, watching Troy, exhaled in her direction.

Troy sighed. "Not fair."

Rosie laughed and clamped the burning tip of the joint between her teeth. She leaned toward Troy.

Troy inhaled deeply as Rosie blew smoke into her open mouth. Clamping her mouth shut, her eyes watering, she gestured Rosie away with a wave of her hand. Rosie sat back but did not return to her side of the seat. She took one more pull on the joint, pinched out the ash and flicked the remainder out the window. Tucking one foot beneath her, Rosie laid a hand on Troy's thigh.

As Troy felt the fingers through her jeans, a dull buzz began somewhere in her brain. Involuntarily, her foot pressed into the gas pedal as the fingers dug into the muscle of her leg. As the grip loosened, she took a deep breath and slowed the truck.

"Do you mind?" Rosie asked as her hand slipped between Troy's legs, pressing against her crotch.

Troy's hands tightened on the steering wheel as her body was jolted by the electric charge emanating from Rosie's fingers. She kept her eyes on the road, forcing herself to concentrate, as she felt Rosie reach beneath the seatbelt and unbutton her pants.

"Speaking   of   accidents ... "   Troy   laughed nervously.

"Just drive," Rosie ordered, her lips against Troy's ear. Her hand slid beneath Troy's shirt, her fingers gliding across Troy's stomach. As her hand closed on Troy's breast, Rosie's tongue skimmed up Troy's neck.

Troy shuddered, suddenly grateful that the road was virtually deserted, that her only concern was keeping the truck somewhere on the pavement. She felt Rosie's hand return to the top of her jeans and

found herself lifting her hips slightly to assist Rosie
in unzipping them.

Rosie leaned into Troy, one arm around her neck.
Her right hand slipped inside Troy's jeans.

"Oh shit," Troy mumbled as she felt a finger
push inside of her, retreat and reenter. Her left foot
jammed against the floorboard, lifting her body
partially from the seat.

Rosie's arm tightened around Troy's neck, her
breasts smashed against Troy's shoulder, as her
hand continued moving assertively.

Troy fought to keep her eyes open and a small
bit of her attention on driving as she felt Rosie's
teeth sink into her neck. A low groan began in her
throat as her body tensed. The need to come was so
intense that Troy felt herself applying a foot to the
brake and jerking the truck off the blacktop. She
pulled onto an overgrown dirt road and found an
abandoned out-building surrounded by gnarled elm
trees. She slammed the truck to a stop and
extracted Rosie's hand from her pants.

Troy took a deep breath to calm her pounding
heart and slowly turned to Rosie. Rosie watched her
expectantly, a small smile on her lips. Troy reached
out and dug her fingers into Rosie's thick, black
hair. Roughly, she pushed Rosie back on the seat
and fell across her, their lips meeting.

Rosie's legs fell apart, one foot on the floor, as
Troy pressed into her, as Troy's tongue plunged into
her mouth. She reached behind Troy, grasped her
ass and shoved her hips into Troy's thigh.

Troy yanked Rosie's shirt away from her body,
her mouth closing around her breast. She felt Rosie's
fingers tighten on the seat of her jeans and thrust

her hips solid!y across her leg. Her lips continued working about Rosie's chest as the motion of her hips became more frantic. The moment before she came her body stilled, every muscle compressed in the effort to absorb the sensory overload. She let the waves flood over her and then, in one final strained effort, let the tension go, her body falling limply over Rosie's.

Troy felt Rosie's hips rise slightly, nudging her back to awareness. Hands were on her back, kneading her shoulders, tracing her spine. She parted her lips slightly and licked the breast cushioning her face.

Troy pushed herself up, unzipped Rosie's tattered jeans and pulled them to her ankles. Shoving her hands beneath Rosie's hips, lifting her slightly, her fingers kneading the soft flesh, Troy began nibbling her way to the top of Rosie's thighs. Rosie threw one leg over Troy's shoulder, her hands closed about Troy's head, pulling her closer. Without hesitation, Troy's mouth opened and her tongue dipped into Rosie's vagina.

Rosie's body thrashed about the seat, her fingers tugging at Troy's hair. Her bare foot kicked at the rear window as her body strained to stave off the approaching orgasm, to prolong the exquisite sensation of Troy's mouth.

Troy felt Rosie's body tense, heard her loud cry echo through the truck cab. Slowly, she released her grip on Rosie's hips, her lips returning to Rosie's thigh, wiping the wetness from her face.

Troy slipped two fingers inside of Rosie and slowly rotated them. She looked up; Rosie's eyes were closed, the lines in her face tight with concentration. Troy picked up the pace of her fingers, pulling them in and out of Rosie, the wetness flowing across her hand.

Troy's hips began rocking in rhythm with her fingers and, going to her knees, she took Rosie's hand, pressing it inside her jeans. Rosie's eyes fluttered open in recognition of her need and, smiling slightly, she wiggled a finger inside of Troy. Her eyes closed again, but the smile remained on her lips as they began rocking together.

Troy shoved herself against Rosie's hand as her own fingers drove into Rosie. She found herself somewhere on the edge between pleasure and pain and, wanting both, pushed herself harder, forcing them both to reach their peak of excitement.

Troy's body jerked, her vagina holding Rosie's finger tight, her muscles constricting painfully. She felt Rosie's own contractions as her fingers were squeezed tightly inside of her. Rosie's body lifted a final time and then she fell back limply. Troy lay across her and, grinding her hips into Rosie's thigh, felt her own body reach satisfaction and relax.

Troy rested her face against Rosie's throat as she caught her breath. Gently, she removed her fingers from inside Rosie and, lifting her hips slightly, allowed Rosie to do the same. She wrapped her arms about Rosie, hugged her tightly and reached to kiss her.

Rosie's eyes fluttered open and she smiled at Troy. "God, I missed you."

Troy grinned. "I could tell. What the hell are you doing out here?"

"I couldn't wait another hour for you to get home." Rosie kissed Troy quickly. "Do you mind?"

Troy laughed. She extracted herself from Rosie's arms and sat up. "Living with you is never dull."

Rosie pushed herself up, leaning against the door. "I thought you liked it that way." Her bare foot slid beneath Troy's shirt, rubbing against her breasts.

Troy's hands wandered up Rosie's leg. "I like you any way I can get you."

"It's getting dark," Rosie observed as Troy's fingers reached the top of her thigh.

"Do you care?"

Rosie shook her head and allowed Troy inside her again. The fingers were gentle this time, merely a reminder of the former intensity.

"Where's the motorcycle?" Troy asked as she continued caressing Rosie.

"Down by the creek, where you picked me up."

Troy leaned to kiss Rosie. "We better get it."

Rosie smiled and nodded. She sat up and began dressing. Troy pulled at her clothes, attempting to straighten the tangled folds. Troy slid behind the steering wheel and waited until Rosie moved beside her, a hand resting lightly on Troy's thigh.

"Did I tell you that I love you?" Troy asked.

Rosie laid her head on Troy's shoulder and sighed. "I know you do."

Troy nodded, turned on the headlights and steered them back toward the highway.

Just Exactly

Molleen Zanger

Closure, she thought, twisting the rearview mirror around so she could see herself better. Closure is what I need. We should have done this years ago. Nine years, to be exact. Nine years. If she could have found the right words back then, what might these nine years have been like?

Futile to wonder. Senseless. She had wasted so much time in the idle speculation over this topic. And it wasn't just time that had been wasted, either. A year's worth of ads in the *Lesbian Link* wasn't cheap. But they'd finally paid off. Tonight she would see Emily again. Tonight she would find just exactly the right words to say and lay it all to rest. Finally. Finally.

The ad read: Emily W., worked at the Baywood in Saginaw '84–'85, call Brat (517) 790-5555.

She sighed, anticipating the relief of banishing this particular blonde ghost once and for all. Again she examined the extremely light-colored hair coming in at her left temple. Could it be . . . nah. Not gray, there was no gray in her family. Well, maybe that one great aunt, the one who never married, but she herself was too young for gray. Wasn't she?

Young. God. They'd been so young. Maybe that was part of the problem.

She settled into the bucket seat. It was way too early to go into the restaurant. Why had she gotten here so early? Emily's voice on the phone. She sounded the same except, maybe . . . no, not tentative . . . what? Wary. She'd sounded wary, even suspicious.

"Brat?" It was Em's own personal nickname for her, an abbreviation of her Polish last name that no one else had ever called her.

"Brat? This is Emily, from the Baywood? I saw your ad, I mean, a friend did and passed it on to me. Are you okay?"

Again it happened. She couldn't speak, couldn't say any of the things she planned to say if this ever really happened, if Emily ever called.

"Brat? Brat? Are you there? Are you all right?"

She said it so concerned, just as if she gave a damn. Just as if. But why the silence? Why the long empty years of not even one fucking word from Em? Still the words wouldn't come, angry words, accusatory words, bitter, betrayed words. She said she'd keep in touch. She said she'd write. Nine fucking years?

No. Anger was not appropriate. Her emotional response was way out of proportion to the reality. Emily had not left her; Emily had simply left. Emily had left before Shelly could find the words to tell her the truth. So Emily could not be blamed for anything. Anything. And Shelly wore a daily regret ever since. Regret over Emily had flavored every relationship Shelly'd tried to have.

"Where are you? Are you in town?" was all she could manage, plus, "I need to talk to you." But she still wasn't honest with Emily. She never even said the word "closure."

"No," Em said, "I'm still in Eugene. But I'm coming home next month for my mom and stepdad's silver anniversary. I'll be there the seventh through the fifteenth. Let's see ... the seventh is Friday. Their party is on Sunday. How about Saturday, Saturday the eighth? Now, where? Oh, I know, is that little restaurant still across from the Baywood? You know, where we used to go for breakfast after work?"

Shelly had to struggle to find any voice at all, so many emotions swirled through her. This was Emily, The Emily, Her Emily. It was her voice and she was coming home and they were going to meet.

"Brat?"

"Sorry. Yeah, the restaurant is still there, different though. Different owners. A couple of dykes and it's gone upscale."

No response from Em.

"Em?"

"Yeah, um, I'm here." The hint of familiarity that had begun to slip into Emily's voice was gone. She became crisply businesslike. "So do you have a problem with that?"

"What, the upscale part?"

"No. The dyke part. Do you have a problem with that?"

"Not at all, Em. In fact, I love it. I go there often, actually. With dates." Well, actually, the "often" was a bit of a stretch. "Occasionally" would have been more accurate.

Emily still hesitated, then said, "Well, okay, that sounds fine. Like, what time? Oh look, let's make this easy: How about eight o'clock on the eighth? Okay?"

"Okay, Em, okay. That sounds great." But she didn't feel great. She felt numb. Up until maybe even last year she might have felt great about seeing Em again, but nine years was just too damn long to carry a torch for someone, a torch that was blinding her to any other possibilities. It was time to end it. Time to say goodbye to Emily.

"Goodbye Emily."

"See you then, Brat . . . Wait. Brat, are you okay? I mean you don't have anything fatal or anything, do you?"

As if you give a shit. I could've died twenty-three times and you would never have even known it. For all you knew . . . "No, Em. I don't have anything anymore."

And she'd hung up. And waited. Hoping. Maybe Em would call her back. Why hadn't she gotten Em's number? Address? Maybe a letter would be easier,

better, even. Now that she knew just exactly the
right thing to say, she was eager to say it.

Eugene. She was still in Eugene. She'd fantasized
that Emily'd spent the last nine years bouncing from
one lesbian paradise to another, playing her guitar
for countless other women at countless other places
where she could be gay openly. That's what she'd
said. Those were her words the day Shelly'd had
none.

"These are my new friends," Em had said, waving
toward the tough-looking, black-leather-clad women
who stood behind her and glared at Shelly. Em had
worn leather, too, but rust-colored buckskin, fringed
and soft. Em was smiling, but only with her mouth.
Her blue-green eyes said something else, something
Shelly couldn't read, didn't know how to read.

"Em?" she'd asked.

"Brat, look, I'm gay. I'm going west with my
friends, to Oregon, to a place we can be gay openly.
Understand? I'll write." And then the leathers had
turned and walked out of the bar, walked out with
Em, walked her right out of Shelly's life.

But . . . but . . . Em . . . wait. That's what I've been
trying to tell you. Me, too, Em. And I'm in love with
you. Wait, Em. Stay. Why would these words not
come out? Why had she waited so long? And where
had these "friends" come from?

Tears slipped down her cheeks and she brushed
them away impatiently. This memory always made
her cry, telling this story always made her cry. And
she was so damned tired of crying.

From where she'd parked she could see the main
entrance to the parking lot, could approach her first

with her sunglasses on to give herself time to check her emotions. Would Em recognize her? How much had Em changed?

She looked again in the mirror before returning it to its proper position, not daring to fantasize anything. Three weeks and nine years was plenty of time to get your shit together. It's not as if they were lovers or anything.

Not that she hadn't wanted to be. Not that she hadn't longed, ached, for Emily. All those nights. Working side by side, flirting. After work, after breakfast, back at her apartment, always at her place because Emily still lived with her parents. All those talks trashing men, except, of course, for their mutual pal Jack Daniels, who kept them company. All that laughter, all those songs, and all that distance between them on the couch, that distance that even Jack could not give her the courage to breach. The air so electric between them, like just before lightning strikes. Gazes that never broke, not for hours. All those yearning silences. How could Em not know how she felt? And how could she have been afraid to tell Em? Did she really think she would laugh at her? Was she just imagining there was something very special between them? Where were her damn words?

Words were her life now. She'd finished college and got the job on the paper. Now she made her living with her words; words paid her rent and had bought her car. Other people came to her when they were looking for just exactly the right word, with just the right connotation. Now, too, she knew just the right words to say to women and how to hold them in her arms. She knew how, just exactly how, to make them . . . smile. But none of them was Em, with her smart mouth and chipped-front-tooth grin, her curly blondish hair that insisted, insisted, on trellising around the bows of her glasses like morning glories. None of them could play silly children's songs on Em's guitar with Em's strong calloused fingers and none of them were as adorably klutzy.

And none of them, Shelly reminded herself with her new determination to be realistic where Em's memory was concerned, none of them could pack away the booze like Em. She was probably an alcoholic now. It was a perversely comforting thought. Emily was probably a lush. Even back then she could drink Shelly under the table. Now Shelly's indulgences were limited to an occasional anchovy pizza, but there'd been a time . . .

It was time, she realized, glancing at her watch. Almost eight. Okay. She'd be the one waiting for Em inside. Appropriate, somehow. But no more, not after tonight. She locked her car and walked across the lot thinking of all the calm, sensible, put-this-to-rest-once-and-for-all closure words that she would say to the one that got away. Because that's all it was, all it had ever been. Fantasy and foolishness. Another thing she'd learned in these nine years was that love is an illusion, nothing lasts, no one lives happy ever after. Happy is a crock and all anyone can count on is their own fingers. She was going to meet an old friend — no, an old acquaintance — for dinner. She was going to see for herself what kind of disaster she had escaped. And she was going to put the immaturity of "what might have been" behind her forever. Resolution squared her shoulders and widened her stride. This dyke was done dreaming.

Through the restaurant dimness she strode purposefully toward the tuxedo-shirted woman at the reservation podium.

"Reservation for Bratowski. For two, non-smoking. My friend —"

She was interrupted by a clatter and soft curse. A woman was standing by a table, trying to mop up the spilled contents of a water glass. A thin slice of lemon lay on the floor. The woman was tall, broad-shouldered, with short blonde hair curling willfully, and glasses, and a chipped-tooth grin which she offered to Shelly as she opened her arms toward her.

"Brat?" the woman said.

Shelly took nine steps toward her and with each step a year of longing and regret fell away. In nine short steps she was, finally, finally, in Emily's arms and they clung together, oblivious of the other diners and of the hostess who was changing the wet tablecloth.

"Em?" they asked each other, "Brat?"

Emily held Shelly's face in her hands, kissing away her tears. Then she pulled away a few inches and looked deeply into Shelly's eyes.

"Brat," she said, "I'm gay. And I'm going away where I can be gay openly. And . . . I want you to come with me."

"No," said Shelly, reaching deep for those just-exactly right words that she had not dared rehearse. "No, Em. No. Don't go. Stay. Stay. Stay."

Especial de la Casa

Karin Kallmaker

What more could I have possibly wanted? I was sitting in a garden restaurant on a sultry May evening in Old Town, San Diego. My meal was going on my expense account. A delicate melody played on a Spanish guitar wafted around my ears. I sat with my back to the tallest hibiscus hedge I'd ever seen; it boasted blooms the size of dinner plates. The heavy scent of the flowers, the aroma of sizzling spices and half a margarita should have put me in a splendid frame of mind.

The problem was, I was surrounded by men. The only other woman at the table was at the far end — conversation with Lindy was impossible. I had gotten all dolled up for what I had thought was a date with Lindy only to find that her co-workers had invited themselves along. I didn't know what to make of Lindy's shrug when they'd proposed joining us (stupid men, not believing two women might want to spend the evening without their company) and so I, stupidly, had said sure, why not.

I only had two nights at this conference. Out of five candidates, I was the lucky analyst my bank had sent to learn the state-of-the-art in bank cost accounting. It wasn't that the conference was so terribly riveting (parts of it were, actually) that made me lucky — it was three days and two nights in sunny San Diego on the bank's wallet. My first night, however, was going to waste.

Excellent margarita, though. The lime was just sharp enough to make me pucker, with a subtle kick from the tequila after the cold, smooth liquid rolled down my throat. I was giving my entire concentration to my drink to avoid joining the conversation around me. Maybe it was the difference between women and men, or maybe I'm just biased, but I didn't think women at a lovely restaurant like this on a gorgeous night like tonight would be talking about theories of overhead allocation.

Lindy and I had sat next to each other at a dreadful session first thing this morning called "Automated Clearing House: Boon or Nightmare?" We'd started whispering to each other when the boredom got to be too much, and, well, she's from

San Francisco. Her hair's short, she's got two different earrings on and no sign of makeup — not that her soft-as-peach-fuzz looking skin needed it. In banking, that attire and a really irreverent attitude toward the Federal Reserve Board practically shouts, "Queer Nation Member." Not that I get up to the City that often — San Jose has plenty to offer. But, well, we clicked. So we sat next to each other for the rest of the sessions for the day. I discovered that in addition to being elegant and wickedly funny, Lindy is sharp as a tack at database manipulation. So we spent the better part of lunch talking allocation models in the hotel coffee shop. *That's* where you discuss allocation models, not in a dreamy, romantic setting like this restaurant.

I glanced down the table and caught Lindy's gaze. She toasted me with a little smile — maybe it said I'm bored, too. Could be. She was, I noted, drinking the same drink — lime margarita on the rocks, no salt. In this light she looked a lot like that dark-haired dream of a British lawyer on *L.A. Law* — absolutely yummers.

Anyway, at the end of the day when she asked me if I wanted to go to dinner in Old Town, of course I said yes. My earlobes had flushed and the backs of my knees had tickled just from the way she smiled. I'd left my room on a cloud, attired in the most dyke-ified outfit I'd brought with me: black jeans and a button-up white shirt adorned with a bolo. In my back pocket I'd slipped my credit card, I.D. and room key. I believe in traveling light when I intend to travel fast. We'd met in the lobby and Lindy had given me a supernova smile. She had to be a lesbian — would a straight cost accountant own tight leather pants and violet silk tunic? Maybe, but I doubted it.

And then this co-worker of hers, still wearing suit and name badge "Hi, my name is Dwayne," butted in, and before I knew it another guy she worked with and three other guys they knew had joined our date, which was obviously not a date anymore. If it ever had been. We had to take two cabs out to Old Town. I sat next to Lindy, making the smallest of small talk, and I tried not to let my leg get too used to feeling her leg next to it. It still felt like surgery when I had to move away.

This doesn't happen to me very often. Okay, it's never happened before. That I wanted someone almost the moment I saw her. That my palms got sweaty just glancing at her as she sat at the end of the table, crunching on a tortilla chip.

"Another margarita?"

I shook my head at our waitress, but I perked up a little. She had a lovely voice, like warm honey. I listened to her describe the specialty of the house to Hi-my-name-is-Dwayne (who then ordered an "inchylada").

What was wrong with me tonight? I wanted to roll languidly in the waitress's voice. When it was my turn I ordered the *especial de la casa,* even though I had no idea what she'd said. Her words had sounded delicious so I took my chances.

God, they were discussing whether legal should be classified as an indirect or administrative cost. I like my job, but when I take off the suit, I shut down that part of my brain. Downloaded, archived, compressed and forgotten. I decided to make a pig of myself on the tortilla chips and salsa. The cilantro and minced scallions smelled wonderful. I didn't smell the hot pepper until after I had already had a large dollop of salsa on my tongue. Yikes, it was hot. But oh how good. Sort of like sex. . . . I realized about then that I didn't have to avoid the conversation. Basically, I was window dressing. The *gentlemen* didn't expect an opinion out of female me. They wouldn't like my opinion anyway, so I felt free to look around. I was glad I did.

Just over the shoulder of the man opposite me, two women were seated alone in a particularly dim section of the restaurant. As I watched I became convinced that they were not only lovers, they were lovers in the midst of *grande passion*. The flickering flame of the candle was nothing to the heat these two women were producing just looking at each other. Silverhair was tracing her finger around the rim of her water glass while Athena (her profile was distinctively Grecian) watched that finger. I found myself equally mesmerized by it.

Silverhair continued to make rings around the rim of the glass. Little by little her finger moved to the inside of the rim, then lower. I found myself not breathing. Athena appeared to be breathing hard. When Silverhair's finger finally dipped into the water inside the glass Athena and I simultaneously straightened in our chairs, uncrossed our legs and took a deep, deep breath. I don't know what else I would have done (my knees did start to slide apart) but my dinner was served and distracted me. I hoped the restaurant was dark enough to hide my vividly blushing ears (I could feel them singeing the side of my head) and my trembling hands.

The *especial de la casa* turned out to be crab, lobster and scallops swimming in a rich mole sauce. As I savored my first delectable piece of crab meat, I found myself — of course — looking at Athena and Silverhair again. Silverhair was now watching Athena. Athena had one hand on her neck, ostensibly stretching her back. Her breasts were thrust forward in her simple white shirt and the candlelight danced across their full beauty. Her stretch completed, she ran her index finger under her collar, then slowly down the inside of the lapel of her shirt, lower, lifting it away from her body slightly. Her finger came to a rest when it reached the first closed button — a tantalizing spot right above the deep shadow between her breasts. Silverhair's gaze was burning a hole in the button. I was sure in Silverhair's mind, the button was gone and Athena was slowly revealing her exquisite softness.

At this point I realized I had stopped chewing, so I swallowed and re-focused on my dinner. I didn't need to look at Athena and Silverhair anymore. In my mind Silverhair was kneeling before her lover's chair, her hands finding their way into the warm shadows of the shirt, then her mouth — oh what a sound I could hear in my head. The sound of her mouth pressing against smooth skin, then rising again, such a soft, delicate sound. The sound of damp kisses. Now the hiss of indrawn breath — both lovers filling their lungs with rarified, passionate air as Silverhair's lips find and encircle Athena's breasts.

My heart was beating up in my ears. Through heat-filled eyes I looked down the table at Lindy, imagining her leaning over me, her hand coming to

my body, parting, opening — and then I realized
Lindy was looking back at me. Somehow I managed
to look away. And found myself staring at Silverhair
and Athena again.

Good God. They were generating enough
electricity to power Rhode Island and parts of
Massachusetts. Silverhair was tracing the rim of her
glass again. Athena languidly reached across the
table and took the glass, raising it slowly to her lips.
She sipped the water (at that moment I wished I
were the water in that glass) then set the glass on
the table. She dipped her finger in the water and
trailed her damp finger down over her throat,
leaving a trembling drop nestled in the notch of her
collarbone. The drop then did what I (and Silverhair
no doubt) was on fire to do — it slowly slid down the
exposed plain of Athena's chest and disappeared
forever into the valley between Athena's breasts.

At this point I didn't feel like eating food. But I
persisted at my dinner, and, having regained a
marginal amount of composure, I glanced back at
Lindy. Lindy was staring fixedly at something. I
followed the line of her gaze to Athena and
Silverhair. They were leaving. Silverhair stood
behind Athena to drape a gossamer shawl over
Athena's elegant shoulders. Athena straightened, eyes
closing briefly, as Silverhair's fingers gripped her
shoulders firmly. I imagined those hands sweeping
down Athena's back, then over her ribs, down,
gliding over Athena's hips, reaching forward.

And when they reached their car, would it be a
while before they started the engine? Would they
sink out of sight, wrapped in each other's arms?
Would zippers slowly give way to eager hands?

Would they strain, gasp and shudder when they first touched the silken wetness of the other? Would propriety lose to passion? Yes to all of it, I thought. I remembered that Lindy had been watching them.

I looked back at her just as she looked back at me. Her eyes were a flamethrower. She sent a column of fire down the table, scorching my body to cinders. I was sure my clothes were melting away. I actually started to get up — I was too far away from her and I wanted to feel her mouth on mine, but then I realized I was trapped between the champion of accelerated tax depreciation and the expert on deposited items returned.

You would think that the banking conversation around me would have ... uh, banked some of my flames. But no, any metaphor will work when you've reached the point I'd reached. I wanted to tell Lindy I was dying to encode her items. I wanted to read her and sort her. I wanted to review her liquidity ratio, plunge into her capital assets, and touch *all* her basis points. And all the while I wanted to maintain high volumes for the greatest productivity possible.

I think, from the way she started to trace her finger around the rim of her margarita glass, that she understood what I wanted to say.

I skipped dessert. So did Lindy. The men all had dessert, so we waited. Finally, long after I was sure I'd soaked through to my chair, we were leaving. Lindy seemed to be making no attempt to talk to me as the group of us drifted toward the taxi stand. Had I misinterpreted her smoldering gaze? Had she been smoldering at one of the men? (I mentally gagged at the idea.)

The first taxi filled. Lindy was in the back against the window. She rolled it down and said to no one in particular, "See you back at the hotel." At that moment something slipped from her hand. The cab pulled away.

"Wait," I called. "You dropped your key."

"Darn," she called back, her voice fading as the cab drew further and further away. "Don't worry, I have a spare. You can give that one back . . . to me . . . later." Then they were out of range.

Later. I supposed I could return it later. Special, personal delivery.

Torch Song

Diane Salvatore

WHEN we finally find Jess's house, with its small amber light above the door, I sense more than see, the towering redwoods on all sides. Through the curtainless front bay window there is the blue shimmer of a television screen and the kaleidoscopic glow of a Tiffany lamp.

Behind me, Aggie stretches — the drive up from San Francisco was nearly two hours — and takes a deep breath of the sweet night air. She gathers our overnight bags, handing me the plant I have brought as a gift. After all, this is a kind of housewarming: before now, Jess has never lived with anyone unless half her clothes were still packed in a knapsack, ready for flight. And yet she has been living with Deb for nearly a year in this house that Deb's wealthy father bought them, a kind of experiment in domesticity that has been startlingly successful.

Aggie and I make as much noise as possible on the stairs, hoping to alert whoever is inside. A woman, tall and slim, with brown, curly hair that falls like a shawl around her shoulders, opens the door. I recognize her from a photo Jess has sent in one of her random letters. "Oh, I'm sorry," she says, smiling through a yawn. "I must have dozed off. I'm Deb," she says, glancing at her watch. "Midnight. Jess won't be home from the restaurant for another hour yet. But, good. We can all get to know each other in the meantime."

She relieves us of one of our bags and leads us through the house to a guest room. There is a homey warmth about the place in the dark wood of the ceiling beams, in the busy white ceramic clutter of the kitchen, in the cared-for look of the plants and wood-burning stove, in the framed photographs of her and Jess and friends arranged on top of the television.

"I hope you don't mind sleeping on a futon," she says, looking uncertain until I quickly reassure her, though I know it will probably be murder on Aggie's back.

"Are these all yours?" Aggie asks, pointing at the far wall which is lined, floor-to-ceiling, with shelves of record albums and CDs. Deb is a deejay, two hours away in San Francisco's gay clubs.

"Yes, I have to stay on top of the business, something like reading all the law journals that come out," she says. For a second I tense, wondering if Aggie, who's a lawyer, will take this as a rebuke. Aggie laughs instead, and I relax, knowing that she has decided she likes Deb.

Back in the living room, Deb shuts off the TV and asks how we're enjoying our San Francisco vacation so far. She and Aggie settle on the couch and I sit in a club chair facing them. Despite having seen her photograph, I am surprised by Deb; in her cut-off jeans and preppy polo shirt, she is less hard-edged than I imagined. She is roughly Aggie's age, but on the couch next to her, Aggie, with her neat, fashionable wedge cut and her tortoise-shell glasses, looks a decade wiser and more mature. There is something adolescent about Deb's leanness, about the way she tucks one leg underneath herself on the couch. She does not appear to be any of the things I once imagined I had to be to keep Jess's attention: untamed, irreverent, undisciplined.

Work seems the safest topic, so we swap progress reports on that front: how my travel writing has allowed me to write off this trip, how Aggie's gotten to argue several major cases in court as lead counsel, how Deb is in enough demand these days that the clubs she deejays for advertise her by name on their flyers. But I know that she also writes her own music, and I ask to hear some. I can tell by her lack of hesitance, as she gets up to oblige my request, that she has none of the false modesty of an amateur. On her way to an arsenal of stereo equipment she passes a staircase that leads to an open loft where, she tells us, she and Jess sleep. Then she clicks a tape into place. "I've been sending these around to labels," she says. "Please be brutally honest."

I listen in silence to the songs while Deb answers Aggie's whispered questions about the technical end of things — whether she writes the music or lyrics first, how the tracks are mixed. I look out the window but it's too dark to see anything past my own reflection. Deb's songs — her voice by turns pleading and demanding — tell tales of toxic love affairs, cheating lovers, people too terrified to trust. And whether it's the night, the place or the music, when I turn back, I'm afraid my voice will crack. "They're beautiful," I manage. "Jess must be very proud."

Deb pushes her hair away from her temples with both hands and arches her back in a yawn. "Yes and no," she says. "It's the lyrics she doesn't like. She thinks I shouldn't waste my time on love songs. She wants me to write songs about stopping racial hatred and world hunger."

Jess, in her unfailingly dogmatic way, had always told me the same thing about the travel articles I wrote. Who needed more information about the best beaches, she had demanded, or whether a four-star restaurant had really earned its stars when there were so many real crises in the world to discuss?

"I try to tell her that when I write music, I go to a very private place," Deb is saying. "And in that private place, there are love songs. Torch songs, she calls them," and I can guess that Jess doesn't mean it as a compliment. "But I don't have to tell you — you know Jess," Deb says, laughing, coming as close to acknowledging our shared history as either of us has dared so far.

Aggie gets up and cups her hand against the dark window. I wonder how much she can see.

Some faraway laughter, drifting up as if from underwater, wakes me hours later. Out the window above our futon, the sky is still black. Aggie is on her back beside me, only her pale bare shoulders above the covers, her face set as though sleep is an effort at which she must work. I lie still, groggily debating whether to get up for something to drink, when I hear a series of moans coming unmistakably from the loft. The sounds register somewhere behind my ribs, triggering memories I have been trying to avoid, and now I am fully awake.

I remember all at once a night, years ago, when Jess and I were at a downtown Manhattan bar; she had had too much to drink and started an argument with someone about how Nicaragua was Vietnam all over again. It wasn't unusual for Jess to spend an entire evening on such a debate, ignoring me. Typically, I would watch from the sidelines, lost in a swill of admiration, impatience, and embarrassment.

This particular night, a woman in tight jeans and elaborate jewelry came up and laced her thin arms around Jess's shoulders, taking Jess's side in the argument. She turned out to be an old girlfriend, also not unusual, but always painful for me, since Jess accumulated ex-girlfriends the whole while she and I were lovers. We both knew that had I pushed her to give them up, I would not have seen her again, and whatever it took to risk such a thing, I didn't have it in me. Instead I pretended to agree with her that monogamy was a heterosexist plot, and had to be satisfied with the hollow satisfaction of knowing that however long the other women drained away some of her affection, she always came back to me.

The three of us — Jess, the ex-girlfriend and I — left the bar and ended up in a Checker Cab headed uptown to Jess's apartment. Jess had managed to leave the place with her drink and was struggling to stand up in the cab, her back pressed against the ceiling, splashing vodka everywhere. The cab driver's jaw was flexing and I registered that stores and buildings were zipping by us in a blur.

Suddenly Jess fell into the seat next to me, wrapped an approving arm around my shoulders, and asked the ex-girlfriend over and over again, "Isn't Laura great? Don't you think she's hot?" My cheeks burned with pride: without Jess, I might have been introduced as an English-major-turned-travel-writer, but at her side, I was perhaps wild instead of cautious, risque instead of proper, contradictory instead of predictable.

The ex-girlfriend got out of the cab some twenty blocks before us, as I recall, and I felt so puffed up with my victory that some of it remains even now, enough that, hearing Jess's laughter and moans spilling over another woman's body, I still feel some mournful twist of possessiveness.

* * * * *

I open my eyes as Aggie is coming back into the
room after a shower. As usual, she is up before I
am. Her short short hair is still slicked to her head;
without her glasses, she has to squint out the
window to assess the weather. The morning fog is
thick, obscuring the tops of the redwoods, which,
Aggie has informed me after reading, can
communicate warnings to each other to protect
themselves against disease. "How did you sleep?" I
ask her.

"Fine," she says, smiling. I put my arms out to
her; I know she is being gracious. In the early
morning hours, while I pretended to be sleeping
soundly, I heard her tossing and groaning, struggling
to find the most comfortable position for her back on
the thin, unyielding futon. "Probably a good idea to
shower now, while the partyers still slumber," she
says, unwrapping the towel she has around her and
slipping into shorts and a blouse.

"Oh, you heard them, too?" I ask, kneading her
lower back when she sits down next to me to tie her
sneakers.

"Hard not to. But, you know, good for them. It's
got to be great. To live out here like this, nothing
but mountains and trees, hours from the city."

"Living from check to check, having no health
insurance," I add.

She laughs. "Well, I didn't say *I* could do it.
Some people wither without pressure. But for now,
I'm enjoying it." She kisses the bridge of my nose,
my chin, then my lips. "I'm going outside to explore.
Happy suds."

She closes the door behind her, and I admonish myself for not leaping up and insisting she wait for me so I can keep her company on her morning walk. It's something we often do when we go on vacation — take the morning to scope out our surroundings, and just be peaceful together before the rushing around of sight-seeing begins. But neither of us has said a word about our neglected ritual; I feel sure Aggie knows I can't concentrate on anything else just now but facing Jess. I'm not sure, though, if Aggie's leaving is an act of generosity or self-protection.

Once in the claustrophobic intimacy of the bathroom, I survey the inventory with frank and guilty curiosity, and feel disappointed to find it completely standard. Moisturizers, blow dryer, brushes of various sizes, lipsticks, tampons, toothpaste, razors, deodorant, Band-Aids, a thermometer and cotton balls crowd the medicine chest, the top of the toilet, the edges of the sink. I hang my nightshirt on the back of the door and wind a large, scratchy towel around me to retrieve from my overnight bag in the bedroom the shampoo I have forgotten there. When I open the bathroom door, I hear footsteps on the stairs, and freeze.

Jess is coming through the living room toward me, doing the stiff-legged shuffle of the recently roused. She is wearing only wrinkled khaki running shorts, and her breasts, full and bobbing, are tan right down to the nipples. Her sleep-tousled hair is both more blonde and more gray than I remember. She stops in front of me, and puts her hands on my shoulders in a way that is part congratulatory, part apologetic. Then she wraps me in a hug. "I knew you'd come," she whispers against my ear, and when she releases me, her nipples are puckered and taut. She's watching me as I lift my eyes from them. Her lips stretch into a smile and she turns and pads barefoot toward the kitchen.

In the shower, my whole body is in an uproar; I am virtually combustible. I let the hot water beat down on me till I feel safely diffused. People say "passion spent" as if there is a finite amount, as if it is used up when it's no longer useful. But it isn't, not always. Sometimes it stays behind, like a lump in your throat. But it's too much to expect my body to accommodate what my mind already knows: it's pointless to still want her, dangerous to even remember.

We all pile into Deb's Honda for the drive to Sonoma County: Jess has promised us a wine-tasting tour. "Put your seat belt on," she reminds Deb, who is driving. "It's *the law.*" I'm not sure whether Aggie has caught the sarcasm of the remark; in the back next to me, she appears too absorbed with the workings of her new camera even to have heard.

"So Gotham goes on without me?" Jess shouts back to me. The sun has come out with a vengeance and we have all the windows down. The wind lashes strands of my hair across my face; I keep yanking it behind my ears.

"Hard to believe, isn't it?" I lean forward and address Deb. "In New York, Jess was only a weekend radical. She actually struggled into a suit during the week, though she always called it the uniform of capitalist oppression."

"Jess in a suit," Deb says. "Nothing short of perverse."

"What exactly did you do?" Aggie asks. This information has caught her attention and no wonder; today Jess looks like the sort of person who is congenitally allergic to suits. She is wearing a pair of cut-off jeans with a hole below the pocket and a purple T-shirt that reads *Stonewall 20*. Aggie is wearing a pair of white, cuffed shorts that the dry-cleaner presses with a crease and a seersucker blouse with buttoned front pockets.

"What they say I did was sell wood flooring to commercial businesses," says Jess, running her hand through her short blonde hair in a gesture that I know betrays self-consciousness. "But what I really did was bust my chops trying to outbid a pack of thieves so my boss could buy a second Mercedes. And then I said, What's a nice dyke like me doing in a place like this? Right after that I got fired. They accused me of sweetening some deals in my favor."

I have never asked Jess if the accusation is true. Part of me is afraid she'd be shocked to hear I believed the company, which she said exploited her and all the other salespeople. And the other half is afraid she'll scold me for doubting the charge, that of course she was right to take her revenge on the company that way.

"Why the hell did you ever take a job like that in the first place?" Deb asks.

"I got greedy, but I got over it. I realized the

new American Dream was never to have to pay
taxes, and since I wasn't rich enough to do that, the
only other choice was to be poor."

Aggie looks out the window at the mountains and
the passing vineyards whose tight green bushes are
planted in remarkably straight rows. I know she's
tensing and I want to throw my arms around her in
gratitude for not taking up Jess's invitation to argue.
I know Aggie is thinking of the years she spent on a
diet of peanut-butter sandwiches and spaghetti,
putting herself through law school. She does not
think of her healthy salary as a crime, but a
well-earned reward.

The moment passes and Jess tells us the names
of the best restaurants to try when we get back to
San Francisco. The one where she is a waitress, I
was surprised to discover when reading the guide
books, is among them. Back in New York, Jess ate
Chinese food almost exclusively. Somewhere along
the way she had developed a democratic and
educated appreciation of all kinds of cuisine, even
that from countries whose politics she doesn't agree
with. Cooking is a new passion of hers I know
nothing about, did not even anticipate. I take it as a
measure of all the things we have neglected to tell
each other over the years, and I feel wounded by the
omission.

The first winery we stop at has a spectacular
view from its backyard garden; there are bushes
with roses the size of cantaloupes, and craggy,
melancholy trees overlooking dark jade valleys. Aggie
hands me the camera with instructions to take good
pictures and she disappears inside the winery with
Deb.

"More shots with no people in them?" Jess asks, suddenly behind me, very close. It's a jab about a trip we made together to Maine one fall to see the color change. I took two rolls of film without a single person turning up in them once.

"Go ahead. Do what you Californians do best," I say, pointing at a bush with gargantuan peach roses. "Stop and smell the flowers."

She stands by the rose bush and grins, not for the camera, I can tell, but for me. "Your turn," she says. "Sit on this picnic table. I want your legs in the shot. Your lovely, mile-long legs."

I climb up on the table, blushing. It seems to me she takes an agonizingly long time focusing. Then I see she is panning my body slowly through the camera lens, starting at my shoulders, moving down to my hips and then around the angle of my legs. Finally she takes the picture and hands the camera back. "Beautiful as always," she says. "Aggie's a lucky woman. Can I say that, or is it too corny?"

I'm too flushed to answer. She is standing close enough for me to smell her skin, fragrant with some woody perfume I don't recall and with a delicate perspiration that I do. "Don't be so judgmental about her," I say, having caught all the little glances and remarks I'm grateful Aggie hasn't. "She doesn't tell you how to live your life."

"I don't mean to. After all, the world is made up of those who are rich, like Deb and Aggie, and those who marry rich, like you and me." She smiles so I know she only wants to tease, not debate. "Don't scowl like that. It breaks my heart," she says, leading me by the hand into the winery.

"Your bleeding heart," I say. She licks her fingertip and scores one for me in the air.

At Hop Kiln, Aggie treats and buys a bottle of Gewurztraminer, which we drink from plastic wine glasses along with a chunk of garlic monterey jack at a picnic table among marigolds and white tulips. When we're done, Jess asks to borrow the camera and she and Deb walk far off to a huge wine barrel with a spout. Aggie and I can see them from the table, posing and smiling.

"Enjoying the guided tour?" Aggie asks.

I smile cautiously, not certain of her question's real intent. "Sure," I say.

"You look a little down."

Before I have a chance to answer, I see Jess swiftly turn and moon the camera as Deb is taking a picture. No one around seems to notice, except Deb, who, from this distance appears as a tiny silent figure bending over to clutch her side.

My cheeks flush hotly. "She was always doing that kind of thing," I say, hearing the apology in my voice. "All her antics were a way of putting the big evil system on notice that she was going to tear it down someday."

"You're disappointed she hasn't done it yet?"

"Yeah, silly as that is," I say, tracing a path with my finger around and around a knot in the wood tabletop. "A part of me always believed that in the end, Jess was going to slay all the world's dragons and still make sure everyone had a good time."

"Seems like too much work for one lifetime."

"Evidently. She seems to have dedicated herself strictly to the good time part."

"People have done worse things with their lives." Aggie smiles, taking off her glasses and angling her face up at the sun, as streaks of auburn appear in her thick brown hair. I look at her with attention, perhaps for the first time the whole weekend. Her friendship can still surprise me this way: the calm and patience at the center of her that's a generosity I don't always feel worthy of. I reach over and touch the back of her neck, warm and familiar in the sun.

Jess and Deb are suddenly back at the table. Jess sits down and hands the camera over, holding my glance for a moment longer than necessary. She starts to say something, then stops and looks out over the valley.

"We'd better head back," Deb says, folding the cellophane wrapper around what's left of the cheese. "I have to get dinner started. Chicken dijon."

"It's her specialty," Jess says, standing up.

Jess is walking among the vegetables in the garden she has planted alongside the house. I am watching from the deck; Deb and Aggie are inside, preparing dinner. "I'm sorry about the way I left New York," Jess says, without warning. "I know it was rotten."

I smile into the sun, which is finally setting behind the redwoods. Jess is letting herself off the hook lightly, but I don't protest even though her exit was, for me, the emotional equivalent of a high-speed train wreck. One day shortly after she lost her job, I called her apartment and a man answered, saying she had sublet the apartment to him. Jess was in California, address and intention unknown. It was months before I heard from her, and when she called, it was just to say "Hi" and tell me about Deb. That was two and a half years ago.

"Look at this goddamn cucumber," she says, running over, red-brown dirt mashed between her toes. "Look at the size of it! And you gotta taste it to believe." She takes a big, noisy bite before holding it out to me.

"Deb is not going to appreciate your delivering half-eaten vegetables for her salad."

"So we won't give her this one. It'll be our secret." She winks.

"Shouldn't it be washed or something?" I say, eyeing the large, knobby cucumber suspiciously, and deliberately ignoring her overtures.

"Jesus, you eat that supermarket stuff that died of chemical poisoning. This," she says, waving the cucumber triumphantly, "is the way this stuff is *supposed* to be eaten."

"Don't tell me you've found God now, too," I say, cautiously taking a bite. It tastes of sunshine and robust soil and green, green grass. "Okay, I'm sold."

She smiles and returns to picking vegetables. "That's what I like about you. You're essentially reasonable."

"As long as I see things your way." She throws a small radish at me. "This is enough for you, then?" I say, gesturing toward the house and the garden.

She straightens up. "If by that you mean, is it enough to waitress and have time for sex for hours on end and time to drink wine and watch TV and love and be loved, then, yeah. It's a whole hell of a lot better than enough. But being happy never figures prominently on anybody's ladder of success, does it? What a joke."

Jess has not completely lost her power to make me feel chastened, small-minded and banal. Years ago, when we were together, it was the exhilaration of challenged assumptions that kept me slightly breathless around her. Now, having been away from her all these years, I summon the energy to disagree. "You used to want to do things in the world. Be heard, make a difference. Now you're out here, just o.d.-ing on hedonism."

I can tell by her clenched jaw that she has heard me. But all she says is, "Look at this lettuce, will you? God, it looks healthy enough to lift weights."

I go down and crouch beside her to watch as she pulls the head out of the ground. Seeing her this way, I realize I never knew how gray and pinched she looked in New York. Her forearms now are brown and muscular, and the fading sun finds the gold in her hair.

The feeling that kept me awake last night suddenly begins to build again: a low-grade ache in the small of my back, in the soles of my feet. We were never really friends, but God, were we ever lovers. Any time words failed us or pointed toward our inevitable incompatibility, we smothered ourselves in each other's touch. And now, kneeling solemnly among heads of lettuce, I barely stopped myself from reaching out for her.

"Hey, you two," Deb appears at the door to call

out, "how long does it take to round up some greens? The dijon sauce is piping hot."

We have eaten our way through salad, a huge chicken, fettucini, and then lingered over truffle cake, and wine, lots of wine. Aggie pushes herself away from the table with a contented sigh knowing that, since she was on cooking duty, she is relieved of cleanup. "It's exhausting living this well," she says. "I gotta turn in. Dinner was perfect, Deb." She slaps Jess on the shoulder in what I know is mock-macho. "You're a lucky woman, Jess."

I steadfastly avoid Jess's eyes and instead pull Aggie down for a kiss. "I'll be in soon, honey," I say. "As soon as everything's cleaned up."

"Thanks for helping cook," Deb says.

"Sleep well," Jess calls after her.

When we hear the guest-room door close, Deb leans across the table to whisper, "I like her. She's very sweet and sincere."

"You mean you don't like ornery types like me anymore?" Jess asks, getting up to seize Deb around the shoulders and bury her face in her neck.

I go into the living room and sink into the couch in front of the television; when I turn it on there's a program about the migration patterns of geese. For a minute, I'm absorbed by the precision of the formations they make in the sky, each bird falling instinctively into place.

"You know," I call into the kitchen, unable to suppress a sudden swell of pride, "Aggie is too modest to talk about it, but she spends every other weekend on pro bono cases to help win asylum for political refugees."

"Wow," Jess says. "A woman with a conscience as well as a checkbook."

"Oh God," Deb says, joining me on the couch. "Sitting down. Does this feel good. Let's do the dishes in the morning."

"You take a break, babe," Jess says. "I'll take care of this mess."

"Don't mind her," Deb whispers while Jess runs the water in the sink. "I know she feels competitive, but she'd let you pull out her fingernails first before she'd admit it."

"I know," I say, feeling weariness creep up my legs like paralysis; the wine and California sun has done its damage. I remember how exhausting it was making excuses for the excesses of Jess's ego all the time, and I wonder for a moment if Deb feels the same way I once did. But it's too late to ask: after only a few minutes of staring numbly at the screen, she closes her eyes, curls up like a cat, and begins to snore softly.

I get up and finish clearing the table. The sun has been down for hours and the house now feels damp. Jess glances past me into the living room and spots Deb on the couch; I put a silencing finger to my lips.

"Guess it's just you and me in the whole world," Jess says softly, making the dishes disappear into the suds.

"I used to feel that way all the time — just you

and me and the whole world. Which of those three let us down?"

Jess picks up the last bottle of wine and empties what's left into her glass. "If I have a little more to drink, I'll think of some way to answer you."

"Deb is good for you. I can tell you love her. Though, if you play the game the way you used to, I bet you keep her guessing."

"Yeah, and Aggie loves you." She swings a kitchen chair around, and straddling the back of it, sits down.

"It's not true, what you're thinking. I love Aggie, too. There's more to be said for being comfortable with someone than I thought possible. Besides, you can't go long distances with someone who's always taking your breath away."

"I'll just call her marathon man from now on."

"The courage of your convictions, Jess. That's what you never had. Unless you consider keeping a cucumber garden a political statement these days." I register a little tremble in my left knee.

The refrigerator hums and Jess's chair squeaks underneath her. "You have every right to despise me. And the way I live."

"But I don't," I say, the threat of tears cutting my sentence short. "I wish I could. It would be simpler."

"I knew you'd come." She leans her chin on her hand and looks up at me. "It kept me going the first few months I was out here, knowing that someone gave a damn if I died in my tracks. It's not that I loved you any less."

I get up and begin scraping food off the remaining plates. Jess has never told me until this moment that she loves me. And now that she has, when it's pointless, disarmed, I punish her by not acknowledging it, certainly not returning it.

"I just felt," she says quietly, swirling wine around in her glass, "that in the beginning you loved me for being different. But in the end, you needed me to be the same."

I suddenly have a flashback of Jess's small apartment in Manhattan, of me unbuttoning her shirt and dragging her down on top of me with an urgency just a shade past desire to something closer to violence. So much clinging and clawing, so many promises made there in her small, unsturdy bed that it used to stun me that she would get up and live whole parts of her life without me.

"I think what disappointed me the most when you left," I say, "wasn't that you were gone, but that you knew I'd never take the chance and follow you." I smile. "We had some crazy times, though, didn't we? Remember your friend who owned the leather club? The one who had the 'S & M means never having to say you're sorry' tattoo across his chest? And that cat of yours that you hated, the one who loved to sit on the windowsill — while you'd shout at it to jump?"

"Oh, God, don't remind me," Jess says, laughing, putting her hand to her heart. Her laughter is contagious and makes me feel dangerously lighthearted. "And then," I press on, "the damn cat finally jumped and everyone told you it committed suicide because it was unloved."

"Yeah, but who ran down twelve flights of stairs to try to catch it before it hit the ground?"

"And the Christmas Eve the palm reader in the Indian restaurant told you you were going to take a trip south before the year was out and I laughed at you for paying ten bucks to hear that — so you made us take a flight to New Orleans the next day, just so it would be true? I nearly missed my deadline on the piece about New England spas."

"You also got the worst hangover of your life," Jess says.

"You hid my aspirin as punishment for doubting providence."

"Just for plain doubting."

I look away from Jess's tanned face, with its new lines around the eyes. "My life with Aggie surprised me at first," I say. "All our friends are couples, either people she knows from the law firm, or I know from publishing. We buy tickets in advance for Broadway shows, only dramas. Aggie always gets the checkbook to balance, and we never take the car anywhere unless the gas tank is full. It took me off-guard, discovering that I was someone who enjoyed constancy. Up till then I'd been measuring my happiness by someone else's standards. I spent years nursing a whole other view of myself as someone who didn't need to make demands on people I loved, who didn't need to have expectations met. I guess I thought if I could be more like you, you'd stay forever."

Jess holds the wine bottle upside down and shakes out the last few drops. "You better go into bed with Aggie, now," she says, looking into her glass, "before I get up and kiss you for all the wrong reasons."

Hours later, when all the food and wine have forced me into a heavy, bloated sleep, I wake up to Deb's voice, singing a sweet sad song. I can't make out the words, but I know it's a love song, and the melody is familiar. In the darkness of the room, I press my body up against Aggie's back and hum myself to sleep.

Aggie puts our overnight bags in the trunk of the rented car and slams it shut. "Have we got everything?"

"Yes, thanks to you," I remind her, grabbing her hand. She was up before all of us, packing, putting coffee on, and — in a gesture that she denied was passive-aggressive — leaving out a dish of milk for the skinny stray cats Jess told us she has been trying to discourage. Over breakfast, Jess has bet us a case of white wine that the sun will be out by eleven, as it always is. It's five of eleven now and still overcast.

"Want to stay another day?" Aggie asks, touching my cheek.

I shake my head. "And make you sleep another night on that futon?"

She laughs and hugs me, and I squeeze back hard. This morning, she woke me with kisses along my collarbone and shoulder. I thought of the redwoods calling out silently to each other, of the geese falling calmly into place.

Out of the corner of my eye, I see Deb and Jess

come down the stairs from the deck. "What's that?" Aggie asks, pointing at the picnic basket Deb is carrying.

"Provisions for the ride back to San Francisco," she says. "Leftover chicken dijon."

We all take turns kissing each other good-bye, and though I am careful to avoid Jess's lips, she deliberately finds mine and kisses me wetly, squeezing me full up against her. "There's something else in the basket," she whispers.

"What?"

"Cucumbers. Consider it a political gesture."

We laugh too loudly and Deb and Aggie shrug good-naturedly at us, like parents who find their teenagers' moods incomprehensible but are grateful, nonetheless, for the good ones. As Aggie backs the car onto the road, I roll down the window. "Looks like you owe us a case of wine. Eleven o'clock and all's cloudy."

"My watch says ten-fifty-nine," Jess yells after the moving car. "Have faith."

As we make the turn onto the main road toward town, sunshine suddenly floods the car. In the rearview mirror, I can see Jess, jumping up and down in the road, her arm stretched up to the sky.

On the Authors

NIKKI BAKER was born in 1962. She is a transplanted midwesterner currently living in Northern California. Baker is the author of three mystery novels published by The Naiad Press: *In the Game* (1991); *The Lavender House Murder* (1992), which was a Lambda Literary Award finalist; and most recently, *Long Goodbyes,* which was released in August 1993. Baker's reviews of contemporary lesbian fiction appear in *Deneuve Magazine.*

JACKIE CALHOUN — the author of *Lifestyles, Second Chance, Sticks and Stones, Friends and*

Lovers — lives in the Fox River Valley of Wisconsin. The mother of two daughters with two small granddaughters, Calhoun focuses her writing on family, friends, lovers, and the environment. She considers her family lake cottage near Wild Rose (Wisconsin) as her real home.

Look for her fifth book, *The Scent of Roses* in 1994. She is presently at work on *Accidental Changes.* All of the above are published or to be published by Naiad Press.

NICOLE CONN — Screenwriter/Director/Producer. Obsessed with Clark Gable, Frank Capra's Black and White period and happy endings, Nicole Conn was a die hard romantic from the age of ten.

Throughout her life as a student, and a four year cross-country trek to follow the bohemian lifestyle of the 'tormented artist', Conn never paused in her love affair with old movies. But as many young romantic artists, Conn fell prey to the easy outs of free living and confused intoxication with inspiration, the excesses of which she addresses in the film, *Claire of the Moon.*

Feeling the need for an altogether new life and new focus she attended Elliott Business College after which she became a Business Manager and Controller for several construction firms. Knowing she could never leave her first love for good, she created Videospectrum, a video company with emphasis on the aesthetic and avant garde.

Proficient in all phases of budgeting, marketing, camera operations, conceptualizing and scripting,

Conn created Demi-Monde Productions, Inc. a company targeting feature film development and production. With a sense of renewal, Nicole was back on the creative track.

Achieving industry recognition as a finalist in the prestigious Academy of Motion Picture Arts and Sciences Nicholl Screenwriting Fellowship, Conn has written one novel, a teleplay and six screenplays that are at various stages of option and development.

Claire of the Moon was a direct result of frustration with the Hollywood system. Conn returned from her last stint there, fed up with the interminable development malaise. Even if it was made for a meager $130,000, it was better than never having done it at all. Sherry Lansing's advice kept metronome vigilance, "If you want to learn how to make a film . . . make a film."

In spite of her innate romanticism, Conn wanted her directorial debut to make a statement. She intentionally did not saccharinize Claire's journey to her sexual identity.

Nicole Conn's desire is to "create films that are not only a risk to make, but a risk to see."

Nicole is currently working on "Cynara," in development as a film. (She describes it as "Howard's End with a lesbian twist.") Her second novel, *The Bottom Line,* will be published by Naiad Press in 1994.

ANITA CORNWELL was born in South Carolina and educated in Pennsylvania. A professional writer for more than twenty years, her work has appeared in *The Ladder, Phylon, Essence Magazine, The Feminist Review, Black Maria, Negro Digest, Motherroot Journal, Sinister Wisdom, Hera, Wicce, The Gay Alternative, Lesbians Speak Out, PGN, Au Courant, Feminary, New York Native, New Directions for Women, Lavender Culture, Top Ranking,* and *For Lesbians Only,* a Separatist anthology, among other publications. Her first book, *Black Lesbians in White America,* a collection of essays and stories, was published in 1983 by Naiad Press. Her second book, a novel for young adults, was published in 1990 by New Seed Press. During the early '80s, Cornwell also turned to playwrighting and is a lifetime member of the Dramatists Guild. In 1990, she began writing crime novels and is a member of Sisters In Crime.

RHONDA DICKSION was born in Los Angeles, California, in August, 1959. After earning a degree in fine and communication arts (easier homework) in 1980, she sold her surfboard, exchanged her Ray Bans for mud boots, and moved to Washington state where she lives with her partner, lover, confidante, teacher, audience, and best friend (the same woman who is dictating this bio) on 13 acres in the Cascade Mountain foothills. She began her cartoon panel, "Lesbian Survival Hints" as doodles on a rainy Sunday afternoon in 1988, and today her cartoons appear in publications across the U.S. She has done two books from Naiad, *The Lesbian Survival Manual* (1990), and *Stay Tooned* (1993). In addition to drawing, Rhonda enjoys taking photographs, making espresso, walking in the woods, sharing meaningless trivia with her partner, taking life easy, and eating pepperoni and pineapple pizza every Friday night.

LAUREN WRIGHT DOUGLAS was born in 1947, in Canada. She grew up in a military family and spent part of her childhood in Europe. Despite professional detours into teaching, journalism, translation, editing, and finance, Lauren has always been writing. Her novels for Naiad Press include *The Always Anonymous Beast,* which introduces private detective Caitlin Reece, and five other novels in that mystery series: *Ninth Life* (winner of the 1990 Lambda Literary Award for Best Lesbian Mystery), *The Daughters of Artemis, A Tiger's Heart,* and *Goblin Market.* A sixth Caitlin Reece novel, *A Rage of Maidens,* will be published by Naiad in 1994. Lauren has also published a science fiction novel, *In the Blood,* and, using the nom de plume of her cat Zenobia Vole, a romance/adventure, *Osten's Bay.* Her short story "What You Want, Sometimes" appeared in *The Erotic Naiad: Love Stories by Naiad Press Authors.*

CATHERINE ENNIS. Hot air ballooning has been the focus of Catherine's research for her fifth book, a romance-adventure novel now in progress.

"Because my shelves and freezers are overflowing, I've stopped gardening for a while. Instead of weeding, I spend as many morning hours as I can drifting with the wind over the beautiful Louisiana landscape. I've also learned to cook 'cajun' and we enjoy foods that we wouldn't have touched years ago. When the roux is right, you should taste my alligator courtboullion."

Now retired, Catherine lives in a rural setting with her lover of twenty years and an assortment of pets.

In addition to teaching for many years, Catherine did art work for medical texts and exhibits.

In comparing past vocations with present avocations, Catherine concluded "When I sit at my desk most afternoons, I'm there to write. Giving my imagination free reign is a labor of love, much more interesting than the rigid requirements of medical art."

Catherine is the author of *To the Lightning, South of the Line, Clearwater, Chautauqua,* and in 1994, *Up, Up and Away.*

KATHLEEN FLEMING writes, swims, walks the ocean and the sound beaches near her home in New York State. After twenty years she has left teaching to write full time and leads writing and anti-bias workshops. Her last novel with Naiad was *Lovers in the Present Afternoon.*

Kathleen Fleming writes: Each year it feels more amazing and urgent to me to write, to love, to celebrate life. In 1993, with the world still as full of terror and wonder as it ever was, it is exciting to be part of the women's community as we strengthen ourselves through our writing, reading one another's words, and myriad other ways of becoming more visible and empowered.

JENNIFER FULTON is thirty-five, writes full-time, and lives in clean, beautiful New Zealand — where the law protects gays and lesbians from discrimination, even in the military. Jennifer is the author of *Passion Bay* and its sequel, *Saving Grace* — romantic adventures set in the South Pacific — both published by Naiad Press. Under the nom de plume Rose Beecham, Jennifer also writes the Amanda Valentine crime series. Of these *Introducing Amanda Valentine* was published by Naiad in 1992 and *Second Guess* will be published in 1995.

Jennifer gains inspiration for her books by reclining in a hot vanilla scented bath, with a long espresso and her favorite opera music playing. It was during one such spell, she penned *The Bride* for this anthology.

NANCY TYLER GLENN was born February 12, 1938 at 8:05 P.M., in Los Angeles, California. The first lesbian she ever knew was her mother, Dorothy, who filled her earliest years with fantasy and song. She learned form and spiritual surfing from her mentor-tormentor, Rachel Rosenthal — the inventor of Instant Theatre and performance artist. At this time she is living in Tucson, Arizona with cat ZahZee (who waddles around) and cat Cooper (who terrorizes every moveable object). Her novel *Clicking Stones* was published by Naiad in 1989. She is currently working on her second Naiad novel *The Collaborators.*

JEANE HARRIS lives with her dachsund Daly in Jonesboro, Arkansas. She is an Associate Professor of English at Arkansas State University. Because of the recent departure of her son Christian for graduate school she is experiencing empty nest syndrome, a condition to which she has reacted badly. She is the author of *Black Iris, Delia Ironfoot* and her short story, "The Road to Healing Heart" appears in *The Erotic Naiad.* She is currently working on the second Delia Ironfoot novel, *Women of the Red Sky,* which is scheduled to be published by Naiad Press in 1995. She was born in 1948 in Elkhart, Indiana.

A note to those who care: Socrates, she of the large rear end, has passed on. She is resting peacefully in Sarah Clem's backyard next to Huggy Bear, Chief and Prissie.

PENNY HAYES was born in Johnson City, New York, February, 1940. As a child she lived on a farm near Binghamton, New York. She later attended school in Utica and Buffalo, graduating with degrees in art and special education. She has made her living teaching in both New York State and West Virginia. She presently resides in Ithaca, New York.

Ms. Hayes' interests include backpacking, mountain climbing, canoeing, traveling, reading, gardening and studying early American history. She picks up abandoned animals along the road and takes them home and keeps them.

She has been published in *I Know You Know, Of the Summits & Of the Forests* and various backpacking magazines. Her Naiad Press novels include *The Long Trail, Yellowthroat, Montana Feathers* and *Grassy Flats*. Her fifth book, *Kathleen O'Donald* is due out in 1994.

MARION L. HEAD is a former Floridian and school teacher. She now resides in the Black Hills of South Dakota and is under/unemployed, depending on the month of the year. She and her partner of thirteen years are building a house in the woods and, most of the time, believe the solitude and beauty of the hills make up for the lack of disposable income.

Marion was born in 1955 and can't understand why she is no longer 25. She has two novels forthcoming from Naiad Press (*Inspiration* in 1995), three more half done in file drawers, and hopes the editing process doesn't hurry the need for bifocals.

MARY J. JONES still lives on the seacoast of Iowa, though after the Great Flood of '93 the joke seems a bit watered down. She is the author of *Avalon* (1991), "Many Seas Away" in *The Erotic Naiad*, and — in 1995 Naiad will publish her contemporary novel, *Red Wine and Honey*.

KARIN KALLMAKER was born in 1960 and raised by loving, middle-class parents. From a normal childhood and equally unremarkable public school adolescence, she went on to obtain an ordinary Bachelor's degree from the California State University at Sacramento. At the age of 16, eyes wide open, she fell into the arms of her first and only sweetheart. Ten years later, after seeing the film *Desert Hearts,* her sweetheart descended on the Berkeley Public Library determined to find some of "those" books. "Rule, Jane" led to "Lesbianism — Fiction" and then on to book after self-affirming book by and about lesbians. Works such as *All True Lovers, Curious Wine,* and *Faultline,* were the encouragement Karin needed to forget the so-called "mainstream" and spin her first romance for lesbians. That manuscript became her first Naiad Press book, *In Every Port.* Now a full-time financial manager in the nonprofit sector, she lives in Oakland with that very same sweetheart; she is a one-woman woman.

Karin is also the contributing editor of *Uncommon Voices,* the bi-monthly publication of the Bay Area Career Women, which is the largest lesbian social organization in the United States. Her essay "When I Grow Up I Want To Be A Lesbian" appears in *Multicultural America: A Resource Book for Teachers of Humanities and American Studies.* In addition to *In Every Port,* she has authored the best-selling *Touchwood* and *Paperback Romance. Car Pool* was published in October 1993. Her fifth Naiad romance will be *Painted Moon.* After that, look for *Wild Things.* Since Karin considers her lesbian readers to be the only mainstream, she intends to write many more.

LEE LYNCH. *Cactus Love,* Lynch's third collection of stories, is slated for release by Naiad Press in 1994. It will be followed in 1995 by *Rafferty Street,* which is both the third in the Morton River Valley series and a sequel to *Toothpick House.* Other Lynch works also published by Naiad: *Old Dyke Tales, The Swashbuckler, Home In Your Hands, Dusty's Queen of Hearts Diner, The Amazon Trail, Sue Slate, Private Eye, That Old Studebaker* and *Morton River Valley.* Her column, "The Amazon Trail" appears across the U.S. as do her feature articles and reviews.

Supporting herself by working in the social services, Lynch lives with her partner in rural Oregon, an area the religious right has targeted for heavy moral shelling. She suggests that although gays are not welcome in the military, we can all become warriors for our rights with the weapons of peace. Write to a newspaper, call a legislator, carry a banner, give a non-gay co-worker a lesbian book for her birthday!

JAYE MAIMAN is the author of three romantic mysteries featuring the private investigator Robin Miller: *I Left My Heart,* the award-winning *Crazy for Loving,* and *Under My Skin.* She is currently working on the fourth book in the series, *Someone*

To Watch. A Halloween baby, she was born in Brooklyn, New York, 1957, and raised in a Coney Island housing project where she spent Tuesday nights consuming blueberry cheese knishes and watching fireworks from a beachside boardwalk. She now lives in Park Slope, Brooklyn, with her two puppy cats and her partner, playmate, editor, co-neurotic, and magic-maker Rhea.

HILARY MULLINS has had little formal instruction in tennis, the sum total of her lessons comprising a week at the age of ten in 1972. Nonetheless, since pairing up with her partner April two years ago, she has become an avid player of lesbian tennis. Her first novel, *The Cat Came Back*, the chronicling of a seventeen year old girl's coming to terms with sexual abuse and her coming out, was published by Naiad in 1993. A self-identified Vermonter, Hilary is a recent transplant to Oakland, California.

LORI A. PAIGE lives near the "famous" city of Northampton, Massachusetts, and will receive her Ph.D. in English in the spring of 1994. Her first historical romance, *Passion's Legacy*, was published by Naiad Press in 1991 and her second novel, *Shadows in the Glade*, is scheduled for publication by Naiad in 1995.

DIANE SALVATORE, a native New Yorker, is the author of, most recently, the novel *Not Telling*

Mother: Stories From A Life. Her first novel, *Benediction*, was a finalist in The Lambda Book Awards' Best Lesbian Fiction category for 1991. Her second novel, *Love, Zena Beth*, was a simultaneous selection of Book of the Month Club and Quality Paperback Book Club, and has been released in four foreign countries. Salvatore also writes for the *Lambda Book Report*. She works in Manhattan as senior editor of a national magazine.

CAROL SCHMIDT and Norma Hair, her partner of fifteen years, live in an old country church they've converted to a home in rural Michigan, near a small Amish community. Both in their early fifties, they moved back to their native Michigan after many years in Los Angeles, where Carol had written a column, "Country Womyn/City Dyke," for the *L.A. Lesbian News*, and co-owned a small business called Words & Numbers with Norma. Schmidt's first novel of suspense, *Silverlake Heat*, was published by Naiad in early 1993, and it will be followed in 1994 by *Sweet Cherry Wine*.

ANITA SKEEN was born in West Virginia in 1946, attended colleges in West Virginia and Ohio, and taught for twenty years in the Creative Writing and Women's Studies Programs at Wichita State University. In 1990 she joined the English Department faculty at Michigan State University where she teaches creative writing, women's studies, gay and lesbian studies, and Canadian literature, and for two years served as the co-chair of the university-wide Task Force on Lesbian and Gay Issues. Besides poetry published in numerous literary magazines, journals, and anthologies, she is the author of *Each Hand A Map* (Naiad Press) and *Portraits* (Kida Press). She has just completed a collection of short stories called *The Summer Camp Stories*, is working on a mother-daughter novel, *Minor Chords*, and a collection of poems titled *The Resurrection of the Animals*. She lives in Okemos, Michigan with her partner of 11 years and an immortal cat, Queen Biscuit I, who has survived 4 dogs, 7 rabbits, a cat named Gravy, and two teenage boys now loose in the world as responsible adults. When she isn't teaching or writing, she likes traveling, camping, hiking, playing tennis, and spending time with friends scattered all over the country.

ROBBI SOMMERS is the author of the best-selling lesbian erotica: *Pleasures, Players, Kiss and Tell, Uncertain Companions, Behind Closed Doors* and the 1994 release, *Personal Ads*. Born in Cincinnati, Ohio, in 1950, she now resides in Northern California. Part-time dental hygienist, mother of three and writer, Robbi candidly admits: "By the end of the day, I'm exhausted. I can barely move from my desk to my bed." Perhaps that's why there's always a strong, sexy woman to carry her there . . .

PENNY SUMNER was born in Australia in 1955 and moved to England to undertake postgraduate studies at the University of Oxford. She has worked as a waitress, librarian, photographer at a dolphin pool, and as a seller of antiquarian books. She currently teaches feminist theory and contemporary writing at a university in the North-East of England. Her first novel, *The End of April*, is published by Naiad and she is working on the sequel, *Crosswords*, to be published early in 1994.

DOROTHY TELL — (born 11/23/39 — San Francisco, CA) Dot and Ruth, her partner of twenty-one years, have moved from the lake to an apartment very close to Dot's day job in Dallas. The daily two and a half hours she previously spent in traffic she now spends writing. Which makes the remaining 800 days until retirement from the jobfromhell, if not easier — at least bearable.

Dot doesn't have her big yellow dog yet, but *has* been seduced by Ru's latest cat, a shrewd and huffy bundle named Kali.

Naiad works by Dot include *Wilderness Trek* (erotic romance), *Murder at Red Rook Ranch* (1st Poppy Dillworth mystery), *The Hallelujah Murders* (2nd Poppy Dillworth mystery) and a short story "Going Up" in *The Erotic Naiad* anthology.

Her next book, a collection of erotica entitled *Certain Smiles* is scheduled for 1994. After that comes the 3rd novel featuring Poppy Dillworth, *The Speaking Rocks Mystery*.

AMANDA KYLE WILLIAMS is the best-selling author of *Club Twelve*, the first espionage thriller to feature a lesbian agent, the Lambda Literary Award nominated *Providence File, A Singular Spy,* and *The Spy In Question.* She also contributed to the first book in this series, *The Erotic Naiad.*

Amanda Kyle Williams lives in Atlanta, Georgia, is professionally involved with a lesbian owned and operated business, holds a senior belt in martial arts and is currently working on the fifth Madison McGuire espionage thriller.

MOLLEEN ZANGER has lived the past three of her forty-five years in the Thumb of Michigan with her mate, her youngest son, three dogs, two cats (one with a triangular pupil in her left eye) and various cacti and succulents. Her first novel, *The Year Seven,* was published by Naiad in the spring of 1993. Presently she is at work on a novel of suspense for Naiad, *Gardenias Where There Are None,* which is scheduled for release in the spring of 1994.

A few of the publications of
THE NAIAD PRESS, INC.
P.O. Box 10543 • Tallahassee, Florida 32302
Phone (904) 539-5965
Toll-Free Order Number: 1-800-533-1973
Mail orders welcome. Please include 15% postage.

THE ROMANTIC NAIAD edited by Katherine V. Forrest &
Barbara Grier. 336 pp. Love stories by Naiad Press women.
ISBN 1-56280-054-X $14.95

UNDER MY SKIN by Jaye Maiman. 336 pp. 3rd Robin Miller
mystery. ISBN 1-56280-049-3. 10.95

STAY TOONED by Rhonda Dicksion. 144 pp. Cartoons — 1st
collection since *Lesbian Survival Manual.* ISBN 1-56280-045-0 9.95

CAR POOL by Karin Kallmaker. 272pp. Lesbians on wheels
and then some! ISBN 1-56280-048-5 9.95

NOT TELLING MOTHER: STORIES FROM A LIFE by Diane
Salvatore. 176 pp. Her 3rd novel. ISBN 1-56280-044-2 9.95

GOBLIN MARKET by Lauren Wright Douglas. 240pp. Fifth
Caitlin Reece Mystery. ISBN 1-56280-047-7 9.95

LONG GOODBYES by Nikki Baker. 256 pp. A Virginia Kelly
mystery. 3rd in a series. ISBN 1-56280-042-6 9.95

FRIENDS AND LOVERS by Jackie Calhoun. 224 pp. Mid-western
Lesbian lives and loves. ISBN 1-56280-041-8 9.95

THE CAT CAME BACK by Hilary Mullins. 208 pp. Highly praised
Lesbian novel. ISBN 1-56280-040-X 9.95

BEHIND CLOSED DOORS by Robbi Sommers. 192 pp. Hot, erotic
short stories. ISBN 1-56280-039-6 9.95

CLAIRE OF THE MOON by Nicole Conn. 192 pp. See the movie —
read the book! ISBN 1-56280-038-8 10.95

SILENT HEART by Claire McNab. 192 pp. Exotic Lesbian
romance. ISBN 1-56280-036-1 9.95

HAPPY ENDINGS by Kate Brandt. 272 pp. Intimate conversations
with Lesbian authors. ISBN 1-56280-050-7 10.95

THE SPY IN QUESTION by Amanda Kyle Williams. 256 pp. 4th
spy novel featuring Lesbian agent Madison McGuire.
ISBN 1-56280-037-X 9.95

SAVING GRACE by Jennifer Fulton. 240 pp. Adventure and
romantic entanglement. ISBN 1-56280-051-5 9.95

THE YEAR SEVEN by Molleen Zanger. 208 pp. Women surviving in a new world.   ISBN 1-56280-034-5   9.95

CURIOUS WINE by Katherine V. Forrest. 176 pp. Tenth Anniversary Edition. The most popular contemporary Lesbian love story.   ISBN 1-56280-053-1   9.95

CHAUTAUQUA by Catherine Ennis. 192 pp. Exciting, romantic adventure.   ISBN 1-56280-032-9   9.95

A PROPER BURIAL by Pat Welch. 192 pp. Third in the Helen Black mystery series.   ISBN 1-56280-033-7   9.95

SILVERLAKE HEAT: A Novel of Suspense by Carol Schmidt. 240 pp. Rhonda is as hot as Laney's dreams.   ISBN 1-56280-031-0   9.95

LOVE, ZENA BETH by Diane Salvatore. 224 pp. The most talked about lesbian novel of the nineties!   ISBN 1-56280-030-2   9.95

A DOORYARD FULL OF FLOWERS by Isabel Miller. 160 pp. Stories incl. 2 sequels to *Patience and Sarah*.   ISBN 1-56280-029-9   9.95

MURDER BY TRADITION by Katherine V. Forrest. 288 pp. A Kate Delafield Mystery. 4th in a series.   ISBN 1-56280-002-7   9.95

THE EROTIC NAIAD edited by Katherine V. Forrest & Barbara Grier. 224 pp. Love stories by Naiad Press authors.   ISBN 1-56280-026-4   12.95

DEAD CERTAIN by Claire McNab. 224 pp. 5th Det. Insp. Carol Ashton mystery.   ISBN 1-56280-027-2   9.95

CRAZY FOR LOVING by Jaye Maiman. 320 pp. 2nd Robin Miller mystery.   ISBN 1-56280-025-6   9.95

STONEHURST by Barbara Johnson. 176 pp. Passionate regency romance.   ISBN 1-56280-024-8   9.95

INTRODUCING AMANDA VALENTINE by Rose Beecham. 256 pp. An Amanda Valentine Mystery — 1st in a series.
                                                ISBN 1-56280-021-3   9.95

UNCERTAIN COMPANIONS by Robbi Sommers. 204 pp. Steamy, erotic novel.   ISBN 1-56280-017-5   9.95

A TIGER'S HEART by Lauren W. Douglas. 240 pp. Fourth Caitlin Reece Mystery.   ISBN 1-56280-018-3   9.95

PAPERBACK ROMANCE by Karin Kallmaker. 256 pp. A delicious romance.   ISBN 1-56280-019-1   9.95

MORTON RIVER VALLEY by Lee Lynch. 304 pp. Lee Lynch at her best!   ISBN 1-56280-016-7   9.95

THE LAVENDER HOUSE MURDER by Nikki Baker. 224 pp. A Virginia Kelly Mystery. Second in a series.   ISBN 1-56280-012-4   9.95

PASSION BAY by Jennifer Fulton. 224 pp. Passionate romance, virgin beaches, tropical skies.   ISBN 1-56280-028-0   9.95

STICKS AND STONES by Jackie Calhoun. 208 pp. Contemporary lesbian lives and loves.   ISBN 1-56280-020-5   9.95

DELIA IRONFOOT by Jeane Harris. 192 pp. Adventure for Delia
and Beth in the Utah mountains.   ISBN 1-56280-014-0   9.95

UNDER THE SOUTHERN CROSS by Claire McNab. 192 pp.
Romantic nights Down Under.   ISBN 1-56280-011-6   9.95

RIVERFINGER WOMEN by Elana Nachman/Dykewomon.
208 pp. Classic Lesbian/feminist novel.   ISBN 1-56280-013-2   8.95

A CERTAIN DISCONTENT by Cleve Boutell. 240 pp. A unique
coterie of women.   ISBN 1-56280-009-4   9.95

GRASSY FLATS by Penny Hayes. 256 pp. Lesbian romance in
the '30s.   ISBN 1-56280-010-8   9.95

A SINGULAR SPY by Amanda K. Williams. 192 pp. 3rd spy novel
featuring Lesbian agent Madison McGuire.   ISBN 1-56280-008-6   8.95

THE END OF APRIL by Penny Sumner. 240 pp. A Victoria Cross
Mystery. First in a series.   ISBN 1-56280-007-8   8.95

A FLIGHT OF ANGELS by Sarah Aldridge. 240 pp. Romance set at
the National Gallery of Art   ISBN 1-56280-001-9   9.95

HOUSTON TOWN by Deborah Powell. 208 pp. A Hollis Carpenter
mystery. Second in a series.   ISBN 1-56280-006-X   8.95

KISS AND TELL by Robbi Sommers. 192 pp. Scorching stories by
the author of *Pleasures*.   ISBN 1-56280-005-1   9.95

STILL WATERS by Pat Welch. 208 pp. Second in the Helen
Black mystery series.   ISBN 0-941483-97-5   9.95

TO LOVE AGAIN by Evelyn Kennedy. 208 pp. Wildly
romantic love story.   ISBN 0-941483-85-1   9.95

IN THE GAME by Nikki Baker. 192 pp. A Virginia Kelly
mystery. First in a series.   ISBN 01-56280-004-3   9.95

AVALON by Mary Jane Jones. 256 pp. A Lesbian Arthurian
romance.   ISBN 0-941483-96-7   9.95

STRANDED by Camarin Grae. 320 pp. Entertaining, riveting
adventure.   ISBN 0-941483-99-1   9.95

THE DAUGHTERS OF ARTEMIS by Lauren Wright Douglas.
240 pp. Third Caitlin Reece mystery.   ISBN 0-941483-95-9   9.95

CLEARWATER by Catherine Ennis. 176 pp. Romantic secrets
of a small Louisiana town.   ISBN 0-941483-65-7   8.95

THE HALLELUJAH MURDERS by Dorothy Tell. 176 pp.
Second Poppy Dillworth mystery.   ISBN 0-941483-88-6   8.95

ZETA BASE by Judith Alguire. 208 pp. Lesbian triangle
on a future Earth.   ISBN 0-941483-94-0   9.95

SECOND CHANCE by Jackie Calhoun. 256 pp. Contemporary
Lesbian lives and loves.   ISBN 0-941483-93-2   9.95

BENEDICTION by Diane Salvatore. 272 pp. Striking,
contemporary romantic novel.   ISBN 0-941483-90-8   9.95

CALLING RAIN by Karen Marie Christa Minns. 240 pp.
Spellbinding, erotic love story ISBN 0-941483-87-8   9.95

BLACK IRIS by Jeane Harris. 192 pp. Caroline's hidden past . . .
ISBN 0-941483-68-1   8.95

TOUCHWOOD by Karin Kallmaker. 240 pp. Loving, May/
December romance. ISBN 0-941483-76-2   9.95

BAYOU CITY SECRETS by Deborah Powell. 224 pp. A Hollis
Carpenter mystery. First in a series. ISBN 0-941483-91-6   9.95

COP OUT by Claire McNab. 208 pp. 4th Det. Insp. Carol Ashton
mystery. ISBN 0-941483-84-3   9.95

LODESTAR by Phyllis Horn. 224 pp. Romantic, fast-moving
adventure. ISBN 0-941483-83-5   8.95

THE BEVERLY MALIBU by Katherine V. Forrest. 288 pp. A
Kate Delafield Mystery. 3rd in a series. ISBN 0-941483-48-7   9.95

THAT OLD STUDEBAKER by Lee Lynch. 272 pp. Andy's affair
with Regina and her attachment to her beloved car.
ISBN 0-941483-82-7   9.95

PASSION'S LEGACY by Lori Paige. 224 pp. Sarah is swept into
the arms of Augusta Pym in this delightful historical romance.
ISBN 0-941483-81-9   8.95

THE PROVIDENCE FILE by Amanda Kyle Williams. 256 pp.
Second espionage thriller featuring lesbian agent Madison McGuire
ISBN 0-941483-92-4   8.95

I LEFT MY HEART by Jaye Maiman. 320 pp. A Robin Miller
Mystery. First in a series. ISBN 0-941483-72-X   9.95

THE PRICE OF SALT by Patricia Highsmith (writing as Claire
Morgan). 288 pp. Classic lesbian novel, first issued in 1952 . . .
acknowledged by its author under her own, very famous, name.
ISBN 1-56280-003-5   9.95

SIDE BY SIDE by Isabel Miller. 256 pp. From beloved author of
Patience and Sarah. ISBN 0-941483-77-0   9.95

SOUTHBOUND by Sheila Ortiz Taylor. 240 pp. Hilarious sequel
to *Faultline.* ISBN 0-941483-78-9   8.95

STAYING POWER: LONG TERM LESBIAN COUPLES
by Susan E. Johnson. 352 pp. Joys of coupledom.
ISBN 0-941-483-75-4   12.95

SLICK by Camarin Grae. 304 pp. Exotic, erotic adventure.
ISBN 0-941483-74-6   9.95

NINTH LIFE by Lauren Wright Douglas. 256 pp. A Caitlin
Reece mystery. 2nd in a series. ISBN 0-941483-50-9   8.95

PLAYERS by Robbi Sommers. 192 pp. Sizzling, erotic novel.
ISBN 0-941483-73-8   9.95

MURDER AT RED ROOK RANCH by Dorothy Tell. 224 pp.
First Poppy Dillworth adventure.   ISBN 0-941483-80-0   8.95

LESBIAN SURVIVAL MANUAL by Rhonda Dicksion.
112 pp. Cartoons!   ISBN 0-941483-71-1   8.95

A ROOM FULL OF WOMEN by Elisabeth Nonas. 256 pp.
Contemporary Lesbian lives.   ISBN 0-941483-69-X   9.95

PRIORITIES by Lynda Lyons 288 pp. Science fiction with
a twist.   ISBN 0-941483-66-5   8.95

THEME FOR DIVERSE INSTRUMENTS by Jane Rule. 208
pp. Powerful romantic lesbian stories. ISBN 0-941483-63-0   8.95

LESBIAN QUERIES by Hertz & Ertman. 112 pp. The questions
you were too embarrassed to ask.   ISBN 0-941483-67-3   8.95

CLUB 12 by Amanda Kyle Williams. 288 pp. Espionage thriller
featuring a lesbian agent!   ISBN 0-941483-64-9   8.95

DEATH DOWN UNDER by Claire McNab. 240 pp. 3rd Det.
Insp. Carol Ashton mystery.   ISBN 0-941483-39-8   9.95

MONTANA FEATHERS by Penny Hayes. 256 pp. Vivian and
Elizabeth find love in frontier Montana. ISBN 0-941483-61-4   8.95

CHESAPEAKE PROJECT by Phyllis Horn. 304 pp. Jessie &
Meredith in perilous adventure.   ISBN 0-941483-58-4   8.95

LIFESTYLES by Jackie Calhoun. 224 pp. Contemporary Lesbian
lives and loves.   ISBN 0-941483-57-6   9.95

VIRAGO by Karen Marie Christa Minns. 208 pp. Darsen has
chosen Ginny.   ISBN 0-941483-56-8   8.95

WILDERNESS TREK by Dorothy Tell. 192 pp. Six women on
vacation learning ''new'' skills.   ISBN 0-941483-60-6   8.95

MURDER BY THE BOOK by Pat Welch. 256 pp. A Helen
Black Mystery. First in a series.   ISBN 0-941483-59-2   9.95

BERRIGAN by Vicki P. McConnell. 176 pp. Youthful Lesbian —
romantic, idealistic Berrigan.   ISBN 0-941483-55-X   8.95

LESBIANS IN GERMANY by Lillian Faderman & B. Eriksson.
128 pp. Fiction, poetry, essays.   ISBN 0-941483-62-2   8.95

THERE'S SOMETHING I'VE BEEN MEANING TO TELL
YOU Ed. by Loralee MacPike. 288 pp. Gay men and lesbians
coming out to their children.   ISBN 0-941483-44-4   9.95

LIFTING BELLY by Gertrude Stein. Ed. by Rebecca Mark. 104
pp. Erotic poetry.   ISBN 0-941483-51-7   8.95

ROSE PENSKI by Roz Perry. 192 pp. Adult lovers in a long-term
relationship.   ISBN 0-941483-37-1   8.95

AFTER THE FIRE by Jane Rule. 256 pp. Warm, human novel
by this incomparable author.   ISBN 0-941483-45-2   8.95

SUE SLATE, PRIVATE EYE by Lee Lynch. 176 pp. The gay folk of Peacock Alley are *all cats*. ISBN 0-941483-52-5   8.95

CHRIS by Randy Salem. 224 pp. Golden oldie. Handsome Chris and her adventures. ISBN 0-941483-42-8   8.95

THREE WOMEN by March Hastings. 232 pp. Golden oldie. A triangle among wealthy sophisticates. ISBN 0-941483-43-6   8.95

RICE AND BEANS by Valeria Taylor. 232 pp. Love and romance on poverty row. ISBN 0-941483-41-X   8.95

PLEASURES by Robbi Sommers. 204 pp. Unprecedented eroticism. ISBN 0-941483-49-5   8.95

EDGEWISE by Camarin Grae. 372 pp. Spellbinding adventure. ISBN 0-941483-19-3   9.95

FATAL REUNION by Claire McNab. 224 pp. 2nd Det. Inspec. Carol Ashton mystery. ISBN 0-941483-40-1   8.95

KEEP TO ME STRANGER by Sarah Aldridge. 372 pp. Romance set in a department store dynasty. ISBN 0-941483-38-X   9.95

HEARTSCAPE by Sue Gambill. 204 pp. American lesbian in Portugal. ISBN 0-941483-33-9   8.95

IN THE BLOOD by Lauren Wright Douglas. 252 pp. Lesbian science fiction adventure fantasy ISBN 0-941483-22-3   8.95

THE BEE'S KISS by Shirley Verel. 216 pp. Delicate, delicious romance. ISBN 0-941483-36-3   8.95

RAGING MOTHER MOUNTAIN by Pat Emmerson. 264 pp. Furosa Firechild's adventures in Wonderland. ISBN 0-941483-35-5   8.95

IN EVERY PORT by Karin Kallmaker. 228 pp. Jessica's sexy, adventuresome travels. ISBN 0-941483-37-7   9.95

OF LOVE AND GLORY by Evelyn Kennedy. 192 pp. Exciting WWII romance. ISBN 0-941483-32-0   8.95

CLICKING STONES by Nancy Tyler Glenn. 288 pp. Love transcending time. ISBN 0-941483-31-2   9.95

SURVIVING SISTERS by Gail Pass. 252 pp. Powerful love story. ISBN 0-941483-16-9   8.95

SOUTH OF THE LINE by Catherine Ennis. 216 pp. Civil War adventure. ISBN 0-941483-29-0   8.95

WOMAN PLUS WOMAN by Dolores Klaich. 300 pp. Supurb Lesbian overview. ISBN 0-941483-28-2   9.95

HEAVY GILT by Delores Klaich. 192 pp. Lesbian detective/disappearing homophobes/upper class gay society.
ISBN 0-941483-25-8   8.95

THE FINER GRAIN by Denise Ohio. 216 pp. Brilliant young college lesbian novel. ISBN 0-941483-11-8   8.95

THE AMAZON TRAIL by Lee Lynch. 216 pp. Life, travel & lore of famous lesbian author. ISBN 0-941483-27-4   8.95

HIGH CONTRAST by Jessie Lattimore. 264 pp. Women of the Crystal Palace. ISBN 0-941483-17-7   8.95

OCTOBER OBSESSION by Meredith More. Josie's rich, secret Lesbian life. ISBN 0-941483-18-5   8.95

LESBIAN CROSSROADS by Ruth Baetz. 276 pp. Contemporary Lesbian lives. ISBN 0-941483-21-5   9.95

BEFORE STONEWALL: THE MAKING OF A GAY AND LESBIAN COMMUNITY by Andrea Weiss & Greta Schiller. 96 pp., 25 illus. ISBN 0-941483-20-7   7.95

WE WALK THE BACK OF THE TIGER by Patricia A. Murphy. 192 pp. Romantic Lesbian novel/beginning women's movement. ISBN 0-941483-13-4   8.95

SUNDAY'S CHILD by Joyce Bright. 216 pp. Lesbian athletics, at last the novel about sports. ISBN 0-941483-12-6   8.95

OSTEN'S BAY by Zenobia N. Vole. 204 pp. Sizzling adventure romance set on Bonaire. ISBN 0-941483-15-0   8.95

LESSONS IN MURDER by Claire McNab. 216 pp. 1st Det. Inspec. Carol Ashton mystery — erotic tension!. ISBN 0-941483-14-2   9.95

YELLOWTHROAT by Penny Hayes. 240 pp. Margarita, bandit, kidnaps Julia. ISBN 0-941483-10-X   8.95

SAPPHISTRY: THE BOOK OF LESBIAN SEXUALITY by Pat Califia. 3d edition, revised. 208 pp. ISBN 0-941483-24-X   10.95

CHERISHED LOVE by Evelyn Kennedy. 192 pp. Erotic Lesbian love story. ISBN 0-941483-08-8   9.95

LAST SEPTEMBER by Helen R. Hull. 208 pp. Six stories & a glorious novella. ISBN 0-941483-09-6   8.95

THE SECRET IN THE BIRD by Camarin Grae. 312 pp. Striking, psychological suspense novel. ISBN 0-941483-05-3   8.95

TO THE LIGHTNING by Catherine Ennis. 208 pp. Romantic Lesbian 'Robinson Crusoe' adventure. ISBN 0-941483-06-1   8.95

THE OTHER SIDE OF VENUS by Shirley Verel. 224 pp. Luminous, romantic love story. ISBN 0-941483-07-X   8.95

DREAMS AND SWORDS by Katherine V. Forrest. 192 pp. Romantic, erotic, imaginative stories. ISBN 0-941483-03-7   8.95

MEMORY BOARD by Jane Rule. 336 pp. Memorable novel about an aging Lesbian couple. ISBN 0-941483-02-9   9.95

THE ALWAYS ANONYMOUS BEAST by Lauren Wright Douglas. 224 pp. A Caitlin Reece mystery. First in a series. ISBN 0-941483-04-5   8.95

SEARCHING FOR SPRING by Patricia A. Murphy. 224 pp.
Novel about the recovery of love. ISBN 0-941483-00-2   8.95

DUSTY'S QUEEN OF HEARTS DINER by Lee Lynch. 240 pp.
Romantic blue-collar novel. ISBN 0-941483-01-0   8.95

PARENTS MATTER by Ann Muller. 240 pp. Parents'
relationships with Lesbian daughters and gay sons.
ISBN 0-930044-91-6   9.95

THE PEARLS by Shelley Smith. 176 pp. Passion and fun in
the Caribbean sun. ISBN 0-930044-93-2   7.95

MAGDALENA by Sarah Aldridge. 352 pp. Epic Lesbian novel
set on three continents. ISBN 0-930044-99-1   8.95

THE BLACK AND WHITE OF IT by Ann Allen Shockley.
144 pp. Short stories. ISBN 0-930044-96-7   7.95

SAY JESUS AND COME TO ME by Ann Allen Shockley. 288
pp. Contemporary romance. ISBN 0-930044-98-3   8.95

LOVING HER by Ann Allen Shockley. 192 pp. Romantic love
story. ISBN 0-930044-97-5   7.95

MURDER AT THE NIGHTWOOD BAR by Katherine V.
Forrest. 240 pp. A Kate Delafield mystery. Second in a series.
ISBN 0-930044-92-4   9.95

ZOE'S BOOK by Gail Pass. 224 pp. Passionate, obsessive love
story. ISBN 0-930044-95-9   7.95

WINGED DANCER by Camarin Grae. 228 pp. Erotic Lesbian
adventure story. ISBN 0-930044-88-6   8.95

PAZ by Camarin Grae. 336 pp. Romantic Lesbian adventurer
with the power to change the world. ISBN 0-930044-89-4   8.95

SOUL SNATCHER by Camarin Grae. 224 pp. A puzzle, an
adventure, a mystery — Lesbian romance. ISBN 0-930044-90-8   8.95

THE LOVE OF GOOD WOMEN by Isabel Miller. 224 pp.
Long-awaited new novel by the author of the beloved *Patience
and Sarah*. ISBN 0-930044-81-9   8.95

THE HOUSE AT PELHAM FALLS by Brenda Weathers. 240
pp. Suspenseful Lesbian ghost story. ISBN 0-930044-79-7   7.95

HOME IN YOUR HANDS by Lee Lynch. 240 pp. More stories
from the author of *Old Dyke Tales*. ISBN 0-930044-80-0   7.95

SURPLUS by Sylvia Stevenson. 342 pp. A classic early Lesbian
novel. ISBN 0-930044-78-9   7.95

PEMBROKE PARK by Michelle Martin. 256 pp. Derring-do
and daring romance in Regency England. ISBN 0-930044-77-0   7.95

THE LONG TRAIL by Penny Hayes. 248 pp. Vivid adventures
of two women in love in the old west. ISBN 0-930044-76-2   8.95

AN EMERGENCE OF GREEN by Katherine V. Forrest. 288 pp. Powerful novel of sexual discovery.   ISBN 0-930044-69-X   9.95

THE LESBIAN PERIODICALS INDEX edited by Claire Potter. 432 pp. Author & subject index.   ISBN 0-930044-74-6   12.95

DESERT OF THE HEART by Jane Rule. 224 pp. A classic; basis for the movie *Desert Hearts*.   ISBN 0-930044-73-8   9.95

SPRING FORWARD/FALL BACK by Sheila Ortiz Taylor. 288 pp. Literary novel of timeless love.   ISBN 0-930044-70-3   7.95

FOR KEEPS by Elisabeth Nonas. 144 pp. Contemporary novel about losing and finding love.   ISBN 0-930044-71-1   7.95

TORCHLIGHT TO VALHALLA by Gale Wilhelm. 128 pp. Classic novel by a great Lesbian writer.   ISBN 0-930044-68-1   7.95

LESBIAN NUNS: BREAKING SILENCE edited by Rosemary Curb and Nancy Manahan. 432 pp. Unprecedented autobiographies of religious life.   ISBN 0-930044-62-2   9.95

THE SWASHBUCKLER by Lee Lynch. 288 pp. Colorful novel set in Greenwich Village in the sixties.   ISBN 0-930044-66-5   8.95

MISFORTUNE'S FRIEND by Sarah Aldridge. 320 pp. Historical Lesbian novel set on two continents.   ISBN 0-930044-67-3   7.95

SEX VARIANT WOMEN IN LITERATURE by Jeannette Howard Foster. 448 pp. Literary history.   ISBN 0-930044-65-7   8.95

A HOT-EYED MODERATE by Jane Rule. 252 pp. Hard-hitting essays on gay life; writing; art.   ISBN 0-930044-57-6   7.95

INLAND PASSAGE AND OTHER STORIES by Jane Rule. 288 pp. Wide-ranging new collection.   ISBN 0-930044-56-8   7.95

WE TOO ARE DRIFTING by Gale Wilhelm. 128 pp. Timeless Lesbian novel, a masterpiece.   ISBN 0-930044-61-4   6.95

AMATEUR CITY by Katherine V. Forrest. 224 pp. A Kate Delafield mystery. First in a series.   ISBN 0-930044-55-X   9.95

THE SOPHIE HOROWITZ STORY by Sarah Schulman. 176 pp. Engaging novel of madcap intrigue.   ISBN 0-930044-54-1   7.95

THE YOUNG IN ONE ANOTHER'S ARMS by Jane Rule. 224 pp. Classic Jane Rule.   ISBN 0-930044-53-3   9.95

OLD DYKE TALES by Lee Lynch. 224 pp. Extraordinary stories of our diverse Lesbian lives.   ISBN 0-930044-51-7   8.95

DAUGHTERS OF A CORAL DAWN by Katherine V. Forrest. 240 pp. Novel set in a Lesbian new world.   ISBN 0-930044-50-9   9.95

AGAINST THE SEASON by Jane Rule. 224 pp. Luminous, complex novel of interrelationships.   ISBN 0-930044-48-7   8.95

LOVERS IN THE PRESENT AFTERNOON by Kathleen Fleming. 288 pp. A novel about recovery and growth.   ISBN 0-930044-46-0   8.95

TOOTHPICK HOUSE by Lee Lynch. 264 pp. Love between
two Lesbians of different classes. ISBN 0-930044-45-2   7.95

MADAME AURORA by Sarah Aldridge. 256 pp. Historical
novel featuring a charismatic "seer." ISBN 0-930044-44-4   7.95

CONTRACT WITH THE WORLD by Jane Rule. 340 pp.
Powerful, panoramic novel of gay life. ISBN 0-930044-28-2   9.95

THE NESTING PLACE by Sarah Aldridge. 224 pp. A
three-woman triangle — love conquers all! ISBN 0-930044-26-6   7.95

THIS IS NOT FOR YOU by Jane Rule. 284 pp. A letter to a
beloved is also an intricate novel. ISBN 0-930044-25-8   8.95

FAULTLINE by Sheila Ortiz Taylor. 140 pp. Warm, funny,
literate story of a startling family. ISBN 0-930044-24-X   6.95

ANNA'S COUNTRY by Elizabeth Lang. 208 pp. A woman
finds her Lesbian identity. ISBN 0-930044-19-3   8.95

PRISM by Valerie Taylor. 158 pp. A love affair between two
women in their sixties. ISBN 0-930044-18-5   6.95

OUTLANDER by Jane Rule. 207 pp. Short stories and essays
by one of our finest writers. ISBN 0-930044-17-7   8.95

ALL TRUE LOVERS by Sarah Aldridge. 292 pp. Romantic
novel set in the 1930s and 1940s. ISBN 0-930044-10-X   8.95

CYTHEREA'S BREATH by Sarah Aldridge. 240 pp. Romantic
novel about women's entrance into medicine.
ISBN 0-930044-02-9   6.95

TOTTIE by Sarah Aldridge. 181 pp. Lesbian romance in the
turmoil of the sixties. ISBN 0-930044-01-0   6.95

THE LATECOMER by Sarah Aldridge. 107 pp. A delicate love
story. ISBN 0-930044-00-2   6.95

ODD GIRL OUT by Ann Bannon. ISBN 0-930044-83-5   5.95
I AM A WOMAN 84-3; WOMEN IN THE SHADOWS 85-1;   each
JOURNEY TO A WOMAN 86-X; BEEBO BRINKER 87-8. Golden
oldies about life in Greenwich Village.

JOURNEY TO FULFILLMENT, A WORLD WITHOUT MEN, and   3.95
RETURN TO LESBOS. All by Valerie Taylor   each

These are just a few of the many Naiad Press titles — we are the oldest and
largest lesbian/feminist publishing company in the world. Please request a
complete catalog. We offer personal service; we encourage and welcome direct
mail orders from individuals who have limited access to bookstores carrying
our publications.